A FEW
Well-Frozen
WORMS

A FEW
Well-Frozen
WORMS

MORE OF THE BERY VEST

Ronnie Barker

EBURY
PRESS

1 3 5 7 9 10 8 6 4 2

This edition published 2014 by Ebury Press, an imprint of Ebury Publishing
A Random House Group company
First published in the UK as part of *All I Ever Wrote: The Complete Works*
by Essential Books in 1999

Originally edited by Bob McCabe
Photographs reproduced by permission of the BBC and Getty Images

The Ronnie Barker Estate has asserted their right to be identified as the authors of
this Work in accordance with the Copyright, Designs and Patents Act 1988

The Random House Group Limited Reg. No. 954009

Addresses for companies within the Random House Group can be found at
www.randomhouse.co.uk

A CIP catalogue record for this book is available from the British Library

The Random House Group Limited supports the Forest Stewardship
Council® (FSC®), the leading international forest-certification organisation.
Our books carrying the FSC label are printed on FSC®-certified paper. FSC is the
only forest-certification scheme supported by the leading environmental
organisations, including Greenpeace. Our paper procurement policy can be
found at www.randomhouse.co.uk/environment

Printed and bound in Great Britain by Clays Ltd, St Ives PLC

ISBN 9780091951412

To buy books by your favourite authors and register for offers visit
www.randomhouse.co.uk

Contents

Early Sketches

All of us reading this have grown up with our own idea of Ronnie Barker. To all of us he is everything: a clipped, trimmed, razor-sharp delivery; a precise, pin-pricked perfection of pronunciation and performance; he is character, he is conviction, he is cartoon; he is broad, bowling-ball-eyed bawdiness. He is British comedy.

However, it is too easy to forget that this genius came with the understated, underplayed bashfulness of the quintessential Englishman.

The delightful, ribald and bombastic early sketches that follow were almost all written by Barker under pseudonyms, for fear of revealing a boastful, 'showbiz' look-at-me aspect. Often he even went as far, when looking over the scripts he had himself written, as to dismiss one or two with a 'He's let us down there' or a quizzical 'I don't understand this line. What's he getting at?'

On one early occasion, Barker – under the pseudonym Gerald Wiley – anonymously wrote a sketch for Ronnie Corbett and actually went as far as encouraging Corbett to reject Wiley's fee of £3,000 as 'too expensive', so keen was he to keep up the pretence and avoid the limelight.

For all the wordplay, wisecracks and wit, Ronnie Barker was ultimately a modest and unassuming writer who wanted the quirks, quips and quality of the writing to speak for itself.

As you're about to discover, there is no doubt that it does.

THE ELIZABETHAN DRAMA

(Early radio piece – 1960)

ANNOUNCER: The scene is a wood near Venice. The chorus enters, and bows low.

CHORUS:
Good gentle people all, hear me I pray.
A tale will I unfold: upon this day
The feast of good Saint Pancras, you will hear
A history that will delight your ear.
'Tis this: two boys, sired by the same good knight
(I trust, in sooth, I am informed aright),
Born at the self-same hour, twins were they named;
Now both, their dead sire's lands and deeds have claimed.
And each have sworn to murder one another
Should either each meet up with either other.
Venutio and Velutio are their names –
But soft; who comes? We'll watch the fun and games.

(He withdraws.)

(Enter Fruitio, a clown.)

CLOWN: Here's a pretty catch of fishes, as the dame said to the ironmonger: for though Velutio is my master, yet I do prefer Venutio, and have done since all proverbial. How can I desert the one, without getting my deserts of the other? Would I were not I, I would! I would I were not that I wished I was; for if I were not that I would not be! Those that do not rise early, get no wenching o' market-days, as the Oracle tells us. Therefore I will resolve to quit my master Velutio, and follow Venutio – or is it turn about, as Lucifer has it. Whate'er it is, I will do it straight. But here comes my master, and with the Doge of Venice. There's company indeed, as they all have it. I'll hide within this bush, and learn little if not much, I trow.

(He conceals himself within a bush.)

(Enter Velutio with Hirsuitio, the Doge of Venice.)

VELUTIO: And there, good uncle, you have all my tale.

DOGE: In faith, good sir, I thank thee much for that. And whither goest thou from hence, to thither?

VELUTIO: To Padua, and thence to Mantua,
by-passing Turin, and Rome's ancient pile,
up to the Bay of Naples, and from thence
cross Africa, and to the farthest shores
of the Antipodes, my chart is set.

DOGE: Take thou provisions, thou will'st need them, straight.

VELUTIO: My thanks to thee, good father; that I will.
And now adieu, for Phoebus' golden steed
e'en now wings down her dappled shadow-show
and wraps the earth in sleep – I must be gone.

DOGE: Then go, and talk no more – it groweth cold.
But stay! who comes from yonder hence to here
moving as if he'd Charon on his back?

VELUTIO: It is my cursed brother, mark, 'tis he!

DOGE: Not Mark, but young Venutio, as I see.
Here, take this cup of poison, which I keep
always beneath my robe in case of thieves,
and make him drink it.

VELUTIO: Nay, I'll use my sword
to settle this encounter; mark me on't.

(He calls to Venutio.)

Thou damned black fiend that once I called my brother
have at thee now, till one shall slay the other!

(They fight.)

FX: *(Long loud scream.)*

DOGE: So brave Velutio falls, and worst is done
But wait – the bodies – there is more than one:
Three bodies? If my brain doth serve me true
we started off the fight with only two!
What of the third? 'Tis Fruitio, the clown!
Whilst crouching in that bush, they struck him down.
O horror! Now my sorrow gives me pause
My life is forfeit to the general cause;
My jewelled dagger now shall pierce my heart.
Let it strike thus!

(Stabs himself.)

And I have done my part.

(Dies.)

(Enter Chorus.)

> **CHORUS:**
> Thus speaks the noble Doge, and nobly dies,
> Now all are dead; each on the green earth lies.
> Thus, gentles all, our entertainment ends;
> But ere I take my leave of you, good friends,
> A cup of wine stands on the greensward here.
> I drink a toast to you – God give you cheer!

(He drinks and gasps.)

'Tis poisoned! And I die! I should have known
had I learnt all the lines, not just my own.
With dying breath, I must announce, with reason,
this is the last play in the present season.

(Dies.)

THE FARCE

(Early radio piece)

ANNOUNCER: This week our critic went to see a revival of the famous farce, A Cuckoo in the Rockery.

CRITIC: Good evening, theatre-lovers. This week I saw an amateur production for a change. I travelled down to Little Shelfont, in Kent, to see the Shelfont Country Club Thespians' production of this famous farce. Strangely enough, I had never seen this play until now; however, one's luck can't last forever, I suppose.

The play was performed in the Old Corn Exchange; it's an interesting thought that this must be the first time for hundreds of years that this historic building has been used for its original purpose – that is, the exchange of corn. For corn it certainly was. Not that I have anything against the amateur; providing he is as good as the professional, he is often much better. But there are amateurs and amateurs. These, unfortunately, were the latter.

My ticket was marked L10. I found row 'L' eventually (it was in between row 'M' and row 'N'). The seat itself turned out to be eighteen inches of wooden school bench, with 'L10' chalked boldly right across the bit where one is supposed to sit. There was nothing for it but to sit on the chalk, and I did so, certain in the knowledge that when I got up again I would have 'oil' on the seat of my trousers.

(Not real oil, you understand, but the word 'oil'.) (Those of you who still don't understand what I'm getting at, please discuss it with the person next to you; but not now!!)

I opened my programme, which seemed to have been printed by an itinerant Indian bookseller, and began to read the interesting misprints. I noted that coffees and teak would be served in the interval; and that the incidental music had been taken from 'Handel's Large', played on the solo crumpet by Mr Higgins. My favourite one, however, was the special programme note saying that the company would like to thank the many willing helpers for all their hard work, especially the big stiff backstage.

But on to the play. The lights in the hall went out suddenly, with a loud click, the curtains half opened to reveal a maid in short black skirt and feather duster, staring in horror at the curtains, which had stuck. They went back and forth a few times, and, when they finally settled, she began to dust. There were seven doors in the set, a bed that folds up into the wall, and what was intended to be a secret cupboard, which for some reason wouldn't stay shut. It clicked open at the most inopportune moments, and everyone on stage gallantly took turns in sidling over and kicking it shut with their feet.

The play itself was quite good of its kind, but it needed bringing up to date a little here and there; the jokes about the Kaiser and the Dardenelles didn't go down well at all.

(The next paragraph is played very fast.)

The plot is fairly simple; a boy and a girl, having been secretly married, because the boy's mother disapproved of the match, arrive at a country cottage to spend their honeymoon. The dragon-like house-keeper, however, doesn't believe they are really married, so she phones the girl's mother, who arrives, indignantly demanding that the girl return home at once. So the young couple pretend they are to be married there and then, and that the vicar is arriving to marry them. They quickly phone up an actor friend, who turns up in about ten minutes flat, dressed as a vicar. From then on, it's anybody's guess what happens. I must admit I lost track of the plot at about this point, just after the maid had got shut in the fold-up bed with the actor, who was pretending to be the vicar. I remember the girl's father making love to the butler, who was dressed as a woman, pretending to be the boy's mother. The vicar, who was pretending to be the actor, lost his trousers while being chased by the housekeeper, and bumped into the girl's father, dressed as a woman, in order to meet the butler secretly, whom he had fallen for when the butler was dressed as the boy's mother. Then on comes the boy, dressed as a woman, and is ques-tioned by the butler, who is now dressed as the vicar, because the actor has now become the housekeeper, who has left in high dudgeon. At this point, the dialogue goes something like this:

(The following played very fast.)

BUTLER: Ah! There you are!

BOY: Ah! So I am!

BUTLER: Who are you?

BOY: I'm a dark horse!

BUTLER: Then why are you wearing a blonde wig?

BOY: That's a fair question!

BUTLER: Do you live here?

BOY: No, do you?

BUTLER: Yes.

BOY: Is this the Vicarage then?

BUTLER: No.

BOY: Then why are you dressed as a vicar?

BUTLER: I'm a visitor.

BOY: No visitors allowed except on Wednesdays and Saturdays. Good morning!

BUTLER: Are you a woman?

BOY: Don't be personal. Look out, here comes mother. Talk about something else.

BUTLER: What else?

BOY: (loudly, as woman) My little Else! She's my eldest, you know! She's such a comfort to me – always brings me my shaving water in bed of a Sunday morning, she does! Dear little Else!

CRITIC: The play hurtled on in this vein for another hour and a half, until everybody was dressed as a woman, including most of the women – except for the maid, that is, who was shut in the secret cupboard, not dressed as anything. Thank goodness they managed to find her a dressing gown for the curtain calls, or we would have been there all night. The play ended happily, and the producer of the company came on, dressed as a man, and thanked us for being a wonderful audience, and said she hoped we'd enjoyed it. I left the Corn Exchange rather dazed, and it was only when I got outside that I remembered I had 'oil' written in chalk on the seat on my trousers. I bent to brush it off, and my braces broke. Still, it didn't matter – the people coming out thought it was all part of the act. Goodnight!

CONVERSATIONS 1

(Variety Playhouse)

ANNOUNCER: An aspect of the British character which continues to stand firm against the march of progress is the complete timelessness of our country life. Machinery now does much of the work that once was accomplished by the honest sweat of the rustic – which means, of course, that the rustic has more time to pursue his favourite pastime – the gentle art of conversation.

A: Evening, Bertie.

B: Evening, Arnold.

A: I reckon we're gonna get some weather afore long, by the look of that sunset. You know what they say, 'Red in the sky, Shepherds' Pie!'

B: Ah. It's gonna be a rough old night all right!

A: Never mind, soon be double summer time, then it'll get lighter. Though I do confess I never do understand it.

B: What? Why, it's simple Arnold – it's a thing worked out by the government to make it light before daybreak, so that we can get more sleep without being woken up in the middle of the night first thing in the morning.

A: Well, my two sisters have to get up and do the milking, and they hate it. The poor old cows don't get enough sleep as it is.

B: Eh? Oh, I see what you mean. But it shouldn't make any difference, Arnold. You just put a couple of hours on in the morning, and take 'em off at night. Just like your trousers.

A: Ah, but the cows don't wear trousers, so they don't understand. And my sisters don't either.

B: Oh yes they do. At least, Sarah does.

A: How do you know?

B: I've seen her.

A: Seen her what?

B: Wearing trousers. Doing the milking.

A: I'm not talking about that. I said she can't understand it.

B: No, I can't understand it either.

A: What?

B: Why she wears trousers.

A: Look, just forget about her trousers for a minute, will you?

B: Well, I'll do me best. What was we talking about?

A: The weather.

B: Ah. It's gonna be a rough old night all right.

A: Ah. Well, I reckon it won't matter what sort of weather it is soon. We shall all be at a loose end afore long.

B: What do you mean, Arnold?

A: Well, I seen in the paper where it says they're doing away with the plough altogether. March of Progress, or summat.

B: What, getting rid of it? The plough?

A: Ah, and you know what that means, don't you?

B: Yes. Us'll have to go and drink somewhere else, shan't us?

A: Ere, I could use a pint of old and filthy now, to wet me down a bit.

B: You'll be wet down in a minute. Look at them clouds. It's going to be a rough old night all right.

A: Ar, us had better get back to the village. Shall we wait for the bus?

B: When's the next one?

A: Thursday.

B: Oh hang it, we'll walk. Ere, I see they be building one of they new-fangled bus shelters on the main road, for when it's raining.

A: Ar, I seen it. That'll never get used.

B: Why not?

A: 'Tis too small. The bus'll never get under it. Ere, I know what I meant to ask yer, Bertie.

B: What's that then?

A: Are you coming to the Annual Muckspreading Festival in the Village Hall on Saturday night?

B: I dunno, what's it like?

A: Ooh, smashing. It's all fancy dress, you know. They do give prizes too.

B: Oh ar?

A: Ar. The squire's wife won it last year – she went as a railway left luggage office.

B: Oh? What did she wear?

A: Tin trunks, and a hold-all. Right boozy do it is, you ought to come.

B: I think I will. Ere, is your sister Sarah going?

A: Oh yes. She's going as a cowboy.

B: Cor! Will she be wearing them trousers?

A: Oh ar!

B: Arnold! You know what?

A: What?

B: It's gonna be a rough old night all right.

CONVERSATIONS 2

(Variety Playhouse)

ANNOUNCER: Another aspect of the British character is the helpfulness and civility shown by representatives of our public services. A typical member of the public, played by Ronnie Barker, approaches the clerk of a coach station ticket office, played by Leslie Crowther, to buy a ticket.

R: Ah, good morning.

L: (Cockney, officious) Morning.

R: Is there a bus to Dingford Stanley?

L: There are buses to everywhere, sir.

R: Oh, good. Well, could you tell me the time?

L: There's a policeman over there, he'll tell you the time. I'm a clerk, not a clock.

R: No, no, I mean the time of the bus.

L: Oh. Let's see. Dingford Stanley, wasn't it? Do you mean the Dingford Stanley near Reading?

R: I suppose so.

L: You suppose so? Don't you know where you're going?

R: Yes. What I mean is, there can't be more than one.

L: Oh, can't there? Do you know how many Newports there are in Britain? Five.

R: Well, I'll settle for the one near Reading.

L: There isn't a Newport near Reading.

R: No, I mean the Dingford Stanley, near Reading.

L: Oh, right. Now then, let's see. Ah! Well. Now then. You don't want to go today.

R: Oh, don't I?

L: No. Should've gone yesterday. There was a special excursion yesterday. Straight through. Only took 25 minutes, four and eight return.

R: Oh, pity. But I've got to get there today.

L: I think you'll be unlucky, mate. Let's see – Well, you can get there, but you'll have to change.

R: Oh, well, that's all right.

L: Right. Which way d'you want to go?

R: What do you mean?

L: Well, you can either change at Locks Bottom, or Opsley.

R: Well, which do you advise?

L: Oh, that's up to you. I'm only here to advise you, not tell you how to get there. I mean, if you change at Locks Bottom, you got to go all round the world to get there. You see, that local bus takes you right through the Gremlies, and back.

R: Oh, well—

L: Whereas, if you go to Opsley, you can wait an hour and a half and pick up the fast Bradbury bus. That doesn't stop at all. It takes a bit longer, but it's quicker.

R: Oh, well – I'd better do that, then.

L: Which?

R: Eh? Oh, er, the fast one. That, er, that second one.

L: Right. Day return?

R: Is it cheaper?

L: 'Course it's not cheaper. You can't have returns cheaper than singles, otherwise nobody would buy singles, would they?

R: No, I mean, is it cheaper than buying two singles?

L: 'Course it is. Otherwise nobody would buy returns, would they? Have some sense, do.

R: Oh, very well. One day return, please.

L: Right, there we are. Seven and fourpence.

R: Thank you.

L: You can't get back tonight, you know.

R: What? Can't get back?

L: No. No connection.

R: But I've just bought a day return!

L: Well, that's your look-out. I asked you which you wanted.

R: Oh, this is ridiculous! What can I do? Is there a train?

L: Train? Oh, well, if you want to mess about with trains, you should have said so. I thought you wanted a bus. Trains is another thing altogether.

R: Look, please, all I'm asking is, IS THERE ONE?!

L: What, a train? 'Course there is. Every ten minutes from Paddington!

CONVERSATIONS 3

(Variety Playhouse)

NURSE: This way, Mr Pettigrew, he's over there, the third bed down.

PETTIGREW: (Lancashire) What, do you mean that big pile of plaster and bandages down there? Blimey, they've made a thorough job of him, haven't they. (Laughs.) Thank you, nurse. (Calling out) Hallo, Bert! I've come to visit you.

BERT: Oh, hallo, Mr Pettigrew. How are you?

PETTIGREW: Oh, not so bad. Don't get up! (Laughs.) Well, well, you're looking very well, what I can see of you! (Laughs.)

BERT: I'm feeling a bit better, thank you, Mr Pettigrew.

PETTIGREW: Here, here, what's all this Mr Pettigrew lark? I'm not your foreman here, you know! Call me Arnold.

BERT: Oh, thank you, Mr Pettigrew.

PETTIGREW: I brought you some grapes, but I ate them on the bus. Saves all those jokes about 'em, doesn't it? I see you haven't collected any autographs on your plaster yet, Bert!

BERT: No, well, it hasn't been on very long.

PETTIGREW: No, well, let me start you off. Now, where shall I sign, on that leg that's hoisted up in the air, or across the top of your head?

BERT: Well, I don't mind really ...

PETTIGREW: Here you are, on the sole of your foot, that'll do. Well now, tell me all about it. How it happened, I mean.

BERT: What, you mean how I fell off the scaffolding?

PETTIGREW: Yes – I was having me tea-break at the time, so I missed it, unfortunately. (Laughs.)

BERT: Well, you know I was working next to the house that the boss bought, don't you?

PETTIGREW: Oh aye, that's where the boss's daughter hangs out, isn't it?

BERT: Yes, well, I happened to look up, and that's what she was doing.

PETTIGREW: What?

BERT: Hanging out.

PETTIGREW: What d'you mean?

BERT: Hanging out of the window. I thought she was falling, and I rushed to help her, and fell off the scaffolding. Turned out she was only cleaning the windows.

PETTIGREW: Ha! I bet you felt a fool, didn't you?

BERT: I didn't feel anything until I came to in here, all done up in plaster.

PETTIGREW: I hear you dropped your lunch-box as you jumped up, and it hit old Charlie right on the head.

BERT: Aye, that's right.

PETTIGREW: How did he feel about that?

BERT: Why don't you ask him? He's in the next bed.

PETTIGREW: (laughing) By gum, it must have been a laugh. How long do they reckon you'll be in here then?

BERT: About six months, I think.

PETTIGREW: Aye, I thought it would be something like that, so I mentioned it to the bosses.

BERT: Oh?

PETTIGREW: Yes – and they agreed with me, to a man.

BERT: What about?

PETTIGREW: Well, they don't want you to feel that you've got to try to hurry back to the job. They told me to tell you that you can take as long as you like to get better.

BERT: Oh really?

PETTIGREW: Yes – you're fired! When do they bring the tea round here?

LAW

(The Frost Report)

A courtroom.

A man (John Cleese) in the dock with a policeman standing at the side of him. The man appears slightly taller than the policeman. The judge on the bench, the counsel for the prosecution and the defence counsel (a lady) are all in evidence.

JUDGE: Arthur James Peterson, you are charged with being too tall in Arkwright Street on the morning of the sixteenth of May of this year. How do you plead?

PETERSON: Not guilty, your honour.

JUDGE: Mr Wigg?

WIGG: *(Prosecutor)* How old are you, Mr Peterson?

PETERSON: Thirty-four.

WIGG: That's a little old to be doing this sort of thing, isn't it? Most people give up that sort of thing when they reach the age of twenty-one. Why do you persist in it?

PETERSON: I don't know what you mean – I've been this height since I was eighteen.

WIGG: Oh. So you've been getting away with it for sixteen years. Have you any previous convictions for this offence, Mr Peterson?

DEFENCE COUNSEL: Objection!

WIGG: Very well, I'll put it another way. Have you ever seen inside a prison?

PETERSON: No.

WIGG: Not even by looking over the wall?

PETERSON: Certainly not.

WIGG: Is it not possible to have entered a prison by walking under the crack in the door?

PETERSON: No.

WIGG: Why not?

PETERSON: I'm too tall.

WIGG: Thank you, Mr Peterson. Call Bernard Botley!

(Bernard Botley enters the witness box.)

WIGG: Now, Mr Botley, tell us what happened in your own words.

BOTLEY: I was walking along Arkwright Street on the sixteenth of May when I saw a man being much too tall outside the tobacconists. I went up to him and asked him what he meant by it, and he tried to cover it up by kneeling down and pretending to be a pavement artist.

WIGG: And what did you do?

BOTLEY: I put threepence in his cap. Well, he was bigger than me.

WIGG: Thank you, Mr Botley. That is the case for the prosecution.

JUDGE: I wish to discuss a point of law with 'Prosecution', so there will therefore be a ten-minute recess. The accused will remain where he is.

PETERSON: Excuse me, your honour.

JUDGE: Well?

PETERSON: I wonder if I might sit down. I feel rather faint.

JUDGE: But I ordered a chair to be brought to you earlier on!

PETERSON: I know.

JUDGE: Well, what have you done with it?

PETERSON: I'm standing on it.

JUDGE: Case dismissed!

AN UNDERTAKER'S PARLOUR

(Frost on Sunday)

A man enters, looks around and sees a sign on the desk which says 'Ring for service'. A bell-push is next to it. He presses it. A loud church bell tolls sepulchrally, three times. The lid of a coffin, which appears to be propped against a wall, creaks open, and a man steps out. He is dressed in black, but with a frilly shirt, a little gay.

UNDERTAKER: Can I help you?

CUSTOMER: (recovering from the shock) Er – yes, I, er, want to buy a coffin.

U: Certainly, sir. (Starts to measure him.) Hmm, I should think you're about a forty-four medium …

C: Oh, it's not for me, it's for my mother-in-law.

U: Oh, I see.

C: I'm choosing one for her.

U: Ah.

C: She's unable to come and choose one herself.

U: I know how it is.

C: She hasn't the time.

U: Not any more, no.

C: She's flat out at the moment.

U: She would be.

C: No, flat out at the office.

U: Well, never mind, we can arrange transport.

C: Transport?

U: For the deceased.

C: (realising) Oh – no, no, she's not dead!

U: Er, look, sir, shall we start again? Can I help you?

C: Yes. My mother-in-law has decided to buy herself a coffin now; she's not dead – she just wants to buy it now.

U: Oh, I see. Oh, yes, sir, that's quite usual these days. Oh well, that makes the whole thing much more cheery, doesn't it?

C: Yes.

U: Makes a change, I must say. I get so bored having to go round with a long face all day. It's nice to have a bit of a laugh now and again, isn't it? Cigarette?

(*Offers the customer a tiny coffin, lifting the lid ... It is a musical box full of cigarettes.*)

C: No, thanks. Bad for the health.

U: Good for trade though. However, now then. First of all, size. What is she, is she a big woman? About my size or smaller?

C: Yes, about your size.

U: Right. I wonder if she'd squeeze into a 14? This one's a 14. Of course, they are cut on the roomy side. I should think she'd manage a 14. Only this one's reduced, it's in the sale, that one. (Looks at ticket on coffin.) You see, that's knocked down to £28 13s 6d.

C: Well ...

U: Or there's this one. (Indicates another.) Of course, it's a question of length. How long would she need the coffin? Apart from forever? (He giggles at his joke.) No, how tall is she, d'you think?

C: Oh, about your height, I should think.

U: No, that would be a bit short on her, that one. We could let a bit into that one, I suppose. Mind you, that's a bit pricey, that one. Made of deal, you see. And as we say in the trade, 'A good deal costs a good deal.' Mind you, it'll last a lifetime. Here (going to another coffin), here's a joke. Special line. (He gets into the coffin and lies down.) This one is specially designed for if you want to be buried at sea. (He sits up, takes two oars from inside the coffin, and pretends to row.) All right, isn't it?

C: (ferreting about among other coffins) What about this one? This is only eleven guineas.

U: What, that one? Oh no, sir, shoddy. Cheap line, made in Japan. No, horrible. I wouldn't be seen dead in it.

C: Well, I'm afraid they all seem a bit expensive – she said something about five pounds.

U: Five pounds? Oh, well now … Here, tell you what, how about having her cremated? (Picks up urn.) Here you are, four, nineteen, six. All one size, fit anybody.

C: Ah, that might be the thing – is it watertight?

U: Why, is she planning to drink herself to death?

C: No. Er – look, the fact is, I'd better tell you. My mother-in-law wants a coffin because she's opening a restaurant and she wants a coffin as a window-box. It's a sort of gimmick.

U: Gimmick?

C: Yes, she wants to grow geraniums in it.

U: Geraniums?

C: Yes. But I think they're more expensive than she thought, so I – er, think I'd better leave it. Thank you.

(He goes.)

(A young man comes in from the back of the shop, with two plates of salad and two glasses, knives and forks.)

YOUNG MAN: Customer?

U: No. Fellow wanted a coffin for a window-box. (Gets a tablecloth from inside a horizontal coffin and lays it on top of the coffin. The young man puts the salads, etc., on it.) Wanted to grow geraniums in it. Geraniums! Not even lilies. Honestly, Cyril, some people have no respect!

(He lifts the lid of a burial urn, takes out a half-empty bottle of wine and pours it into the glasses while Cyril begins to eat.)

A GREENGROCER'S SHOP

'B' is just finishing serving a woman, tipping Brussels sprouts into her shopping bag. 'A' enters, and approaches 'B'.

A: 2lbs of King Edwards, please.

B: Right guv. (He weighs them out.) Lovely, these are.

A: Yes, they look excellent. Could I have them gift-wrapped, please.

B: Eh?

A: They're a present for someone.

B: Oh, oh, er—

A: You know – bit of coloured paper, nice fancy box, something of that sort. Makes all the difference, doesn't it?

B: Oh, it does, guv, yeah. I don't know what I've got …

A: Well, leave it for the moment, there's some more things I want. Er – have you got anything suitable for an old aunt?

B: Er – well—

A: Sits on her own a lot and doesn't do much?

B: How about some prunes?

A: No. I don't think so. Hardly the sort of thing one gives as a present, is it? A prune. No – I know. A cabbage. That's always acceptable, a nice big cabbage.

B: Right – how's that one?

(Shows him cabbage.)

A: Fine, she'll like that. Now then, Mummy.

B: Mummy? Your mummy?

A: Yes. She's so difficult. She's got everything. Absolutely everything.

B: Tomatoes?

A: No, I gave her those last year.

B: Oh.

A: She's still got some left.

B: I've got it. What about a nice avocado? Perhaps a pair?

A: An avocado is a pear.

B: No, I mean two avocado pears set in straw, side by side. Sort of presentation case.

A: It's not a bad idea.

B: (showing him) Look at those. They'd do anybody's mother proud, they would.

A: (looking at them) You haven't got any white ones, have you?

B: White ones? You don't get white ones, not with avocados.

A: Oh, you see, she lives in Cheltenham. I don't know what the neighbours might think if they found out she'd got a couple of black avocados in the house.

B: They're green – dark green, these.

A: Yes, I suppose they are. All right. I'll take them – it's about time she learned to be a bit more broad-minded, anyway. Now then, Uncle Willy.

B: Ah. What's he like?

A: Well, he's a very heavy smoker.

B: What about a few artichokes? That would be a laugh.

A: (laughing) Yes, it would, that's marvellous.

B: Hearty Choke. Heavy smoker. You see? Arti-choke! (He coughs and splutters.) Choke! Hearty ... how about a marrow?

A: Yes, all right. Now, do you send vegetables by wire?

B: No.

A: No Interveg, or Cauliflora, or anything like that?

B: No.

A: Only I've got these relatives in Australia and they miss their spring greens at Christmas.

B: Don't they get spring greens in Australia?

A: Only in the summer, you see. That's the way it works out. Well, never mind. Have all these items sent round to this address, would you. (Gives him a card.) Nice to get one's Christmas shopping done all in one go, isn't it?

B: Yes, isn't it?

(A goes, and immediately returns.)

A: I am silly, bought all those things and I haven't got myself anything for lunch today. How much are the chrysanthemums?

BORED MEETING

(Frost on Sunday)

Four old men at a board meeting. They all look alike. One – Mr Green – is asleep.

RB: Now gentlemen, we have called this meeting because the shareholders are worried the company is not paying enough attention to improving and modernising the production lines. Southern Safety Pins Ltd is a well-established firm, and sales are steady. However, there is room for improvement and we have to discuss ways of increasing the shareholders' dividends – not to put too fine a point on it.

RC: But surely, Hopkins, if we don't put too fine a point on it the safety pin won't do up. And that's your export trade up the spout. That would be fatal.

JONES: How about making the spout more rounded? I'm sure that by and large people prefer a rounded spout.

RB: Well, large people would, certainly. I should have thought it was a question of individual taste.

RC: I disagree. It doesn't matter what things taste like, as long as it says 'Delicious, mouth-watering and fresh' on the packet. Mark my words.

JONES: That's not a bad idea. Mark the words in red on every tin. They'll sell like hot cakes.

RC: Perhaps we could install ovens in the supermarkets to keep the cakes hot. That would put us streets ahead of our competitors.

RB: Well, I suppose street-trading is certainly something to be considered. Although our conditions of licence would probably put the tin hat on that.

RC: Hardly likely to increase trade, I would have thought. I mean if I saw a man standing by an oven in the street with a tin hat on, I'd think it was a little queer.

RB: Well, they could wear a little notice saying 'I am not a little queer.' And they could push things through letter-boxes, which would appeal to the housewife.

RC: Yes, letter-boxes are certainly worth looking into. Perhaps as an experiment, we could try it out in certain key places.

JONES: Well, the best key place I know is under the mat, by the back door.

RB: True. You know, these keys could open up all sorts of possibilities with the house-owners.

RC: And if we did get the owners to open up their houses, the public could be admitted at a nominal fee – and we'd beat our competitors on their own ground.

RB: I think it will work – and not only on our own ground, but when we are playing away as well. Of course, we need someone to really get the team up to scratch. The question is, who's best?

RC: He's a footballer. Georgie Best.

RB: Then he's the very man! Appoint him to the board, and get the public to open their houses.

RC: Do you think we can do this? Get the public's houses open?

RB: What's the time?

RC: Ten to twelve.

RB: Is it? Oh yes, they must be open by now. Come on, I'll buy you one. (They all get up and wake Mr Green.) Come on, Green, the pubs are open.

RC: We're going to vote Georgie Best on to the board. (Mr Green gets up.)

JONES: Well, that's that then.

RC: Yes – nice to feel you've got something done, isn't it?

RB: Quite. All you have to do is get round a table and talk about it.

(They go out to the pub.)

DOCTOR'S ORDERS

A bedroom. A girl in bed. A doctor enters.

DOCTOR: Well, now, your mistress tells me you're not feeling well, Sarah. What seems to be the matter?

SARAH: Doctor – I'm not really ill.

DOCTOR: But Lady Frampton phoned me and said, 'My maid is ill – come at once.'

SARAH: I'm all right. She owes me six weeks' wages and I'm not getting out of bed until she pays me.

DOCTOR: She owes me for the last eight visits I've made ... Move over.

(He gets into bed beside her.)

COCKNEY WOMAN

COCKNEY WOMAN: I'm leaving you – do you hear? I can't stand your criticising any more. 'I'm thoughtless, I'm forgetful, I don't take any notice of you, I'm not interested in you' – well, if that's what you think, I'm off. All I've ever thought about is you. I've devoted the best years of my life to you. But if you think I'm going to stay here and be told I'm thoughtless and forgetful and disinterested, then you've got another think coming, Bert Thompson!

COCKNEY MAN: Tomkins! TOMKINS!

MAGIC RING

MAN: (holding ring) Magic Ring, O Magic Ring, grant me, grant me, just one thing. Make my wife twice as pretty, twice as smart, twice as intelligent, and twice as sexy as she is now!

(Enter ugly, untidy, stupid, frigid woman.)

WOMAN: Oi! Yer dinner's ready when yer want it.

MAN: My God! It works!

(He rushes to her and clasps her to him.)

AA

(Frost on Sunday)

A rather plain, dingy office, RB on the phone.

RB: Hello. Alcoholics Unanimous. No, well, it's similar, madam, we are a new group unanimously dedicated to removing the menace of alcohol. Well, there are two differences – one, we are a local group, so we know the trouble spots ... places like the Women's Institute meeting, and the back of the Scout hut; and two, it'll cost you three quid to belong, payable to me, George Jones. (A tall girl enters and leans over him to put typing into the 'in' tray.) That's to cover my expenses. I've got some pretty hefty overheads. No, no appointment, just turn up, and I'll help you to stamp out drink. What do you do for a living? Oh, grape treader – well, you've got a good start. See you later – bye.

GIRL: (She lisps.) There's a gentleman to see you, sir – he wants to join. He's outside.

RB: Is he sober?

GIRL: Seems to be.

RB: Well, show him in. And Miss Pringle, you'll have to do something about your breath.

GIRL: My breath, Mr Joneth? What's the matter with them?

RB: No, your breath. It smells of peppermints. When you work for Alcoholics Unanimous and smell like that, people will think you've got something to hide. Try a few spring onions, will you?

(She exits. A knock. RC peeps round the door.)

RC: Is this the AA?

RB: Well, something very similar – come in, sit down. You wish to join us, sir?

RC: Yes.

RB: That will be three pounds, sir.

RC: Oh, thank you – I had a job finding you, actually, up all those stairs. Not very well signposted, this office, is it? (Gives him the money.)

RB: We make it a rule to keep the whole thing as discreet as possible, sir.

RC: Quite right. Quite right. Otherwise you'd have everybody becoming a member, wouldn't you. Better to keep it a bit select. Now, I've brought my provisional licence, my birth certificate ...

RB: Oh, don't get me wrong. We're not choosy. Any drunk who comes in off the street can join.

RC: Oh, really?

RB: Oh yes, that's part of our policy.

RC: Ah. Well, I haven't read your policy, actually, but there are one or two points you could enlighten me over. Now say, for instance, I get stranded somewhere in the middle of the night – do you come out and collect me?

RB: Well, if you phone us, we can talk to you and offer you advice, sir.

RC: But you don't actually send someone to take me in tow and get me back home?

RB: No, we haven't the staff, there's only me and Miss Pringle, but we can provide comfort and consolation.

RC: Oh – nothing more than that?

RB: Well, Miss Pringle has been known to provide a little more than that on occasion, but that's an optional extra between you and her. But we'd certainly get you back on the right road.

RC: Oh, talking of the right road – do I get a handbook?

RB: You wouldn't need a handbook with Miss Pringle, she knows where everything is, sir.

RC: No, I mean one of those with the good hotels in it. Because my wife and I plan to do quite a bit of touring round the hotels, once we've joined.

RB: But surely, sir, an organised tour round the hotels with your wife might be inclined to stimulate the urge.

RC: Well, I think, as a matter of fact, that's what she's hoping.

RB: No, no, the urge to drink.

RC: Oh, I see. Oh, no, I don't agree with drinking and driving. Unfortunately it runs in my family. My auntie drove my uncle to drink.

RB: Did you bring your car tonight, sir?

RC: Yes – d'you want to have a look at it?

RB: No, sir – a car is a car. They're all lethal weapons. Miss Pringle always says – the only place to be in a car is the back seat – when it's parked.

RC: Ah, yes – that's a point. Would I be covered in the back of a parked car?

RB: With Miss Pringle you would, yes, sir.

RC: Miss Pringle seems to be the mainstay of this organisation.

RB: Well, I do the paperwork and she's the field officer, sir. She's better in the field than on the desk, as it were.

RC: But is she able to cope? I mean, if I suddenly got a flat in Acton High Street, what would happen then?

RB: Oh, she's not proud – she'll sleep anywhere.

RC: I'm suddenly not sure I'm doing the right thing ...

RB: Of course, there are lots of other ways we can be of use – for instance, if you suddenly started giving your wife a good hiding, we'd come over and help you.

RC: Oh, it's quite a comprehensive service, isn't it? That comes under damage to a third party, I suppose. Come to think of it, I'd probably need a bit of help – she's a big woman. What about fire and theft?

RB: Well, I suppose if you did start thieving and setting fire to things, we'd see what we could do – tell me, how much do you drink?

RC: Me? I don't drink. Never touch a drop.

RB: You what?

RC: Never a drop.

RB: Then why do you want to join us, sir?

RC: This is the AA, the Automobile Association, isn't it?

RB: No, no. This is Alcoholics Unanimous.

RC: Well, my wife's given me the wrong address. Hang on, she's outside ... (Goes to door.) Elsie! You've given me the wrong address, dear.

(Elsie enters, an enormous woman – very drunk.)

RC: Where did you get this address from, love?

ELSIE: The two new vicars gave it to me, outside the saloon bar of the Eight Feathers.

(She takes a nip from a hip flask.)

RC: (sighing) Look, talk to her, will you? If you can't get anywhere, I'll ring the RAC and get her towed away.

(He exits.)

TALL STORY

(Frost on Sunday)

An employer is sitting at a large desk. Secretary enters.

SEC: Mr Green has arrived, sir. Do you still wish to see him?

BOSS: (looking at watch) He's four hours late. All right, wheel him in.

(Secretary goes, and returns with Mr Green.)

SEC: Mr Green, sir. (She goes.)

BOSS: Sit down, Mr Green. (Green does so.) I wouldn't have thought turning up four hours late for an interview for a job was awfully wise, Mr Green.

GREEN: No, sir – but I've had a most amazing morning. I set out on time, but I'm afraid I ran out of petrol and got a puncture.

BOSS: Both at the same time?

GREEN: I got a puncture in the petrol tank. And I started to walk to the nearest garage, and this little old lady offered me a lift, and I accepted, but we hit a pebble in the road and crashed.

BOSS: Crashed? Into a pebble?

GREEN: Well, we didn't crash, we fell off.

GREEN: Fell off what?

GREEN: Her bicycle. She hit a stone and I fell off. The crossbar.

BOSS: Ladies' bicycles don't have crossbars.

GREEN: No. Well, she was riding a man's bicycle.

BOSS: I see. Go on, Mr Green.

GREEN: Yes. Well, she was rather shaken up, so I called in at the pub to get her a brandy.

BOSS: Ah!

GREEN: And something to keep her warm. And, as luck would have it, there in the pub I saw an old man in a fur coat.

BOSS: A fur coat? In this weather?

GREEN: Quite. I thought it was a fur coat. But it turned out to be a chimpanzee.

BOSS: In the pub.

GREEN: In the pub. So I went back to the old lady with the gin and lime, but when I got outside ...

BOSS: I thought it was a brandy.

GREEN: What?

BOSS: I thought you got her a brandy.

GREEN: Ah, no. I went into the pub to get a brandy but she said she would prefer a gin and lime.

BOSS: Aha.

GREEN: So. When I got outside, she'd gone. So I returned to the pub, whereupon the chimpanzee insisted on buying me a drink.

BOSS: I believe they are quite generous, as a species.

GREEN: Well, of course, I was amazed! I mean this chimpanzee chatted away, and asked me where I was going, and I said I was going for this interview, and he said he'd always wanted to work in advertising.

BOSS: And did he buy you a drink?

GREEN: Well, no. He said he didn't carry money around with him – and do you know why?

BOSS: No pockets.

GREEN: Exactly. And I said, 'It's not often one meets a chimpanzee in a pub like this.'

BOSS: And he said, 'I'm not surprised, with these prices.'

GREEN: And when I left, he followed me and asked me to get him into advertising. And the conductor wouldn't let us on the bus, and so I had to walk all the way here, and that's why I'm late.

BOSS: I see.

GREEN: And all this is absolutely true, I swear it.

BOSS: Ah. Well that's a pity.

GREEN: A pity?

BOSS: A great shame. You see, this organisation is looking for a man with a fertile imagination – and for a moment, when you were telling that story, I thought we'd found him. If the whole thing had been a pack of lies, I would have offered you the job right here and now.

GREEN: Oh, well, I accept your offer.

BOSS: What?

GREEN: I made the whole thing up. Actually I overslept. My alarm didn't go off.

BOSS: I thought as much.

GREEN: Well, do I get the job?

BOSS: Get out.

GREEN: But you said ...

BOSS: Get out, don't waste my time. Two things I insist upon in this company – efficiency and honesty. And I don't think either of those are your strong point, Mr Green.

GREEN: No, please – I was telling the truth – I only said about over-sleeping to get the job – and I really did have a puncture and fell off a ladies' bicycle and ...

BOSS: Out! (He propels him to the door.)

GREEN: (going) It was all true!

(Boss shuts the door, sits down and presses the buzzer.)

BOSS: Next applicant, please.

(A chimpanzee enters.)

LATE DEVELOPER

(Frost on Sunday)

RC and mother: at breakfast. RC is a man of twenty-four, but dressed as a boy of seven.

RC: Mummy, how old am I?

MOTHER: Be quiet, darling, and eat your breakfast.

RC: But I want to know, mummy.

MOTHER: You're seven, darling.

RC: That's what you always say, but I don't think I am. I think you've made a mistake.

MOTHER: Listen, David. I'm twenty-four, and I had you when I was seventeen so you must be seven. Twenty-four take away seven equals seventeen. Aren't you doing takeaways at school yet?

RC: Yes, I'm doing takeaways at school. I'm top of the class in sums. I'm also the only one who shaves.

MOTHER: Well, darling – you're advanced, that's all.

RC: Yes. And so's Miss Perkins.

MOTHER: Your teacher?

RC: She keeps cuddling me.

MOTHER: Cuddling you? Where?

RC: All over.

MOTHER: No, I mean, in front of the whole class?

RC: Oh, no.

MOTHER: Oh, good.

RC: She takes me behind the blackboard.

MOTHER: Oh. Well, you must just tell her you don't like it.

RC: I do like it. I love it. I can't get enough of it.

MOTHER: Really, David – that's not nice.

RC: Yes it is. It's wonderful! I look forward to it.

MOTHER: Now that's enough. Eat your breakfast. And what about those crusts? Come on.

RC: (after a pause) I think I'm about twenty-four.

MOTHER: How can you be twenty-four if I'm twenty-four?

RC: Perhaps you had me when you were nought.

MOTHER: You can't have a baby when you're nought.

RC: Well, perhaps you're older than twenty-four. Perhaps you're forty-four.

MOTHER: (outraged) How dare you! You know very well I'm a member of the 'Under-thirties' Social Club. It's a very exclusive club, and terribly difficult to get into. They wouldn't let me be in it unless I was under thirty.

RC: No, I s'pose they wouldn't. Ah, but just a minute ...

MOTHER: Aren't you going to be late for school, darling?

RC: There isn't any school – it's Saturday.

MOTHER: Oh, good.

RC: It's not good. It's horrible. I was looking forward to a nice cuddle behind the blackboard.

MOTHER: Well, you'll just have to wait till Monday, won't you?

RC: Yes. Monday's pink sweater day. Miss Perkins looks super in her pink sweater. It points straight at you over the desk.

MOTHER: I don't want to hear another word about it, do you hear? Now, Mrs Anstruther will be bringing Johnny round in a minute to play. You'd better get washed.

RC: Why's he coming? (Lighting a cigarette.)

MOTHER: I'm going out. It's my 'Under-thirties' coffee morning – you know that.

RC: He's so babyish. He always wants to play with my rotten old train set and he doesn't even fancy Miss Perkins, and he's nearly eight. (Flicks ash into plate.)

MOTHER: Don't flick your ash on your plate, dear, there's a good boy.

RC: Anyway, he's so little. Every time we play leapfrog, I squash him.

(Doorbell.)

MOTHER: That'll be Johnny – go and let him in, dear.

RC: All right. (He goes out.)

(The phone rings.)

MOTHER: Hello – yes? Speaking. Oh, hello, Mrs Thirkell. What? (Enter RC with Johnny, a boy of eight.)

RC: Johnny's mother says he's got new trousers on.

MOTHER: (covering phone) Go and play, dear. I'm on the phone.

RC: Come on, Johnny, let's go out on our bikes. (Taking Johnny's hand, he leads him out.)

MOTHER: (into phone) Sorry – what? What do you mean? Resign from the club? Why? Oh. Oh, I see. Yes. May I ask who told you? Oh, did she. Very well, I resign. Yes. What? Yes, yes, I don't want to discuss it! (She slams down the phone and bursts into tears. Enter RC.)

RC: Johnny's fallen off his bike and split his trousers. What's the matter?

MOTHER: I've had to resign from the 'Under-thirties Club'. They've found out I'm forty-four. The vicar's wife saw the church records.

RC: Forty-four? But then ...

MOTHER: You are twenty-four.

RC: Twenty-four? Hey! That's old enough to get married, isn't it?

MOTHER: Yes.

RC: Hey! I can marry Miss Perkins, can't I?

MOTHER: Yes. If she'll have you.

RC: Oh, she'll have me all right. Hey, I'm going round to tell her now. (He goes to the door. Mother is sobbing quietly.) Hey, mummy. (Coming back to her.)

MOTHER: Yes, dear?

RC: When you're married, do you still get toys from Father Christmas?

(Mother flings her arms round him, with a fresh flood of tears.)

CRINOLINE SKETCH

(Frost on Sunday)

A girl in a crinoline, in a corner of a Victorian garden. Evening.

J: (off) Mary? Where are you?

M: I'm here, John. In the rose garden.

(J enters.)

J: Mary, my love.

M: John, my own dear one. (He kisses her hand.) What brings you here, on this night above all others?

J: What do you mean, dearest?

M: Much as it pleases me to see you, know you not that it is considered by many bad luck to see the bride on the eve of the wedding?

J: But, dearest, I shall see you tomorrow. All of you. (passionately)

M: John!

J: In all your glory! That milk-white skin, that divine waist ...

M: Are my blushes not to be spared at all?

J: In truth, I cannot contain myself – that dainty ankle – oh, that ankle!

M: (laughing) I have more than one ankle, John dear!

J: You may remember that I have only seen one of your ankles, Mary – and the thought of the other one is driving me mad!

M: I assure you, it is much like the first.

J: But don't you understand – I want to see your ankles together.

M: (teasing him) Always, John?

J: (enflamed) Oh, Mary, Mary. There is one thing I must know. Just now, I walked from the house across the lawn, treading carefully through the daffodils so as not to crush their dainty petals – searching for you. And I wondered – Mary – am I the first?

M: Good heavens, no. The gardeners are up and down there all day. In gumboots.

J: Mary – I mean – am I the first – with you? Am I going to be the first?

M: Oh, John. Dearest! What a question. (Sincerely) Yes, John. You are. And you will be the last. The only one, John. No other man shall ever receive so much as a glance from me, dearest John. I am yours and yours alone. Always.

J: Oh, Mary, my dearest love. (He kisses her hand again.) And now I will leave you to your thoughts. I must away to prepare myself for tomorrow, and our blessed nuptials. Goodnight, my own true love – may you pass the hours peacefully until we meet in church.

(He goes. RC comes out from under the girl's crinoline.)

RC: I thought he'd never go!

(He grabs the girl and they fall, giggling, to the ground.)

SINISTER PARTY

(Frost on Sunday)

A party. Seven or eight people stand drinking and chatting quietly. 'A' is standing on his own, looking a little lost. 'B' approaches him.

B: Good evening.

A: Oh, good evening.

B: Enjoying yourself?

A: Yes, thanks. (Pause.) My girl is powdering her nose.

B: Nice people, aren't they?

A: Girls? Oh yes, I like girls, I've always ...

B: No, these people here. Nice people, aren't they?

A: Oh yes, very.

B: Don't let 'em fool you.

A: What?

B: Don't let 'em fool you. They're all crooks.

A: What?

B: International crooks. Murderers and thieves, all of 'em.

A: I don't believe you.

B: See that fellow over there? (Indicating a bishop.) Light-fingered Leonard. One of the world's cleverest silver-thieves. Always dresses as a bishop – hides the loot in those baggy trousers. If you kicked him in the seat of the pants he'd sound like Lyons Corner House.

A: Nonsense. He's a bishop.

B: Try it, go on –

A: Certainly not.

B: See that woman over there? (Indicating thirty-five-year-old, elegant female in cocktail dress.) Muriel Manderson – international drug trafficker.

A: She looks perfectly respectable to me.

B: She's hooked on the stuff herself, you know. If you were to lift up her skirt you'd see her thighs are covered in needle marks.

A: How ever could you know that?

B: I used to clean windows at the Cairo Hilton.

A: The where?

B: The Hilton, Cairo. Yes, covered in needle marks, her thighs are. Tell you what, if you pull her skirt up I'll kick the bishop in the trousers, all right?

A: Look, this is all nonsense.

B: It's not, my friend, it's not nonsense, I can assure you. Look over there. (Indicating rather burly businessman.) Itchy Luke. See that bulge in his pocket? That's his blackjack. He'd hit you over the head with that as soon as look at you. Sooner.

A: Good grief!

B: That fellow there. (Another man.) A. J. Slaughter. Murders to order. Enjoys it. The thing that worries me is, what are they all doing here? Tonight?

A: Well, I must be getting along ...

B: Not so fast. I need your help. I've got to get this lot behind bars. My superiors want blood.

A: Your what?

B: My superiors. They want blood.

A: Well, they're bloody well not having mine.

B: (crowding him) Listen! There's a phone on the table there. Dial 999. I'll keep them talking, distract their attention. Remember, I've got this trained on you. (He indicates a bulge in his jacket pocket.)

A: (picking up phone) Hello – Police, please. Hullo, Police? I wish to report a desperate gang of thieves and murderers at number 29 Kensington ...

B: (roaring with laughter suddenly) Ha! I really got you going there, didn't I? You took it all in, didn't you? Marvellous! You ought to have seen your face ...

(He tails off as he sees the woman lift her skirt and take a gun from her stocking. Her thigh is covered in needle marks. The businessman has a cosh in his hand. The other man has a knife. They, and the other guests, all advance on A and B. As the bishop approaches, with a revolver, we hear the rattle of silver in his clothing.)

RAILWAY PLATFORM

(Frost on Sunday)

A country station platform. RC and RB meet. They are dressed as conventional stuffy Englishmen. Each carries a weekend case or holdall.

RC: Hello, Ted.

RB: Hello, Jack.

RC: I didn't see you on the train.

RB: I was at the other end today.

RC: Thought it wouldn't be like you to miss it.

RB: Mm. Never have up to now, Jack. I saw you get on, but I couldn't reach you. Damn non-corridor trains.

RC: Cold this evening, isn't it?

RB: It is. It is cold.

(They both remove their overcoats and put them on the ground beside them.)

RC: How long have we got to wait for the connection?

RB: Ten minutes, if it's on time. Try and get into the carriage near the engine – in the warm. (They are taking off their jackets.) What sort of day did the stock market have?

RC: We were pretty lively today – everything's coming down, you know.

(RC drops his trousers and steps out of them.)

RB: Well, it's inevitable, isn't it?

(RB also removes his trousers.)

RC: People haven't got the money to play with (unbuttoning his shirt), not with the tax system in this country. (Removes his shirt.) They'd have the shirt off your back if they could.

RB: It's criminal. (Removing his shirt.) I've certainly got nothing to spare these days. It's hard enough trying to make ends meet. And the wife's no help, either. (Delving into his bag.) Always spending money on some ridiculous item of clothing. (He brings out of the bag a lady's hat with a veil and puts it on.)

RC: That's just like a woman, isn't it? (He takes out a mini-skirt from his bag and puts it on.) It's my daughter that's ruining me. Never out of the boutiques, spending a fortune. Takes absolutely no notice of me. (Taking out a ladies' sweater and putting it on.) Does exactly as she thinks fit. No one would believe that I was the man of the house. (Taking off his socks.)

RB: (During this has pulled up his light-coloured socks so that they become girls' knee-length ones.) It's the modern generation, Jack. (Takes frilly mini-dress out of his bag.) You can't tell them anything. They just do things for kicks, nowadays. (He steps into the dress and pulls it on.)

RC: We never know where she is at night. (He has rolled his socks into balls.) Worries me to death – there are some very odd people about, you know, Ted. (Tucks his socks under his sweater to make bosoms.)

RB: (getting high-heeled shoes out of his bag.) Quite. Still, I suppose we were considered odd when we were young. (Putting on shoes.)

RC: (also putting on high-heeled shoes.) Yes. We probably seem terribly dull and staid to them, just going about our business in the normal manner, travelling up on the train to work, day in, day out, always the same. I would say our lives must appear pretty colourless. (He reaches into his bag and puts on a wildly colourful, jazzy hat.)

RB: Well, I seem to be about ready. Are you? (Takes handbag out of case.)

RC: Yes, I'm ready. Bit of a nuisance all this, isn't it?

RB: Yes. Still, we live in hopes. Perhaps one day they'll build a gentleman's lavatory on this station.

(They walk round a corner and into a door marked 'Ladies'.)

ASK NO QUESTIONS

(Frost on Sunday)

An office.

JENKINS: Good morning, Mr Braithwaite. Sit down, won't you?

BRAITHWAITE: Thank you.

J: Now, Mr Braithwaite, the labour exchange has sent you round for a job here, and I'd just like you to help me fill in this questionnaire – just a routine thing we do with all prospective employees. Just take down Mr Braithwaite's replies, will you, Miss Legge?

MISS LEGGE: Ready, sir.

J: Now then. Full name?

B: George Pip Pip Pip Braithwaite.

J: Pardon?

J: I see. Address?

B: 41 Whizz-Bang-Crash Gardens, Potted Shrimps, Sussex.

J: Potted Shrimps? Where is that?

B: It's a suburb of Horsham. Just beyond Ponky-Doos, on the Bedstead Road.

MISS LEGGE: Ponky where?

B: Doos. Ponky Doos.

J: Age?

B: Forty.

J: Ah, thank you.

B: Inside leg 31.

MISS LEGGE: I beg your pardon?

B: Not at all. I enjoyed it.

J: Previous experience?

B: 26½.

J: Now, Mr Braithwaite, details of your previous experience.

B: Oh – er – three years in the grunt business – shining up tapioca for use in barrel organs. Left there because of the parrot stuffers. Then I spent a short time going bang for a deaf drummer in the London Symphony Orchestra. Chewed parsley for Rolls Royce for a time, joined the Foreign Office as a bucket-balancer, and finally unscrewed my leg and fell over.

J: Thank you. Oh, one final question. What would you say was your main ambition in life?

B: To form a National Naked Ladies' Choir and travel round the country, bringing music to millions, and enjoyment to the deaf.

J: Right. Well, I think that's all we need at the moment, Mr Braithwaite. We'll be in touch. Thank you so much.

B: Not at all. Good day.

J: Good day.

MISS LEGGE: Good day.

(He exits.)

J: Well, Miss Legge?

MISS LEGGE: Well, I had the feeling that he didn't want the job.

J: Oh dear. Well, who can we get as prime minister?

MARRIAGE BUREAU

(The Corbett Follies)

The waiting room of a marriage bureau. A man is sitting underneath a sign which says 'Why be lonely? The Wedwell marriage bureau will find you a mate.' He is reading a copy of Girls Monthly. *Another man enters. They eye each other. The second man walks to a sign that says 'Love is just around the corner.' He looks round a corner, but appears to see nothing. He turns back and looks around him.*

RC: Er – excuse me.

RB: Yes?

RC: It's over here.

RB: Is it?

RC: No – men over here. This side. Women that side, men this – see, there's the sign. (Points to a sign saying 'guys' and 'dolls' with arrows pointing to either side.)

RB: Oh, sorry. I thought that meant toilets. (He sits next to RC.)

RC: Do you want the toilet?

RB: Who, me? No, I … er, I don't want it.

RC: Oh.

RB: Not at the moment.

RC: No, quite.

RB: Is that all there is to read – Girls Monthly?

RC: Oh, I just pinched this from the other side. The only ones this side are Do It Yourself. If I could do it myself, I wouldn't be here. (They laugh a little at his joke.)

RB: No. You're hoping to find someone too, then?

RC: Yes. Bit embarrassing, isn't it?

RB: It is rather. What sort of thing are you looking for?

RC: Oh, something about thirty-five, attractive, well-built. Interested in music, ballroom dancing and fly fishing.

RB: Reckon you're going to be lucky?

RC: I don't see why not. There must be some girl around with those qualifications somewhere.

RB: Yes. I don't know about the fly fishing.

RC: Ah, no, well that's more of an acquired taste, isn't it? I hope she'll acquire a taste for that in due course. What about you?

RB: Oh, you know, early thirties, petite; fond of gardening, desire to see foreign parts, able to ride tandem, with long, flowing hair.

RC: What colour?

RB: Oh, white, preferably.

RC: White hair?

RB: Oh, I see. I thought you meant skin. No, brunette, definitely. You can't trust blondes. I had a blonde girlfriend once. Dyed.

RC: Oh, I am sorry.

RB: No, no – dyed her hair.

RC: Oh, I see.

RB: It all came out in the finish.

RC: What, just fell out, you mean?

RB: No, no, it came out that her hair was dyed. I found out.

RC: Oh, really. How? (Interested.)

RB: We lived in the same block of flats and I went into her bathroom by mistake once.

RC: (more interested) Yes?

RB: Yeah, and there it was.

RC: What, you mean—

RB: Yeah. Bottle of peroxide.

RC: (losing interest) Oh.

(The door opens. A woman enters and sits opposite them. She is very tall and large, and about forty, with dark hair. Attractive, but rather forbidding in appearance.)

RB: (to RC, lowering his voice) Here, I wonder if she's one.

RC: What?

RB: One of the ones for us?

RC: Ooh – I hope not.

RB: She's more your type than mine.

RC: No, no, not my type.

RB: You did say well-built.

RC: Not that well-built. I mean, she's built like a block of flats, isn't she? I mean, it wouldn't just be a question of getting married, would it? I mean, you'd need planning permission, wouldn't you? Anyway, she's too old.

RB: I should think she's about thirty-five.

RC: What, round the leg? Look at 'em!

RB: Don't you like long legs?

RC: Yes, I like long legs, yes, but they're enormous. I'd have to run to keep up with them.

RB: I wonder if she's any good at fishing.

RC: She ought to be. She's built like a trawler.

RB: She's got a nice face.

RC: Yes, but I'd never see it, would I? I'd always be down here some-where. (He indicates his chest.)

RB: No, you're exaggerating. Here, go and get her to stand up and measure yourself against her.

RC: Oh, she'd like that, wouldn't she? Put her at her ease, that would, wouldn't it?

RB: No, I mean – say you think she's sitting on your hat and see where your head comes up to.

RC: I can't.

RB: Go on, she wouldn't know.

RC: All right then. (He crosses to girl.) Er, excuse me, I think you're sitting on my head. My hat. (The girl smiles, embarrassed, and stands up.) Ah, no. It's funny, it was on my head when I left home. (Puts his hand on top of his head.) It's a cap with a long peak, like that. (He slides his hand across his head indicating long peak at the front and also measuring where he comes to on the girl.) Sticks straight out in front like that. (He finally touches the girl's chest.) Sorry you've been troubled. (He returns to his chair.) There you are. You saw where I came up to, didn't you?

RB: Yes. Very nice.

RC: It's not nice at all. What's nice about it?

RB: Well, it's somewhere to stand under when it's raining.

RC: It's all very well for you.

(The door opens and a tiny, thin, flat-chested girl with glasses enters. About twenty. Brunette with long, straight hair. She sits down next to the large woman.)

RC: Hello, this must be yours.

RB: Eh?

RC: Yes, there you are. Petite, brunette, long, flowing hair.

RB: Oh. No, no. She's only a kid.

RC: That's all right. You'd have a young wife longer.

RB: She'd have to be longer than that. She's about four foot nothing. (The girl is peering at a travel magazine.)

RC: Look what she's reading. She's got a desire to see foreign parts.

RB: She'd be glad to see anything, I should think, the way she's peering through those glasses. Blind as a bat.

RC: Well, you wear glasses.

RB: That's what I mean. Imagine us in the morning. Both looking for each other. Anyway, she's too skinny.

RC: You'd save quite a bit on food. And mini skirts.

RB: She couldn't wear a mini skirt.

RC: Why not?

RB: They're supposed to be nine inches above the knee. She hasn't got nine inches above the knee. And can you imagine her and me on a tandem?

RC: Oh, I don't know – she looks quite athletic.

RB: It's no good being athletic if your feet don't reach the pedals, is it? Anyway, I want someone with a bit of weight to keep the back down going round corners. And where would we do our courting?

RC: How do you mean?

RB: Well, I share a flat with three other blokes. I couldn't take a girl with a figure like that back there – they'd laugh at me.

RC: She's probably got a flat too.

RB: That's what I mean. Two of the flattest I've ever seen. She's like a bean pole. You could grow beans up her.

(The door opens and a gorgeous red-headed girl enters. About twenty-eight to thirty. Beautifully built, about 5'6" tall.)

RB: Ah. Now that's more like it. That's mine.

RC: No, no, that must be mine. Well-built.

RB: No, that's definitely me. Long hair.

RC: You said dark. She's red-haired.

RB: Well, it's dark red.

RC: She's not petite! Anyway, I was here first.

VIKKI: (going to inner door) I'm rather late, I'm afraid. Sorry to have kept you all waiting. I'll be with you in a second.

(She goes into office and closes door.)

RB: Oh, pity.

RC: Yes.

RB: She's on the staff.

RC: Yes, just our luck.

RB: I was already picturing us having dinner together.

RC: I'd got further than that. I was in a taxi, tearing back to her place. And you were nowhere in sight.

(The office door reopens. Vikki emerges.)

VIKKI: Mr Arnold Winterbourne?

RC: Yes?

VIKKI: Your date for tonight is Miss Lesley Johnson. Is Miss Johnson here? (Looking at ladies.)

RB: Er – excuse me.

VIKKI: Yes?

RB: Mr Leslie Johnson.

VIKKI: I beg your pardon?

RB: I'm Mr Leslie Johnson. That's me.

VIKKI: Oh dear, there must have been a mistake …

RC: You mean to say – you're my date?

RB: Well—

VIKKI: I'm awfully sorry—

RC: So he and I have been sitting here wasting our time. You being late has practically ruined our evening.

VIKKI: How do you mean?

RC: I'm supposed to be taking him to the Odeon and we'll have missed half the picture already. (To RB) Come on!

(They exit, chattering.)

THE TWO OF THEM

(Written as audition piece – credited to 'John Cobbold')

Four chairs, placed together, represent a park bench. All props, other than these chairs and the boy's newspaper, are mimed.

On the right-hand end of the bench sits the girl, knitting. The boy enters and the girl looks up and speaks.

SHE: That was a quick walk.

HE: I went by bus.

SHE: You went for a walk on the bus?

HE: I wanted to go through the park to the fountain. It is too far to walk both ways, so I caught a bus there. Perfectly logical.

SHE: Why not walk there, and get the bus back, when your feet are tired?

HE: Because I wanted to be there quickly. At the fountain. Then, by the time my feet got tired, I would be back.

SHE: And here you are. Well now, let's see what is in the picnic bag. (She picks up bag of food and begins to lay things on the bench, one by one.) I've brought some pâté, some of those little tomatoes, some blue cheese and that lovely crusty French bread from the corner shop. How does that look?

HE: What are you talking about?

SHE: What?

HE: What are you talking about? There's nothing there. You're just pretending – there's no food there, you're just miming it.

SHE: I was only playing.

HE: Really, Louise, you're so stupid sometimes. Just get it into your head. We haven't any money. We haven't eaten since yesterday morning. We're living rough. We should never have got married. I know it's my fault, but stupid jokes like that are in very poor taste. It's just a question of taste, of which you seem to have very little.

(She begins to cry, quietly. After a moment or two, he moves up to her.)

HE: Don't cry. (He puts his arm around her.) Louise, don't cry. You're upsetting that policeman. (This makes her giggle through her tears.) I still love you. We'll get something to eat from somewhere. Here, I'll tell you something. When F W Woolworth first arrived in New York, he had one nickel in his pocket. But he invested it very wisely.

SHE: How?

HE: He put it into a phone box, phoned his father and his father sent him half a million dollars.

(He opens his paper and reads, holding it up in front of him. She hits it, making him jump.)

HE: You frightened me to death!

SHE: Let's do something.

HE: Like what?

SHE: Go to Hyde Park and throw bread at the ducks.

HE: Only one thing wrong with that. We haven't any bread.

SHE: All right, we'll throw stones at them.

HE: Not very ladylike.

SHE: It wasn't very ladylike of you to shout at me just now.

HE: I'm not supposed to be ladylike. I'm a man.

SHE: I don't see why that should make a difference. Why is it always women who have to be ladylike? Why can't it be men sometimes?

HE: Anyway, it's impractical to go to Hyde Park for another reason.

SHE: What, may I ask?

HE: We're not in London, we're in Paris.

SHE: Of course we're not. If we were in Paris, we'd be speaking with a French accent.

HE: Not if we were speaking in French. We would sound ordinary. No accent.

SHE: All right, supposing one of us was English, the other French.

HE: Then one would speak (he puts on French accent) like so. Mademoiselle, I have always admired you from a distance ...

SHE: Wrong. One would speak ordinarily, the other would be all (puts on exaggerated English accent) I say, how fraightfulleh ripping, old sport, don't you know.

HE: (cutting in) Not vagrants! Vagrants don't talk like that.

SHE: Oh, phooey.

HE: Phooey? Where are we now, America?

SHE: No. Phooey. I just felt like saying phooey. Phooey, phooey, poo-ey fadooey. I'm tired of being a tramp, anyway. Where did you leave the car?

HE: Marble Arch. (Goes behind his paper again.)

SHE: That's miles. Let's get a cab.

(He makes a noise like a taxi approaching, stopping, ticking over.)

SHE: There's one, stopped at the lights.

(He makes the noise of it starting off again, then driving away.)

SHE: That was very good. Do you often do funny noises?

HE: Morning, noon and night.

SHE: Good job we're not really married.

HE: Yes. Still, it's worked out well, us being together, hasn't it?

SHE: Most of the time, yes. I'm sorry I made you angry.

HE: I wasn't really angry. I'm sorry I made you cry.

SHE: I wasn't really crying. It's been a good, working relationship, yes. But I think the time has come to end it all.

HE: End it all? But why?

SHE: There are others, waiting.

HE: I suppose so. All right, how do we do it?

SHE: Pick up two chairs each, bow to the people, and walk off – come on!

(They do so.)

'NEXT PLEASE'

(Lines from My Grandfather's Forehead)

RB: Well, here we are then. Quite full. There's a seat over there. That's it. Now let's see – one, two three ... (counts quickly) ... eighteen. Give 'em five minutes each, that's an hour and a half. Huh, what a prospect.

Staring at this lot for an hour and a half. Look at 'em. They all look so miserable. I suppose it's the thought of sitting looking at the others for an hour and a half. It's funny, though, none of 'em look ill. You'd think they would do, being as they're at the doctors. You'd think they'd at least try and look ill. They're not, though. None of 'ems making any attempt to look ill. There's a bloke over there actually smiling. He'll have to go. Not one of 'em looks the slightest bit ill – except that chap over there with his head covered in bandages. He looks ill. He looks half dead, he does. I bet he's not smiling underneath that lot. (Whistles through his teeth for a moment or two.) Now then – I'd better learn who's come in since I did, otherwise I shan't know when it's my turn. Three of 'em. There's the woman in the red hat, the woman with the fat legs and the bloke with the pipe. That should be easy to remember. Red hat, fat legs and pipe. Easy. The criminal was last seen wearing a red hat, fat legs and a pipe. Red hat, fat pipe and legs. Red legs, fat hat and pipes. A hat, red fat and pipe legs. Wait a minute, there's another coming in now. How am I going to remember him? He's too ordinary. Absolutely undistinguished. Completely anonymous. He must be the ordinary man in the street. I wish he was in the street, then I wouldn't have to try and remember him. Ah well. Here, there's a man reading a magazine upside down over there. Perhaps he's blind. Yes, either he's blind or he's dead nervous. 'Course he may be Australian. Yes, that's what it is. He's a blind, nervous Australian. It's so quiet in here. Why don't people talk to each other in the doctor's? Dead quiet it is. You could hear a hypodermic needle drop in here. I bet they'd like to talk to each other – they just daren't because it's not done. That woman with the fat legs is bursting to talk. She's absolutely bursting, she is. P'raps that's why she's here. 'Good morning, Doctor. I have come to see you because I think I'm going to burst!' 'Let's have a look at you, madam. Would you mind touching your toes? Thank you. Ah yes, I can see what's the matter with you, yes. Your garters are too tight. All the fat's rushing to your head. Hold still, I'll just cut through your suspenders, that should do it. There. Oops. Sorry! Now what's happened? What? Well, how was I supposed to know your roll-on would shoot up over your head? Just a minute, I'll just cut a couple of eye holes in it so you can see. No, I know that hasn't cured you of being fat, but at least no one knows who you are now. Come and see me in a week and I'll take the stitches out of your gusset.' (Giggles to himself.) What a carry on. I can't wait for her to go in and come out with her corset over her head. Ooh! There goes the flashing light. Next one in.

Good idea, that flashing light. Lights up with the doctor's name. Dr Harvey. Good, that. Here! Dr Harvey? (Chuckles.) Well, that's the biggest laugh of the morning. I'm in the wrong surgery.

SPORTS NIGHT

(Lines from My Grandfather's Forehead)

RB: Well, now the games are about to begin, the players are lining up and it promises to be a most unusual game, this, because, as you may have heard, both teams have promised, actually sworn, there will be no foul play, no roughness of any sort. The game is going to be played purely on skill alone, gently and skilfully, no punching, tripping or kicking the opposing team. Pure football. And that's why they've agreed to a lady referee for this match only. And she's on the pitch now, looking very attractive in tiny shorts and a low-cut jersey. A fine figure of a woman, this Miss Nora Pinks. And she's about to toss the coin to decide which way the team will play – and she tosses the coin – and, ooh dear, it's gone down the front of her jersey. The two captains are just looking to see whether it's heads or tails – and – apparently it's standing on end. Now, they've retrieved it, tossing again now and – yes, Miss Pinks is bending down to pick it up, and it looks like a definite tail. Yes, it's a tail. Now she's about to blow her whistle any minute – she takes a deep breath, and ... *(Sound of whistle.)* And no one kicked off. They were all watching her take a deep breath. Ah, now they've finally kicked off; and we'll now see just how polite they can be to each other – a long ball out to Jones – Jones to Huntley – intercepted very delicately by Hall, Hall right down the field to Blenkinsop, who dribbles daintily round Jerry Taylor, taps it to Wright; all very polite at the moment – they're all moving very gracefully. Wright tripping lightly down the field, and loses the ball to Jones, who flicks it to Taylor, and it's –

(Piano: 'Pas de Quatre' from Ruy Blas (Meyer-Lutz) – comes in under. (RB's commentary is now in time to the tune.)

RB: Taylor to Jones–
Jones back to Wilks –
Tackled by Hall –
Put into touch –
Throw in by Huntley out to Wilks
And Wilks to Billy O'Shea
Blenkinsop intercepts the ball
And taps it lightly out to Wright and
Wright puts the ball across to Hall
But Huntley heads it away
Taps it gently across the line for a corner kick.
Jones pirouettes –
Taking the kick –
Slips in the mud –
Flat on his back –
Huntley comes up and takes the corner.
Wright leaps up in the air,
Misses the ball and knocks Miss Pinks who
Tries to duck and splits her trousers.
Blenkinsop tries to head the ball but
Wilks is right in his way.
He boots it under the crossbar making the score one nil.
(Sound of cheers then two short blasts on whistle. Music continues.)
RB: Miss Pinks waves her arms
High in the air
Down fall her shorts
Up goes a cheer ...

(Piano stops. Sound of long blast on whistle.)

RB: Good gracious – it's all over – it's all over! Miss Pinks, the referee, has called the game off! Well! Well, that's the first time I've known a game abandoned because of good visibility!

Piano: to end.

The (Almost) Silent Comedies

It is surprising that Ronnie Barker, for many the master of the verbal, the linguistic, the perfectly pronounced prose and the master monologue, should also have been sublime when orchestrating the silent, visual joke. Picturing perhaps the Marx Brothers, one imagines either the physical, larger-than-life performer of Harpo and Chico or the snappy, sassy, cynical wordplay of Groucho. In Barker we had the best of both, his visual instinct never so perfectly illustrated as in the two (almost) silent comedies on show here.

From the opening scenes of French maids, monacled old generals and swanee-whistled underwear, both *The Picnic* (1976) and *By The Sea* (1982) have a simple, saucy, seaside postcard feel that is uniquely British. In re-reading the descriptions of dropped ice-creams, mistaken identities, bosoms, beach balls and ballyhoo, one is instantly transported to a world of Ektachrome colours, rosy cheeks and Bamforth picture postcards.

For true *aficionados* it is worth noting that – on first viewing – the BBC took against *By the Sea* and brought in a new producer, Alan J.W. Bell, to recut and even reshoot scenes to salvage the film. It is a credit to Ronnie Barker's sublime writing and masterful depiction of a simple, pre-Fall Eden England of sandcastles, sunhats and sauciness that Bell didn't reshoot a single moment. He simply reordered the scenes and added a jaunty score by the BBC legend Ronnie Hazelhurst. The rest he left to the brilliance of Ronnie Barker's visual instinct and the wonderful cheekiness of the Corbett/Barker performance.

The British Bank Holiday getaway will never be more appealing than this.

THE PICNIC

The Picnic (credited to Gerald Wiley) and *By the Sea* ('by the author of *Futtock's End* and *The Picnic* and concerned with a similar group of characters') were produced in 1976 and 1982 respectively, as spin-offs from *The Two Ronnies*. Featuring Barker and Corbett, with a host of others, they were further opportunities for Ronnie to explore the almost-silent comedy, or as he put it, 'Grumble and grunt' films. 'The *Picnic* was much more exciting to me than either of the other two,' recalls Ronnie, 'because I wanted to capture the feel of that far-off childhood summer. That sort of feeling you remember of slight weirdness … in *The Picnic* you have a sort of Edwardian picture. It's a situation that's unreal to most people and that's what I liked about it. And you had this man who just sort of rode over everyone and behaved how he wanted to and everyone just sort of fitted in. I loved that kind of thing hugely.'

Although unnamed in both films that man was, once again, Lord Rustless.

The English countryside. A sunny morning. England at its prettiest. We hear a cock crow. A shot rings out. The cock croaks, and perishes.

An English country house. A milk float is coming down the drive. It stops, the milkman gets out, with his crate. Close-up on the crate. It contains one bottle of milk and eleven bottles of champagne.

Cut to the doorstep as he exchanges the full bottles for similar empties – one milk, eleven champagne.

Inside the house. A pretty maid in a black uniform walks along a corridor, carrying *The Times* on a silver salver. She passes the butler, who carries breakfast on a tray. As she passes him, she steals a small piece of bacon from his tray with her free hand. He looks disapproving. They pass on. The maid walks to a door, knocks, goes in. She is followed by a stupid-looking retriever dog.

The bedroom. Dominated by a large four-poster-bed, with curtains all round it. They are fully closed.

The maid approaches the curtains. A hand *(belonging to the General)* comes out, takes the newspaper. Then the hand re-emerges, grabs the maid, and drags her head first behind the curtains. The dog looks on, wagging his tail. After a few squeals and guffaws, the maid backs out again, rather dishevelled, and tuts her way out of the room.

The General appears from out of the bed – night-shirt, monocle. He yawns, and exits to an adjoining bathroom. The dog sits down. A loud loo-chain is heard, and a wheezy flushing. The General emerges, drying his hair with a towel. The dog does a double-take *(reverse film!)*.

The breakfast-room door. Silence as the General approaches it. He opens it – cacophony. Loading of plates, high-pitched chatter. He goes in.

We cut to a very crowded picture of the rest of the household. The General's sister, Fern, clutching a large piece of knitting and needles in one hand, trying to fill her plate from the entrée dishes. Clive, the eldest son, has managed to get some bacon on to a plate, and is just about to add an egg when the plate is whipped away by a very old man with a toothless grin. Fern's companion, Edith, a plain girl who doesn't believe in make-up, but who does believe in eating *(although she is thin)*, reaches across and blocks Clive's view of the buffet-table, and manages to drop her pendant into his egg, and a large well-developed 'bird' *(who is obviously on Clive's wanted list by the way he behaves towards her)* nearly pokes his eye out with her sweater as she thrashes about in search of a succulent kidney. A close-up of Clive's desperate face.

At the table, the General sits with a packet of cornflakes and a bottle of champagne. He starts to pour cornflakes into a bowl. A small horrid boy passes behind him. The General greets him affably. The boy pokes out his tongue at him. The General shrugs, takes foil off the top of the champagne.

Cut back to the fight around the sideboard. The bird is much in evidence, wearing an extremely brief and cheeky pair of bright red shorts. A crash of a knife is heard as one is knocked on to the floor. The bird bends to pick it up. The General reacts to this vision, and the cork pops out of the champagne bottle in his hand. He doesn't even notice.

The bird and Clive sit down at the table.

The General pours champagne on his cornflakes and tucks in. The noise around him is still deafening.

Cut to the kitchen. Silence. The butler and the maid are preparing food for the picnic, which is to be the event of the day. They stand primly side by side, cutting and buttering bread. They are surrounded by tomatoes, cucumbers, strawberries and other fruits – and cold meats and pastries.

Cut back to the breakfast – tremendous noise again. Clive and his bird are eating. Peeping out from underneath the table, the stupid-looking dog. Clive's hand comes into shot and feeds it a piece of bacon. Underneath the table, we see the bird's shapely limbs. The dog's tail, wagging with pleasure, is tickling her legs. Above the table, she reacts towards Clive, thinking he is doing it. He smiles back at her, then, putting his finger to his lips and pointing under the table, tries to indicate that he is secretly feeding the dog. She mistakes him completely. Underneath the table again, we see the bird's hand appear, holding a fork. The tail is still tickling her. She jabs Clive's leg hard. Above the table, he leaps up, and shoos the dog away angrily. The bird smiles sweetly at him.

The kitchen. The butler is slicing a large radish into a very fancy shape. Big close-up as he cuts a beautiful pattern in it. The maid looks on. He smiles, pops it on top of a pile of sandwiches. He then picks up a picnic-basket, and exits. The maid takes the radish and puts it into her mouth, crunching it up.

The breakfast-room again. The old lady knitting, reading *The Times* and drinking coffee. On the floor, the dog spies the ball of wool, grabs it, races out of the room. After a few seconds, the knitting is suddenly whisked away from the old lady. She doesn't notice immediately, however, and carries on knitting thin air – then realises.

The corridor. The dog rushes round the corner with the ball of wool in its mouth, followed eventually by the piece of knitting *(which is about eighteen inches square)*. As the dog disappears round the next corner, the butler appears, sees the knitting going along on its own, and steps on it firmly.

Round the corner, the dog is pulled up so sharply that he slithers all over the place on the shiny floor.

Back at the knitting, the butler has his foot firmly planted on it. Round the corner comes the old lady. She stares in disapproval at the butler, who sheepishly hands over the knitting. It has a large black footprint right across it.

Outside the house. An enormous old open-topped *(convertible)* car. The butler is loading things into the boot. The picnic party come streaming out of the house. The General, who carries a shotgun; the old lady, knitting; the small boy, with small bow and arrows; Clive, with tennis racquets and perhaps a butterfly net; the bird, in her plain red shorts and overflowing sweater; the companion, with a black umbrella; and the dog.

The old lady gets in front, and the bird and Clive, with the companion and the boy, in the back. The dog leaps in after them. There is obviously not enough room, but they eventually get settled. The General, who is the last to get in, sticks his shotgun into a piece of rope which is obviously holding the offside back door together *(in fact the companion perhaps had to climb over it to get in)*. He looks round, everyone is ready. He slams the driver's door shut, the shotgun goes off bang, and, in close-up, the offside back tyre collapses. Groans from all, and everyone piles out again as the long-suffering butler removes the spare wheel.

The screen is 'wiped' in the old-fashioned way, and we find the butler just removing the jack, as the others all pile back in to the car. The General waves, and the car pulls away from camera, up the drive. Out to the maid, waving. We go with her as she walks to where the butler is astride an old motorbike. She mounts the pillion, and they too set off for the picnic.

The car is going along, through some pretty countryside. A wide shot – then we follow it as it goes round a hidden bend. It passes a loaded hay-cart, jogging along between the meadows on either side. We see the cart from the front – the old yokel driving it waves as the car overtakes it and goes past camera.

Now we are with the motorbike again. A close shot of the butler and maid, then a static shot, as they zoom away from the camera, round the same hidden bend, out of sight. Three seconds pause, and then a crash.

A close shot of a spinning motorbike wheel in the hedge. A front shot of the yokel getting off his cart. He walks into the motorbike's shot – looks over the hedge. From his point of view we see quite a steep drop down. There, under the bushes, two sets of legs. He runs out of shot. We pick him up as he scrambles down the slope towards the two bodies. He grabs the girl's legs and rolls her over onto her back. It's the wrong girl; she sits up and slaps his face. Her lover, too, sits up and glares. Cut back to the yokel retreating towards the camera by the motorbike on the road. He turns, and stares past camera. A reverse shot. The butler's and the maid's legs are sticking out of the hay at the back of the cart.

The maid's knickers are very much in evidence. She is slightly higher than he is in the pile of hay. The yokel moves forward, and, from another angle, starts to haul the maid out by the feet.

Back at the car. It stops at a pretty country pub, nothing elaborate, and not too pseudo-Tudor, but a real, friendly place, with little tables and rustic arches outside. Everybody gets out of the car, and occupy the chairs and tables. Clive goes inside to get the drinks. There are three yokels playing dominoes at a table. The General takes a photograph of them *(as he raises his camera and clicks, we freeze frame and go to black and white for a couple of seconds)*. The old lady sits down next to them, watching their game and knitting.

The three yokels: one has a cigarette, one a pipe, and one a pint of ale. There are ashtrays at each corner of the table. As they play, each one puts down his pipe, or pint, or cigarette on his left. Having played, they sometimes pick up the wrong object – but they still smoke or drink it, apparently without noticing.

Clive appears with drinks. A pint of Pimms, loaded with mint and fruit, for the General, a sherry for the old lady, lager for himself, and orange juice for the other three. In close-up, hands come in and take all but the sherry. This Clive takes over to old lady. She acknowledges it with a smile. The local on her left drinks it in one, and puts it on the other side of him. The old lady picks up the pipe, which is on her right, and puffs at it.

The General is at another table. He has a wooden penny whistle, and is showing it to the small boy. The boy, however, is not at all interested in the General's tooting. He pokes out his tongue and leaves the shot. The General swigs his Pimms, and continues to toot.

At another table, the bird is with Clive, and the companion girl. The bird excuses herself, leaves the shot. We see the back of the car. She comes from behind camera, opens the boot, finds her vanity-case, and bends over it, rummaging about.

Cut to the small boy, with a pea-shooter. He fires. Cut back to the bird. She is hit fair and square in the shorts. She leaps up, rubs her rear end, and, taking an aerosol from her vanity-case, sprays the surrounding area.

As she bends to return it, however, the horrid boy fires again. Again she leaps up, but this time she looks round suspiciously.

Cut to the General, still holding his penny whistle.

He waves it at her in a friendly fashion. She stalks over to him, and breaks his whistle in half. He is nonplussed. She leaves the shot. The General, not knowing quite what to do, drinks a vase of flowers instead of his Pimms. He fails to notice the difference. He even chews one of the flowers.

The butler and the maid sail by on their motorbike, looking a bit the worse for wear. They disappear up the road, as all the guests once more board the car.

Cut to a very pretty wide shot of a country road. The car goes past camera. Reverse shot as it goes away, entering a tiny village. Inside the car, Clive leans forward and whispers in the General's ear. The General nods. The car pulls up outside a couple of old cottages, with a passageway between. Clive gets out, and walks to the back of the houses, through the passage. The others wait.

At the back of the house, the owner is watering his garden with a hose. Clive speaks to him, and the old man indicates an outside loo at the bottom of the garden. Clive moves smartly to it, and shuts himself in, as the man now concentrates on watering the flowers on the opposite side of his garden.

At the car, the occupants are amazed to see a great jet of water issue from the side of the house, landing on the flowers. The General decides to take a photograph of the phenomenon. *(Freeze frame – black and white.)*

In the back garden again, Clive emerges from the loo, just as the owner turns off his garden tap. Clive thanks him.

From the car, the jet dies down, and Clive appears round the side of the house, smiling uncertainly.

A beautiful meadow, by the river. A romantic wide shot shows us that this is the picnic-ground.

The car pulls in at the five-bar gate, drives across the meadow, and stops very near the river.

In a closer shot, everyone gets out. The butler and the maid rise from where they have been sitting waiting under a tree, and approach the car. The General gives him instructions as to where he wants the picnic; Clive and the bird wander off together across the meadow.

The butler begins to take all sorts of strange things out of the car – including large, ungainly things: a gramophone, ice bucket on a stand, card table, croquet set, deck chairs, screen, etc. Far more than the boot could in reality hold.

Clive and the bird in a field. She is looking for blackberries in a hedgerow. He sits near her, on the grass, his back leaning against an old post. We tilt up, to see that it is a notice-board saying, simply, 'Danger'. He suddenly notices the sign, gets up, looks all round – he can see nothing dangerous. He shrugs his shoulders. The sign falls and hits him on the head.

The butler and the maid are laying a vast tablecloth on the grass. With a croquet mallet he bashes down the bumps in the ground that stick up through the cloth. One of the bumps moves about. It eventually emerges as a hedgehog. *(Or a rabbit – try both.)*

Clive and the bird are walking in a field, away from camera. The bird suddenly turns and looks. A reverse shot of a large bull, glowering. Then, from the bull's point of view *(perhaps over a dummy bull's shoulder)* we see the two of them run in opposite directions. A close shot of the girl's bright red shorts as they run away. A shot of the bull. A close shot of Clive, scrambling over the fence – turning and looking. A wide shot – the girl disappears behind a large tree. A shot of the bull, sauntering *(or trotting)* towards the tree. The girl, in close-up, looks towards Clive. Clive points to her bright red shorts, and then points to his own trousers. Indicates that she should remove them. The bird looks vacant. The bull looks interested. A yokel approaches, on the other side of the field, and looks over the fence. Clive demonstrates again with a mime movement, then in desperation drops his own trousers a little. A woman going by on a bicycle stares. He pulls them up again. The young yokel grins. However, the girl has got the message, and goes behind the tree. In a second or two, the shorts are thrown out. They land in front of the bull. *(The rest of the shot is up to him.)*

Cut to Clive. He looks relieved. Cut to the yokel – he looks astounded. The girl dashes out from behind the tree, wearing G-string briefs. With a yell, the yokel leaps over the fence and gives chase. A wide shot as they whizz across the field. A close-up of the bull staring at them.

Back at the picnic, all is now laid out. The General has built a fire of newspapers and sticks. He has perched a kettle on it. He tries to light the fire, but the matches keep going out: as they do so, he throws them over his shoulder. Now a wider shot, to include, behind him, a box with wood-straw in, which had contained champagne bottles. Close shot of an apparently dead match landing on it. The straw suddenly lights. Back to the wider shot. The General places the kettle on the box instead, with the air of a man who has done a good job.

The others wander over to the tablecloth and sit down around it. The old lady, the companion, the boy, the dog, too. A bizarre picture, with all the strange props around them, as the butler and the maid begin to serve the sandwiches, etc.

Further down the riverbank, a fisherman is fishing. Clive and the bird walk past him, towards camera. She is now wearing round her waist part of a yellow plastic bag – the sort that has farm fertiliser in. It crackles very loudly as she walks. The fisherman reacts, and 'shushes' her, glaring his disapproval.

The picnic. The butler hands the boy a kipper on a plate. The boy waits until no one is looking, then slings it into the river. Close shot as it lands, and floats.

Clive and the bird arrive back. She sits down amidst tremendous crackling. Clive explains to the General. The General looks interested.

The fisherman. He suddenly realises that he has got a bite. He reels in; on the hook is the kipper. He reacts.

The General takes a hard-boiled egg from a basket of about seven or eight. He bangs it against a plate to crack the shell. It cracks the plate. He stares, and puts it back *(close shot)*. In the same shot, another hand comes in and takes the same egg. It is the old lady. She bangs it on a plate. The plate cracks. She puts the egg back.

Clive is feeding the dog, taking bits of meat out of the sandwiches, and throwing the bread away over his shoulder. The butler looks disapproving. He stands behind Clive, picks up the bread, exchanges it for bread round another piece of meat. He gives it to the maid to offer it to Clive again. When the maid has gone, the butler eats the unsoiled pieces of bread. We see Clive do the same thing again, and the maid again picks up the same old pieces of bread, and takes them back to the butler. This time distracted by the bird *(we see a shot of her in her rather revealing fertiliser bag)* he puts the new bread inside the old bread, and eats the meat himself. The maid enters Clive's shot, but this time he shoos the dog away, and eats the bread sandwich. He takes a hard-boiled egg, bangs it on the plate. The plate cracks. He puts back the egg. The General witnesses this, takes a felt-tip pen from his pocket, picks up the egg and makes a large asterisk on the egg, followed by a full stop. The full stop pierces the egg; it bursts. It is uncooked.

A pretty shot of the dog chasing butterflies – and, then, once again, we see the fisherman. He has tied a line to his toe *(he wears open-toed sandals)* which is attached to his rod, at present reposing in a cleft stick. He lies back and prepares to snooze. Cut to a motor launch – it surges by with a great noise. Cut to fisherman, close – he is dragged out of shot. A wide shot as he is pulled feet first into the water with a great splash.

The old lady is pouring tea. She pours some for the General, who unnoticed by the old lady throws it over his shoulder and fills his cup from a hip-flask. She then puts sugar into the General's cup, and offers him milk. He declines, reaches out of shot, gets a soda siphon, and squirts soda into his cup. The old lady looks surprised. The General deposits the soda siphon by his feet, but it falls over.

Clive and his bird are hitting a tennis ball to each other. She reaches up to return a high ball, and her plastic bag slides down to her knees. The old lady looks embarrassed. So does Clive. The General stares. He is holding a bottle of champagne. The cork pops out on its own. He hands it to the companion, who gets rather wet. The bird goes to pull up the bag again. The General takes a photograph. *(Freeze frame – black and white.)*

The companion is handed a meringue on a plate by the butler. In a wide shot, we see the General and the others interested in the game. Close-up of the General's foot and the soda siphon. The General kicks it – it squirts at the meringue which shoots off its plate. It bounces off on to the grass in another close shot.

Clive misses a ball, it bounces away in the direction of the tea table. Clive runs towards the group, looks around, spots the meringue. A close shot as he picks it up from the grass. Wider as he serves it, and it bursts into smithereens. Close-up of him, covered in bits – more floating down on him.

Now a very wide shot of the whole scene. The picnickers are wandering away towards the further reaches of the river. In the foreground, the maid and the butler are tidying up, but have hardly started. The butler says something to the maid, who nods, resignedly. The butler walks off to some bushes beside the river.

Cut to the group *(minus the small boy)* walking towards camera – enjoying the walk, and chattering to each other.

Cut to the fisherman, soaking wet, but determined to fish. He stands up, and prepares to cast.

Cut to the butler in the bushes. He faces camera, bushes at chest height – and also bushes behind him. He is obviously about to relieve himself.

Cut to the small boy. He is in another bush, with a bow, and arrows with rubber suckers. From his point of view he can see the butler. Then from another angle we can see the fisherman, who is now seen to be just the other side of the bushes from the butler. The fisherman casts his line. Cut to the butler. His expression changes as his toupee is whipped off his head by the fishing line. He clasps his bald head, amazed. Cut to the small boy; he shoots an arrow. We hear a plop.

Cut to the butler. He has an arrow stuck to his head.

A close-up of the maid, tidying up. She looks up; suddenly her face changes, she looks horrified.

We cut to her point of view. A herd of black cows is approaching the picnic area. Alone, she panics, rushes to the car, and starts to pull up the hood. Another shot of the cows, getting nearer.

A wide shot of the butler chasing the boy. Suddenly, they both stop. A quick close-up of each as they stare.

Cut to the picnic area. Cows everywhere. Eating, trampling – various shots of the destruction. The maid's face peers, terrified, through the car window. A wide shot of everyone hurrying towards the picnic area. They shoo the cows away. A close-up of some reeds, near the river. Pan up. The fisherman is preparing to go home. He stares at, first the kipper, and then the toupee. His catch for the day. Disgruntled, he throws them back into the river, and walks dejectedly away.

Cut back to the picnic. The cows have gone – everything is packed away – the boot of the car is still open, although the passengers are all settled into their seats. The butler is picking up the last of the paper serviettes, bags, etc., and putting them into a larger dustbin-liner bag, which is already very full. He looks round – everything is tidy again. He puts the sack in the boot, slams it shut. He gets on to his motor-bike, the maid mounts pillion, and off they go.

The General gets into the driving seat, and slams the door. The boot immediately springs open, in a close shot. Then, in wide shot, the car pulls away, and the rubbish is distributed all across the field as the car bumps its way out of the gate and heads towards home.

It is evening. The sun is setting on a beautiful day. A shot of the countryside – the car goes through frame.

They pass the pub. The three yokels still sit there. The picnickers wave – no response. We go closer and see that the yokels are all asleep.

The house. The car approaches down the drive and pulls up. It is twilight. Clive and his bird move towards the house, she still crackling in her fertiliser skirt. From the front we see Clive, in a two-shot, make a jocular remark, and put his hand behind her. We hear a swift 'crackle-crackle' as her skirt betrays what his hand is doing. She reacts as if to admonish him, but then changes her mind, runs the tip of one finger through his hair, and smiles. They go into the house; he is looking very hopeful.

The General and the old lady totter towards the house. The maid passes them, the General stops her and whispers in her ear, points upwards, and makes drinking movements. She nods, and goes on in. The small boy and the dog also overtake them. Finally a shot of the butler, loaded with baskets, etc., from the boot, enters the house, with a long-suffering expression.

Outside the General's room. The maid is about to enter, with a large brandy on a tray. The butler approaches, with an armful of dirty tablecloths from the picnic. He gives them to the maid, takes the tray and enters the room.

Inside the room. The General's hand comes out from the four-poster curtains, takes the brandy, and withdraws. A second later, the hand returns the empty glass. It then grabs the butler by the wrist and drags him inside. A scuffle, a shout, a crash of the tray, and the butler emerges: and the General's face, apologetic.

The outside of the house, a moonlit night. The lights go out one by one. An owl hoots somewhere in the middle distance. A shot rings out. The owl gives a screech, and a flutter of feathers. Silence. The last light in the house goes out.

BY THE SEA

A Film without Dialogue

By the author of *Futtock's End* and *The Picnic*.

And concerned with a similar group of characters. May, 1981.

1: A view of an empty English beach – early morning.

2: Now a view of the promenade, with tall houses at the back.

3: Then a shot looking down the long, straight street. A milk float: a milkman delivering in the street. A boy, walking, delivering newspapers. He whistles. A postman, on a bicycle, delivering letters.

4: A shopkeeper, pulling down an awning, opening up. He puts goods outside, fruit, etc. We hear the cries of seagulls.

5: A handyman arrives at the gate of a house. He goes up a long path, to where a grim-faced woman is scrubbing a step. She warns him not to tread on the clean step. She gives him some letters to fix on to the gate – they are resting on a piece of cardboard, and are arranged to say 'Mon Repos'.

Woman shuts the door, and handyman goes back to the gate, trips over a geranium pot, spilling dirt on to the path. He also spills the letters. He picks them up and tries to rearrange them. They say 'Prom Nose'. He looks puzzled. The milkman passes him, walks through the dirt from the geraniums, and leaves his muddy footprints on the step. As he goes, the woman comes out – stares at the step, annoyed. The man at the gate has rearranged the letters. They now say 'Ponse Mor'.

The woman is cleaning her step again. The postman now goes in, steps in the dirt, and delivers letters. The woman comes out, and is furious. She gets her bucket again.

The paperboy approaches the handyman: he stops and looks, and helps to rearrange the letters. They now say 'Poor Mens'. The boy goes up the path. The woman has just finished the step. She shuts the door.

The boy delivers a paper and goes, and she opens the door immediately. She fumes. Her face is hideous with anger.

6: Another shop, in a row of shops a sign being put outside, on a stand-up sandwich board. It says 'Ladies high fashion, upstairs'.

A scruffy-looking cleaning lady is putting it out.

Next door, a butcher's shop. He puts out a similar sign. It says 'Fat spring lamb – try one.'

The two signs, close together, read 'Fat ladies spring high, lamb-fashion. Try one upstairs.'

7: A man stops, reads the sign, and looks up at the upstairs window.

Traffic in the high street is beginning to build up.

At the traffic lights, a lorry has stopped. A motorcyclist arrives on its right.

The lorry driver, staring across at the two signs outside the shop, stubs out his cigarette on the crash helmet of the motorcyclist, and drives off.

8: A vicar, selling flags from door to door, approaches the handyman. He stares at the lettering the man has nailed on to the gate. It reads 'Some porn'.

The vicar shakes his head – no, no, no. He walks up the path, through the dirt, knocks at the door and gets the bucket of water full in the face.

The door is again shut.

9: The railway station forecourt. The noise of trains.

RB appears at the entrance, puts his hand to his mouth and calls 'porter', but we hear the two-tone hooter of a diesel train. The porter comes over, happy that RB only has one bag. But round the corner come the rest of the family – RC, the girl, the aunt, the boy, the companion, and the little tiny frenetic dog. They all have enormous cases, golf umbrellas, etc. The porter loads them all on to a trolley. RB indicates to the porter that a car has been ordered for them – a big one. Ah, here it comes now. It is a hearse. They all bundle into the car – the little dog leaps all over everybody, licking their faces, etc. The luggage goes into the boot. The car drives off, leaving one suitcase revealed on the pavement. The car reverses: after a moment, it drives off again. The suitcase has now gone, but the dog is left on the pavement. The dog runs after the disappearing car, yapping at it.

10: The hotel. The car arrives at the front entrance, near the revolving door. RC is carrying a lot of luggage, and gets jammed into one section – the rest of the family go in after him – he keeps going round, stuck. RB is the last to go in, but just before he does, the redhead comes out, in a bikini, and beach bag. RB goes right round, and hurtles out again staring after her. RC whizzes round and round. RB stops the door with a jerk – (RC, inside) – a crash of luggage. The little dog trots up (having run from the station). RB is about to re-enter. He sees a sign on door – 'No dogs'. RB picks up the little dog, puts him into a string bag he is carrying, covers it with a towel and goes into the hotel.

11: A bedroom door. A notice, roughly written, hung on the door. 'Caution – electrical re-wiring in progress.' A pathetic maid points this sign out to RB. They enter.

12: Workman's tool-bag, and wire, etc., on the floor. RB looks round at the room, nods, looks at the bed, tests it with his hands, then flops back on it, bounces up and down. Pathetic maid watches him. RB bounces some more, indicates that the maid should bounce too. She shakes her head. He bounces some more. An electrician sticks his head out from under the bed, glaring. RB reacts.

13: Another bedroom. RC and a young porter. RC tips him, looks around, sees a pretty view of the sea through the window – he indicates it with a wave of the hand. 'Very nice.' The porter leaves. RC puts his suitcase on the bed. The pretty view drives away – it is painted on the side of a truck. It reveals a brick wall.

14: Another bedroom. The companion has just changed into a sweater. She adjusts it, then scratches uncomfortably.

She starts to unpack from the open suitcase, still scratching. She picks up a pack of biscuits – they have burst, scattering crumbs on everything in the case. She keeps scratching. She continues to scratch for the rest of the holiday.

15: A wide corridor. RC walking towards camera. The aunt comes out of a door, and just beats him into the toilet. Above the door, a large sign lights up 'Engaged'. He stands – looks round, and straightens a picture on the wall. RC sits on a chair opposite the door – the chair is spindly and small. One of the arms of the chair comes off in RC's hand. He tries to put it back; it falls off. He looks round – then breaks the other arm off to make it look like an ordinary upright chair. He puts them both inside a huge grandfather clock. It strikes, frightening him. He goes back and sits on the chair; it folds flat like a hinge, depositing RC on the floor. He gets up, bends it straight again, stands it carefully against the wall, and sits on the small coffee table next to it, which is sturdier. He looks at the sign; it now says 'Finished'. He reacts, then looks again. It says 'Standing up'; he reacts. Now it says 'Washing hands'. We hear the tap running. He stares. It says 'Flushing'; he reacts as the chain is pulled. It says 'Leaving', and out comes the aunt – gives him a stare, and leaves the shot.

16: RB's bedroom door. RB comes out, leaving door ajar. The string bag comes trotting out. Companion, approaching, sees it, picks it up, and goes off with it.

17: RB approaching the toilet door. A gong is heard; close-up on the toilet door. It says 'Lunch'. RB sees it, reacts.

18: The front of the hotel. The party are leaving for the beach, carrying all the various things they will need for the day. The aunt has lots of carrier bags, etc., about her person – the companion carries the string bag with the dog in.

19: They walk along the street and pass the handyman with his letters on the gate. He has just nailed up 'Po Sermon'. RB looks at it – points to it, and laughs. The handyman looks daggers, as RB demonstrates what it is to the others (a dog collar and a chamber pot, in mime). As they move off, he starts to take the letters off with a claw hammer.

20: The beach. Some pretty establishing shots, evocative, golden summer-day scenes.

21: Our party troop down on to the sand and sets up camp near the promenade wall. RC, the girl, the companion and the boy all immediately strip off, revealing swimming clothes beneath. RC in a singlet top, with stars on, and a striped bottom-half – the American flag design.

The girl in high-cut cheeky one-piece. Companion in very modest thing with wide shoulder straps. The boy in trunks. They all give their wristwatches to the aunt, who puts them all up one arm, on top of her own. The boy bounces his beach ball. RC is complimenting the girl on her costume, and the beach ball hits him on the side of the head. They all then rush off into the sea.

22: RB is settling into a deckchair with *The Times*. A shot of seagulls, circling overhead. RB reacts as something hits his newspaper. He looks up, then screws up the page he was reading, picks up the paper, and starts to read again. Another splat. He screws up the page again, muttering angrily.

23: RC and the girl are in the water, splashing about. The beach ball hits him on the side of the head again. He looks annoyed.

24: RB is now surrounded by screwed-up newspaper. He looks up into the sky, annoyed. Another splat. He deliberately puts his newspaper on the sands, puts all the other screwed-up bits on to it, wraps them up (still leaving part of the newspaper on the sand) and moves to a nearby waste-bin to put them in. While his back is turned a tiny child, led by an older one, drops a large lump of vanilla ice-cream out of its cornet on to the newspaper. RB returns. Stares at the newspaper. Close-up of blob of ice-cream. He looks up into the sky, amazed, then puts up a large golf umbrella over him, as quickly as possible.

25: A small woman in a bright flowered sun-dress is blowing up a plastic lilo. She has her back towards the camera. The aunt, watching her. The woman, again – she looks fatter, her dress looks tighter – and she's still blowing. The aunt looks surprised. Back to the woman again – she is now enormous and is still blowing. The aunt again, amazed. The woman again, her dress is ridiculously tight. Suddenly there is a loud bang, and she disappears. Her dress floats down, with the lilo, on to the sands. The aunt is puzzled.

26: The boy is at a kiosk on the promenade. He buys two large lumps of candyfloss and a gas-filled balloon: it is black, painted like a savage cannibal, and has a feather stuck to it. It floats upright. He exits with his purchases, eating the candyfloss.

27: RC and the girl are coming out of the water, he chasing her. A beach ball hits him. He is furious, pulls out the plug, and deflates it, jumping on it. A large hairy man enters the shot, watching him. That's mine, he indicates. RC has to sheepishly blow it up again.

28: The boy has just given RB a stick of candyfloss, when the girl arrives, and flops down on a slatted plastic sunbed. She lies on her stomach, looking away from RB. The companion, playing with the little dog. She throws something for it to fetch, and it rushes out of frame. The girl on the sunbed. The little dog rushes underneath her sunbed and out again. It obviously tickled her and she jumps up in alarm. She looks round. RB laughs and gesticulates with his candyfloss. She looks daggers at him, thinking it was him, and puts her towel underneath the bed as a barrier to further mischief.

29: The aunt and the companion are walking along the shore, gathering shells. The aunt sees one in the water, and plunges her arm in to get it. It comes out with all the watches dripping wet. The companion looks aghast.

30: The boy, carrying his balloon in one hand and a bucket in the other. He is behind RB's deckchair, where RC has left his clothes. He looks round, then quietly fills RC's jacket pockets with sand, sniggering to himself. Then he takes a good-sized live crab from the bucket and puts it into RC's shorts pocket. In order to do this he anchors his balloon by hooking the wire hook on the end of its string on to the bottom rung of RB's deckchair.

RB in deckchair. The little dog runs in, grabs the girl's bright-coloured knickers, which are on her pile of clothes behind RB's chair. RB grabs the dog, takes the knickers from it, looks at them, not knowing what to do with them, hangs them behind him on the top of his deckchair. He settles back; suddenly beside him, the balloon looms into shot. RB reacts violently, scared. The boy, laughing. RB grabs the string and hangs it on the top of the deckchair also. A close-up as we see the wire hook go through the leg-hole of the knickers.

The boy, pretending to busy himself with building a sandcastle.

The aunt comes back, together with the companion. The aunt gets out a tiny little canvas fold-up stool, puts it next to RB, preparing to sit on it. RB puts down his candyfloss on it, just before the aunt sits.

RB, aunt and companion. RB hears a mosquito – and so do we – it buzzes round. RB slaps his leg (trousers rolled up), aunt hits out, then slaps her own arm. The companion slaps her legs and body. The mosquito can be heard to stop and start throughout this. They are all slapping like mad, except the girl, who still lies face down on the sunbed. RB hearing the mosquito stop, looks round, spots it: it has landed on the girl's bikini bottom. RB swats it. The girl leaps up, annoyed, and slaps RB's face. RB puts his hand to his face, finds the squashed mosquito – the girl had killed it. He looks pleased, and thanks her. She, however, stalks off.

31: RC, a little way off, lies on the beach. Eyes shut sunbathing. A close-up – he smiles happily. A load of water is poured on to him by the girl from a child's bucket. She giggles, and runs off. He chases her out of shot, with the bucket which she has dropped.

32: The aunt is still sitting, but packing her bags up. The companion emerges from beach hut, having changed. Her dress is partially tucked up in her knickers at the back. She goes behind the beach hut, and wrings out her costume with her hands. The front of the beach hut. RC is searching for the girl. He hears the water being wrung out of the costume. He listens: it stops. Behind the hut, the companion shakes out the costume, and goes round to the front again. As she emerges, RC sees her skirt tucked up. He peeps round the back of the hut, sees the puddle in the sand. He looks nonplussed. He re-emerges – sees (33) the girl – she ducks down behind a wind-break erected on the sand. (34) He runs to the sea to fill his bucket. The beach ball hits him. He fills the bucket, and leaves shot. (35) The wind-break. RC creeps up to it, pours water over the top. It is the big hairy man again. He makes to chase RC, who bolts for it.

36: The aunt and companion, packing up. Aunt stands up, and the candyfloss causes the tiny canvas stool to stick to her seat. She looks around vaguely for it, but soon gives up. RB sits asleep. Aunt gives him a nudge, to say they are going. RB jumps, and this shakes his deckchair, which dislodges the gas balloon. It starts to rise up in the air, and it takes the brightly coloured knickers with it. They stare at it as it goes.

The girl returns and watches in consternation. She picks up her T-shirt and, as she puts it on, whispers in RC's ear. He looks pleased, but she points a finger at him, admonishingly: and he understands that she means she needs an undergarment. He immediately offers his shorts to her. She gets the aunt and companion to hold up two towels, to change behind.

RB is still watching the knickers, now floating quite a way up. He chuckles. The girl emerges wearing RC's shorts.

The boy's face, waiting.

Suddenly the girl leaps about – the crab is using its pincers. She yells and dashes behind the beach hut. The shorts are thrown out. In close-up the crab emerges and sidles off. RC, grabbing the shorts, dashes behind the hut as well. Returns with the shorts over his head. The companion arrives with the girl's skirt, and gives it to the blindfolded RC, who gropes his way back to behind the hut. The beach ball hits him on the side of the head. He pauses, then continues round behind the hut.

37: A wide pretty shot of the sea, panning round to see the whole party walking away from camera going back to the hotel. The little dog, on a string. The companion, with her dress still tucked up. The aunt, still with the stool stuck to her. RC with his pockets full of sand.

38: The sunlit water splashing round the iron supports of the pier. Then a shot of the pier entrance and the arrival of the party. They wander on, chatting and laughing. The boy has a beach ball which he bounces. The girl wears short shorts, RC in the same jacket as yesterday.

39: A shot of RC, as he walks along, from behind. His pockets are bulging, still full of sand, and he feels the weight of them, then plunges his hand into them and realises why he feels so heavy. He stops, and empties one of his pockets out onto the floor.

40: The sand trickles through the gaps in the floorboards. Below, on the sand under the pier, a woman is making sandwiches. She has spread peanut butter onto a slice of bread. She puts it onto a plate a little to one side of her. As she spreads another piece, we see sand trickling onto the first piece. She, without noticing this, puts the second piece on top of the first, cuts through it once diagonally, and hands it to her husband. He takes a large bite, and chews and we hear the sound effect of his gritty chewing. He is not a pretty eater.

41: Up on the pier, RC has emptied the other pocket a few feet from the first one. Again, the sand trickles through the boards.

42: This time it lands in the mug of tea on the other side of the man. His face, as he chews the sandwich – then he takes the tea, stirs it, and drinks. He resumes chewing – but the grinding sounds louder than before.

43: The party have now reached the comic photographers. We see a large board with holes cut out for people's heads, and grotesque painted bodies. An enormous fat woman in a pink two-piece bathing suit, and a little skinny man in shorts and vest. Two people have their heads through the holes, they have their photos taken, and emerge – an enormous fat woman in a pink two-piece, and a little skinny man in shorts and vest. RB reacts, then indicates to RC and girl that they should go into the other cut.

This represents a tall figure in a one-piece bathing costume, accompanied by a tiny child in a sun bonnet. RB indicates – girl in tall body, RC in baby's body. RC shakes his head, takes girl's hand, goes behind board. The others all watch, except boy, who has wandered off. RC suddenly emerges in the very tall body, and the girl in the baby's body. The photographer prepares, and RB sidles round the back of the boards, with his camera.

The girl is crouching with her bottom in the air, and RC is standing on tiptoe on a box. RB photographs it, the photographer does the same. RB's picture is a much funnier sight.

44: The boy is at a stall or kiosk, buying sweets. He sees, and we see in close-up, a packet marked 'Keyhole blacking – amuse your friends. A riot.' It has a badly drawn picture of a boy with a keyhole-shaped mark on one eye. The boy buys a packet, opens it; it contains a jar of black cream. He moves off, as the aunt and companion arrive at the stall. They stare at the vulgar ornaments, etc., on the stall. The companion is trying to read a naughty postcard in the revolving rack.

The aunt, on the other side, looks at them, and keeps revolving the rack, so that the companion has to walk round with it. She eventually cracks her head on the side of the kiosk wall, knocking her glasses awry.

45: The boy is busy smearing all the 'What the butler saw' machines with his eye-black. He sniggers.

46: The aunt is buying a cruet in the form of a girl's boobs (these are items actually on sale at seaside resorts). It is pink and vulgar.

47: RB saunters up to a curtained booth saying 'Madame Rosie Lee – fortune-teller' in bold lettering. On going closer, RB sees a notice, written in magic marker, saying 'Closed owing to unforeseen circumstances'.

48: He wanders across to the 'What the butler saw' machines. He places his eye to the hole, and we hear it whirring. He takes his eye away – he has a black ring round it. He smiles, not knowing of its presence. Behind the machines, a workman has just taken the back off an old machine, repairing it. RB moves to this machine, puts in money, and we see what he sees – a young couple smooching on a seat behind the machine. Suddenly the aunt looms into shot, which gives RB a shock. He peers round the side, and realises.

49: RC and the girl, on their own, standing eating toffee apples, talking. RC leans back on a post – the post cracks at the base, and the post, which is supporting a board on which hangs a lifebelt, tips over towards the pier rail, dislodging the lifebelt. The lifebelt falls in the water. RC looks over the rail, dismayed; he becomes more dismayed as we see the lifebelt immediately sink. As he watches, his toffee apple drops off its stick. He watches it fall, and stares at the stick.

50: RB, boy and companion sitting in sheltered glass compartment on pier. Aunt approaches with ice-cream cones. They all move up to accommodate her, as she sits, handing out the cones. A wider shot, to reveal that RB is now sitting on something. He gets up, and we discover that it is a tiny old lady. RB apologises, and gives her his ice-cream as she hobbles away. He then takes the boy's ice-cream, and eats it. As they sit, people pass by.

All the men have one eye black. RB laughs – then aunt shows him, in her pocket mirror, his own eye. He gets out his hankie – the aunt takes it, spits on it, and cleans up his eye. The girl and RC return. RC has a black circle in the middle of his forehead.

51: The rifle range. Little ducks being shot by an expert. The party arrive, and RB and RC decide to have a go. A sign says 'New – 12-shot rapid repeater rifle – 60p'. RB points to it, and is given a gun. Another sign says 'Small bore, 10p'. RC points to this one, and is given another sort. RB opens fire, demolishes a row of prizes –

plates, mugs, little pandas, perfume, etc., before he can stop the gun. The stall-keeper rushes over, RB takes £10 note from pocket, apologetically, and hands it to the man. RC, at the other end, is about to shoot when the beach ball hits him on the side of the head. Angry, he turns, and shoots the beach ball as it bounces away. It goes bang, and falls dead. Everyone, except the boy, gives a round of applause.

RB, also congratulating RC, when he suddenly sees floating across the sky in the middle distance the black balloon with the girl's knickers hanging from it. He fires, and scores a direct hit. The balloon bursts, and the knickers drop to the ground.

52: They land on the head of a vicar, sitting reading near the pier on the sand. He looks up in surprise, to see two girls leaning over the rail, laughing at him. He also catches the eye of a middle-aged woman sitting a little way off. He mops his brow with the knickers, and puts them in his pocket.

53: The boy is buying another beach ball, of a different colour, from the stall. He runs to catch the rest of the party up.

54: They get to the entrance, the vicar is seen talking to one of the two girls, who wears a tight skirt. RB watches as the vicar, holding out the knickers, asks the girl if they are hers. The girl shakes her head and produces her own knickers from her handbag. RB watches as she minces away on her high heels.

55: They pass the handyman at his gate. On the gate is now nailed 'No' – on the ground the letters say 'Mopers'. RB looks – shakes his head – indicates it's all wrong. Then handyman has had enough. Tight-lipped, he goes into the garden, fetches his tool bag, kicks the letters for six, slams the gate, and marches off.

As the gate slams, the letters 'N' and 'O', which are in a curious art-nouveau style, swing sideways and form the figure 20. RB stares at this, nods satisfaction, and hurries after the retreating party. The sun is setting.

56: The dining room at the hotel. A large oval table. The waitress is setting up paper napkins placed all round the table. She suddenly sneezes violently, and blows them all over. She takes one, and blows her nose on it.

57: RC, hurrying along the corridor. He sees the same picture, crooked again. He straightens it. Out of the door comes the aunt, and they go out of frame together.

58: The party arrive and sit at table. RC seats girl, then goes to sit next to her, but RB, who is near the chair, sits on it first. By then the others are already seated, so RC has to sit between the companion and the aunt. RC looks daggers from across the table. RB and girl in animated conversation, ordering wine from a waiter. RC looks jealous, but the waitress blocks his view with an enormous menu. It completely covers RC. The aunt and companion peer in at it from either side. RB and girl giggling together. RB pointing out that they can't be seen by RC. A two-shot as they laugh and point, which becomes a three-shot as RC walks in from the back. RB, surprised, looks across at menu – aunt and companion fold it up, revealing RC's empty chair. RB looks under table, realises. RC goes to get another chair, while RB explains to girl what happened.

RC at another table, picks up upright chair, walks away. Only the back of the chair goes, leaving the rest. He comes back into shot, dumps the chair back, takes another and leaves shot again. RC sits on the other side of girl. The waiter brings the wine. RB tastes it, nods, waiter starts with companion, pours large glasses to everyone, in a clockwise direction. The bottle runs out just before it reaches RB; they all say cheers and drink, except RB, who orders another bottle. The aunt is talking to the waitress, indicating the large 'à la carte' menu. The waitress walks out of shot, comes back with a small card, which says 'Table d'hôte'. She hands it to the aunt, and blows another rasp-berry on her nose. Aunt orders for all. The waiter returns with another bottle. RB tries it, nods – it goes round again, and runs out at the same place. RB orders another bottle. They all say cheers again.

The redhead walks in, looking terrific, and sits at a nearby table. RB spots her, and while RC is talking to aunt RB asks girl to change places with him, so he can sit nearer the redhead's table. The girl does so, and the maid arrives, with the 'starters' – pâté, featuring a large lettuce leaf on each plate. RC notices the girl has changed places – RB indicates the redhead. The maid puts down RB's starters, and sneezes, blowing RB's lettuce leaf off the plate. She picks it up off the table, and as she walks away absent-mindedly wipes her nose on it and puts it in her pocket.

The waiter brings another bottle. RB tries it, nods, and the waiter goes round again, starting with the girl, then the companion. RB indi-cates to RC that he is willing to change places. He does so just in time for the waiter to arrive. This time RB gets the wine, but it runs out before RC gets any. They start to eat the pâté – it is awful.

Boy pulls a face – aunt looks askance at it, drains her wine glass, tries again. RC hates it. Aunt pushes hers away, to her left. RB, looking round at the redhead, leans his right elbow into it. He turns back – the pâté drops to the floor.

RB tastes his – revolting. He cuts it up, sticks his fork into it a piece at a time, and transfers it to his jacket pocket. He also puts a bit into RC's jacket pocket while he's about it. A shot of the redhead, noticing this, and smiling.

The waitress is carrying a tray towards another table. A close-up of the tray – it contains a bowl of tomato soup. She sneezes, violently, as she walks away. A close-up of her face – it is covered in spots of soup. She looks as though she has the measles. RC is talking animat-edly to the girl. He whispers in her ear. She shakes her head, regretfully but firmly. He suggests something else, whispering again. Again she shakes her head. He catches RB's eye. RB shakes his head, meaningfully.

The waitress arrives with a large dish. They stare at her measles – and all decide to leave. They've had enough. They all rise, and make their way out. RB stands up, steps on the pâté on the floor, and slips head first into the redhead's low-cut dress, with a resounding splat. She looks surprised, he doesn't know whether to look sorry or pleased.

59: A close-up of RC, standing, waiting. Girl behind him – we pan down a row of the party's faces. The boy, the girl, the aunt, the companion, and RB. We widen to see they are in a Chinese takeaway restaurant. The Chinese assistant starts to hand RC packets of take-away food; RC's face registers joyful anticipation.

60: Next morning. The sand dunes, near the beach. The companion sits on a fold-up chair, the aunt sits on the ground. She is spreading honey onto slices of bread and butter. The little dog tries to eat a piece, but is shooed away from the plate. It returns, and grabs a bit. The companion gets up to get the dog, and the aunt, at the same time, picks up the plate and puts it on the companion's chair behind her. The companion immediately sits again, fussing the dog. She then throws the bitten piece of bread for the dog, who chases after it. She gets up again, and follows it out. The aunt, having spread some more honey, goes to put it onto the plate – the plate is there, but now empty.

61: RB is walking along the dunes. He suddenly sees the redhead, changing among the long grass. She wears a sun-top of some sort, and a long wrap-around skirt. RB stops, interested. She removes the skirt, revealing little shorts. RB's interest increases. She starts to remove shorts. RB is watching through a telescope. She finishes removing shorts. RB is watching through binoculars. She is now in brief briefs. She starts to remove them. RB is hit by the new beach ball. He staggers, and looks again through the binoculars; we see the back end of a sheep. RB removes the binoculars, revealing two black-ringed eyes. He looks disgruntled, and taking a hip flask from his pocket takes a hefty swig. His mouth now has a black ring round it too.

62: A shot of the companion, wandering along the shore, with slices of bread and butter stuck to her slacks.

63: RC and the girl – a quiet corner near the dunes. RC is trying to fix a tall beach umbrella into the sand, but it is rather rocky, and the umbrella isn't easy to fix. He eventually sticks it in, rather precariously. The girl is already spreading suntan lotion on her body. As RC sits down next to her, she hands him the lotion and rolls onto her stomach, indicating he should oil her back. He sits up, looks at her recumbent form, then turns away to pour the oil into his hands. As he turns, the umbrella falls over, one edge of it dropping neatly between him and the girl. He turns, and spreads oil over the outstretched pale pink skin of the umbrella in a circular motion. It dawns on him that something's wrong. His hands are covered in oil. He lifts the umbrella off the girl, who laughs, and lies there. He picks up the bottle of oil, and it shoots up out of his slippery fingers and lands on the girl's back, drenching her in oil. He tries to spread it around, but gets his hand slapped. He gets up, picks up the umbrella, raises it upright again. It collapses on him, shutting him inside.

64: The aunt is where we last left her. With her, the boy, the companion and RB. They are eating sandwiches and drinking coffee. The girl arrives, glistening with suntan. RC, in shirt-sleeves and trousers, is covered in oil stains all over his front, from top to toe. RB looks askance at him, wondering what they have been up to. RC is handed a cucumber sandwich from a plate. He takes it. RB is drinking tea. RC makes a face as he tastes the oil on the sandwich. The aunt offers him the cruet, which she bought at the vulgar stall. He stares, then takes out one of the boobs. His fingers are so slippery it immediately shoots into the air. It lands in RB's large teacup as he is about to drink, splashing him with tea. He fishes it out, not knowing where it came from, or what it is. He looks at it, then looks at the companion, eyeing her flat chest.

65: On the green the donkeys are giving their rides. The boy riding ahead. The girl, going quite fast, bouncing up and down with RC watching from his position on the donkey. Immediately behind her, we see the redhead, in her long skirt and sun-top, riding more slowly. RC passes her and from his point of view we see the redhead, whose sun-top is very revealing. Cut back to RC – he is now sitting backwards on his donkey, to get a better view of the redhead.

66: A train-whistle is heard – we are now on the miniature railway. The party, except the companion and the girl, are all on board, and about to set off. RB is found to be sitting on the same old lady again, and apologises. The train sets off, and RB sits beside the tiny lady – squashing her between him and RC. The train takes us past the miniature golf course, which, although sparsely attended by golfers, has quite a lot of people sitting about, picnicking, sunbathing, etc.

The train arrives, and RB and RC part company with the aunt and the boy.

67: RC and RB get a club and some balls each from the little kiosk.

68: The aunt and the boy are seen approaching the boating lake nearby.

69: RB drives off, swiping at his ball.

70: In the hotel grounds, a crash of glass, somewhere behind the hotel. In a very wide shot, we hear terrible Italian swearing. The tiny figure of a chef appears, brandishing a large knife at the sky. We see the companion, in her bathing suit, sit up and stare. Then she lies down again, and we see she is sunbathing in the grounds, near a row of ornamental railings. A shot of the sunshine through the railings.

71: RC is showing RB that he must drop a ball behind him over his shoulder. RB does so, and RC then plays his first shot, a much more professional effort. He marches off in the direction it went. RB plays his ball; this time no crash.

72: RC comes over a rise, we pull back, to show a fat man, asleep on his back, in a bunker. RC stares, as he sees that his golf ball has come to rest in the fat man's navel.

73: RB is looking for his ball in the rough. He sees a ragged-looking boy throwing stones at a notice board on the edge of the course. He goes over and tells the child to stop, pointing at the notice. Cut to the notice – it says 'It is forbidden to throw stones at this notice board'. RB suddenly stops and wonders why the board is there at all.

74: RC is standing very gingerly astride the fat man, and he plays a perfect delicate shot off the man's tummy, without disturbing him at all. Very pleased with himself, he follows it with his eyes, stepping back to do so. The ball rolls into a hole. With a sigh of self-congratulation, RC walks straight across the fat man's stomach, and leaves the shot. The fat man sits up with a yell.

75: The redhead, in an amazing bikini, is playing golf, too – on her own. Her ball is on the green, and, just before she putts, she tucks another ball into the back of her bikini pants, to save holding it – it is the only place to put it. She goes to take up her position to putt. RB appears, still looking for his ball. He sees the back view of the redhead

– and sees the ball in her bikini. He walks over and removes it; she turns round, and he is surprised to see that it is her. He waves the ball at her, demonstrating that he had lost it. She shakes her head, says she herself put it there. 'Oh sorry,' says RB, and backs away. She smiles, and continues her game.

76: RB comes round a tree, finds a couple having a picnic. There, in the middle of a cream cake, is his ball. Apologetically he retrieves it.

77: RC is about to hit a ball, when he sees RB in the distance, sucking cream off his golf ball. He is puzzled.

78: RB drops the ball behind him over his shoulder. It hits the bald head of the picnicking man, who glares at RB. RB grabs his ball from the tablecloth, and retreats hastily.

79: RC watches all this with interest.

80: RB's hand sticks a golf tee into the ground in close-up, then, in a wider shot, places the ball on it, but proudly over his shoulder. A close-up reveals that it is in fact a hard-boiled egg. RB stares at it, then back at the picnicker. He cracks the egg by tapping it on his club and peels away the shell.

81: Then, as RC watches fascinated, RB, in the distance appears to be eating his golf ball. RC cannot believe his eyes.

82: The aunt and the boy are sitting in a little boat – the boy is driving, the aunt has a packet of assorted biscuits. She tries one, doesn't like it, throws it over her shoulder. She does the same thing four or five times. We cut wide, to see that the boat is being followed by at least twenty ducks.

83: The cry of seagulls is heard, as RC prepares to strike a ball. He hits it hard and high. A squawk, and a seagull drops from the sky onto the fairway. RB gives him the thumbs-up sign, and he too hits a ball.

84: Back at the hotel, the companion is still sunbathing, with her transistor radio playing 'Fingal's Cave'. This effectively drowns the noise of RB's ball, which bounces along the terrace, and into a cup of tea which stands on the ground near to her. She looks at her watch, takes from her handbag a pill box, and removes a large white pill, which she puts onto her tongue. Picking up the cup of tea, she takes a good gulp, and swallows. The surprise on her face shows us she has swallowed the golf ball.

85: RC strikes another ball, another squawk, another seagull drops onto the grass. RB applauds.

86: The companion picks up her towel, and her radio, and stands up in the sunlight, yawning. She catches sight of her arms – she is sunburnt, in stripes, where she has been behind the railings. Her legs and back are the same – she looks like a pink zebra.

87: The redhead and RB are returning from the golf course, towards the little kiosk where they return the equipment. They walk through the frame chattering. Behind them comes RC, with his brace of seagulls hanging from his golf club, which he carries proudly over his shoulder.

88: The hotel terrace. In the foreground, the redhead lies on a low lounger. Pan and tilt to reveal the whole party chattering away about the day's events. They are in jolly mood and each has a drink. The aunt is telling the companion about the biscuits and the ducks. RC is telling the girl about the seagulls and holds them up to prove it. RB then tells the aunt about the hard-boiled egg. The aunt, meanwhile, is pouring herself a Guinness. The redhead tells them all about the ball in her bikini. The companion tells RB about the chef and the broken window pane. RB indicates 'it must have been my ball' and helps himself to whisky and soda as he talks. He puts the glass to the wrong side of the siphon, and presses – the soda squirts onto the redhead's recumbent midriff. She squeals, and RB mops her up with his handkerchief, wringing it out into his glass, and toasting everyone with it.

The sun is setting.

89: The big grandfather clock in the corridor of the hotel. It strikes eleven, and at the same time makes terrible wooden clumpings and bangings.

The maid is walking past it, she opens the door on the front of the clock, and extracts the two arms of the chair that RC put there.

It continues its slow striking without further encumbrances.

90: From the silence of the corridor we cut to the noise of the residents' bar. The clock on the wall says eleven o'clock. A cuckoo pops out, and cuckoos. From off camera somebody throws beer at it, soaking it. It comes out again, but quacks like a duck. The whole party, plus the redhead (but minus the boy) are leaving the bar, waving goodnight to each other – the aunt and companion go off in one direction, RC and the girl go upstairs, while RB and the redhead linger a little.

91: RC is rather the worse for drink, and the girl half supports him with her arm as they walk along the corridor. He reaches the picture – it is straight. He puts it crooked. They arrive at the girl's door. She plants a loud kiss on his forehead, but he whispers something in her ear – and she, pretending to be very shocked, 'tuts' loudly through her teeth and playfully slaps his face several times in rapid succession. She then turns on her heel, goes into the room, and slams the door. All the leaves on a rubber plant on a nearby table fall off. RC registers this. Having done so, he wanders off. We see him enter his bedroom and close the door. Immediately, round the corner comes RB and the redhead. Her room is next to RC's. RB says good night. She kisses his cheek. He whispers in her ear. She indicates with fingers and wristwatch 'five minutes' and disappears inside. RB sits on a chair and looks round. He sees a picture of a grim-faced woman on the wall opposite. He looks round for somewhere to flick his cigar ash, finds nowhere, so flicks it on the table. Cut to: picture – the woman looks very angry – her eyes wide. He reacts – then carefully brushes up the ash into the palm of his hand, and puts it in his pocket.

Cut to: picture. It now looks benign, smiling approval. RB nods at it. He applies his eye to the keyhole. His eye now has a black keyhole mark on it. The door clicks open a fraction. In close-up, a bare foot appears. The camera tilts slowly up, revealing a bare leg protruding from a filmy négligé – up and up – arriving eventually to reveal the redhead's hair in curlers, and her face covered in white cream. She kisses him goodnight on the cheek, and waves, then closes the door. He is left with a black eye and a white cheek. He considers for a moment, then strides off round the corner.

92: RC is in his bedroom. He has put on a pair of gaudy pyjamas, and is arranging his teddy bear in his bed. He looks at it; and punches it in the eye. He is obviously disappointed.

93: RB, hurrying along the corridor. He carries a hand-written note. He looks round, and then, kissing it, shoves it under RC's door by mistake. RC, in his room, sees it appear, and quickly opens it.

94: In close-up we read, 'You are such a little darling, I can't resist you. I must see you tonight XX.'

RC: Delighted – quickly scribbles or the back of it, and returns it under the door.

95: Outside the door RB reads it. It says – 'Climb in my bedroom window – third from left XX.' RB is delighted, hurries off.

96: Outside the back of the hotel it is dark. Round the corner comes the companion, carrying the front of a large ladder. RB follows up in the rear: she wears a plain dressing-gown, he a voluminous knee-length night-shirt. He also carries a bottle of champagne.

97: They look up – there is the lighted window, open, but with curtains closed.

98: RB leaves the companion to hoist the ladder, while he takes the foil off the champagne. The ladder is secure, he indicates that she should steady the ladder by standing on the bottom rung, while he mounts it. Up he goes. A shot of her, looking up – then a shot of RB'S night-shirt, seen from below. The companion reacts in embarrassment, and turns to face frontwards. RB, as he ascends, has the champagne under his arm. The cork suddenly pops out, and hits the companion on the head, followed by a shower of champagne. RB, on the ladder, throws the bottle away.

99: A crash as it hits a cucumber frame.

100: Outside, in the street, a policeman hears the crash, and, torch in hand, goes round the back to investigate.

101: The companion, standing facing front on the ladder, is approached by the policeman. RB, from above, sees him, and starts to descend. The companion, looking embarrassed. Suddenly RB's night-shirt descends over her head. With a squeak, she fights her way out of it amid reactions from the puzzled policeman and the assaulted RB.

102: In RC's bedroom, he now wears a white silk dressing-gown and is rehearsing a torrid embrace with a lamp-standard.

103: There is a tap at the window. He goes to it and plants a passionate kiss on the figure on the ladder, which happens to be the policeman.

The shock of this makes RC give the policeman a shove, and we see the ladder fall away from the window, still containing a policeman.

104: They both crash into the bushes below. RB and companion rush to his aid, and help him to his feet. Apart from losing his helmet, he seems little the worse for wear. He gropes around in the bushes, and solemnly picks up a plastic flowerpot and places it on his head, before reaching for his note-book.

105: The big black car stands glinting in the morning sun, outside the hotel. RB is supervising the luggage being put into the boot by the chauffeur. Out from the hotel come the aunt and the boy, followed by the companion, who carries two suitcases, plus the little dog on a lead round her wrist.

She dumps the two suitcases down side by side, and they open like bookends, spilling out their contents all over the pavement. She and RB put the clothes back in, RB holding up a bra for inspection, snatched away by the embarrassed companion. When the clothes are in and the cases are shut, a yapping is heard.

The companion looks at the dog's lead and traces it back to one of the suitcases. The case is opened again, and the little dog pokes its head out. She ties the dog's lead to the back bumper of the car, while she, yet again, packs the suitcase. The chauffeur, meanwhile, is putting away the other case. RB is chatting, with his head inside the car, talking to the aunt. A sports car horn is heard. RB looks up, as we hear a screech of brakes. It is the redhead, in a bright green open sports car. She has pulled up just behind the big car.

RB waves, and she indicates, with a toss of her head, that he should come with her – pointing to the passenger seat. RB says, 'Who, me?' The redhead nods. RB, without more ado, reaches into the big black car, and produces a string bag. We see, in close-up, that it contains a bottle of champagne and a large orange alarm clock.

He makes straight for the sports car, gets in, gives the redhead a peck, and she starts the engine.

RC and the girl come from the hotel, just in time to see the green sports car do a U-turn and roar off down the road. They look at each other, smile, and the girl gets into the car, RC putting a friendly helping hand on her shorts.

He takes a last look at the retreating sports car, and gets in, shuts the door.

The big black car begins to glide away. The little dog, in close-up, is pulled out of frame, and as the car drives away from the camera the little dog bounces about behind it down the long straight seaside road.

The Poems

From his sublime monologue 'The Ministry for Poetry' (*'It's Margaret Thatcher's brainchild this – our venerable Prime Misses; I'll tell you if you'll all pin back your aural orifices'*) to the swift couplets of the much-loved two-hander 'The Case of Mrs Mace' (*'He's been shot at Oxshott. Bagshot got him with a slingshot full of buckshot'*), Ronnie Barker's gift for rhyme has always played a huge part in his work. On show here we have eleven of Barker's flights of fancy, from the short and silly to the dramatically daft.

Pure poetry was never Barker's stock in trade, more a hobby an agile mind did to keep itself sharp and entertained, as much for himself as for others.

Interestingly, in 2001, aged 72, Barker took it upon himself to while away an idle hour improving the punchlines of the great poet Edward Lear. Disappointed at Lear's habit of using the same word to end the first and last lines, Barker crossed out many last lines and added his own cheeky rejoinders. He wrote an introduction to the hand-annotated edition, explaining his whim in true Lear style:

> *There was an old fossil named Lear,*
> *Whose verses were boring and drear.*
> *His last lines were worst – just the same as the first!*
> *So I've tried to improve on them here.*

The book went up for auction in Gloucestershire and fetched £3,600, described on the auctioneer's website as 'an extraordinary and unique item, associating two British masters of comic language and wordplay'.

Barker's *Open All Hours* co-star David Jason talks fondly of his work with Barker – whom he referred to as The Guv'nor – and revealed in an interview that poetry was something Barker wrote and handed out to friends in the same way others might send cards or flowers.

He tells the story of an episode of *Open All Hours* that needed several minutes cutting to get it down to a half-hour. He watched as many of his best lines were trimmed and left on the cutting-room floor, feeling that all he was being left with were 'feed lines' to Awkwright's gags. The following day he received a handwritten mock-Shakespearean sonnet, full of comedy thee's and thou's, which ended:

> *The future will provide thy need*
> *Till then be content to be a little feed*

– a poetic nod from The Guv'nor that it was the laugh that was important, not who got it, and a sign of how much Barker valued Jason's performance.

Barker died just two months before his long-time friend and co-star David Jason received his knighthood, although Jason cherishes the poem Barker sent him upon the announcement of his gong, which ends:

> *'Arise, Sir David,' she will say,*
> *The sword upon your shoulder lay.*
> *I raise a glass filled to the brim*
> *And truly say: 'Good Knight from him.'*

GOODNESS

> Good place,
> good weather,
> good views,
> good sand,
> good digs,
> good table,
> good waiter,
> good band,
> good wine,
> good soup,
> good fish,
> good duck,
> good brandy,
> good night –
> good girl,
> Bad luck.

THE LURE OF A LADY'S FAN

The world of fashion and of fad
Of elegance and élan
Has never created a wittier whim
Than the lure of a lady's fan.
This simple weapon has caused the rout
Of many an army man;
I've seen them wobble and go weak-kneed
At the sight of a lady's fan.
When they chance to meet in the steaming heat
Of a street in Old Japan,
There's many a sailor led astray
By the wave of a lady's fan.
Who knows how many heads of state
Have strayed from the master plan?
Or how many diplomats succumbed
To the touch of a lady's fan?
She will simper from behind it
She will twist it and unwind it
She will wiggle and rotate it if she can –
She will open it out wide
Or she'll snap it shut and hide
Behind the flutters of her fascinating fan.

GENEROSITY

He gave her this, he gave her that,
A brand new car, a Paris hat.
He gave her dollars, gave her pounds.
His generosity knew no bounds.
He spent it all, became flat broke;

She thought it all a great big joke.
To him the joke was not so funny –
He had to marry her for his money.

PRISCILLA JONES

Priscilla Jones had great big knees
Yet never ceased to show 'em –
Like champagne bottles stood on end
Each one a Jeroboam.
Although her friends all called her plump
She thought her shape perfection;
She crossed her legs at the flower show
And won the Marrow section.

THE SAME POEM

A ROMANTIC'S VIEW

Gold is the colour of my true love's hair
As she raises up her glass
And the candle shines through the red wine's glow
And the evenings gently pass.
Green is the colour of my true love's eyes
Eyes that I can't resist,
They glow through the smoke of her cigarette
Like jade through the morning mist.

A REALIST'S VIEW

Red is the colour of a June-bloomed rose
When plucked from its briar's posy –
But red is the colour of my true love's nose
When she's been at the Rouge or the Rosé.
Yellow is the colour of the dawning sun

That creeps where the frost still lingers,
But yellow is the colour of my true love's thumb
And brown is the colour of her fingers.

THE SALES

I've just had a very nice day
At the Sales,
It's a day that I always enjoy –
I rang up the office and
Said I was ill,
Then had lunch with that
Patterson boy,
Then off to the Sales, it was
Ever such fun
And I got quite a lot of nice things:
A lovely pink girdle, a
Really tight one,
With that big thick elastic that 'pings'.
And a green thing with bows *(they had several of those)* and a
    white thing with drapes like a goddess.
And a black thing with strings, and a blue thing with things –
    and a red thing with straps, and a bodice.
Can't wait 'til tomorrow, to go to work, and walk in dressed up
    like a toff!
But after today I'm so tired – oh well, I'll ring up for another
    day off!

ISN'T THE WATER WET?

FIRST CHORUS:

Isn't the water wet?
Isn't the sunshine hot?
Isn't the man with the ices nice

And hasn't he got a lot?
Don't the nights get dark
Nights I'll never forget –
Ain't the winkles wonderful
And isn't the water wet!

SECOND CHORUS:

Isn't the water wet?
Isn't the sky ber-lue?
Nobody here but people
And nothing but things to do.
Don't the boys look grand?
Sights I'll never forget –
Ain't the cockles a caution
And isn't the water wet!

THIRD CHORUS:

Isn't the water wet?
Isn't the ocean deep?
If the sand was all swept up
Wouldn't it make a heap?
Sailors with ship-shape shapes
Shapes I'll never forget –
Ain't the mussels marvellous
And isn't the water wet!

THE TYPESETTER'S STOP-GAP

In penny novelettes, it was customary always to include a 'filler' story or poem which got pushed around from one page to another, throughout the magazine, wherever there was a space to fill. Here is such a poem ...

1: Oh Mary, meet me by the gate
   I swear my love be true
   And fain would tell you of my great
   (*continued on page 2*)

2: Oh Mary, Mary, hear my song
   Come walk the woods with me
   And I'll plant kisses all along
   (*continued on page 3*)

3 Oh Mary, Mary, say you'll be
   Within my arms once more
   And I'll again caress your warm
   (*continued on page 4*)

4: If only you will stay with me
   Beyond the beaten track
   I know our love affair will be
   (*concluded on the back*)

THINGUMMYJIG

My hair was a mess
Till I talked to young Bess
Who had prickly hair, like a pig;
But I've noticed of late
It's full-bodied and straight
Since she washed it in THINGUMMYJIG.
So I talked to young Di
Whose hair was so dry
That it crackled and cracked like a twig;
Now it glows with a sheen
That is almost obscene
Since she washed it in THINGUMMYJIG.
So I bought some from Boots
And I massaged my roots
Just like they did, with THINGUMMYJIG –
Now just look at mine!
See it sparkle and shine!
Don't you think it looks fine? It's a wig.

MAIN LINE

When I sit in railway carriages, I often think of all the
    marriages
Whose first few blissful moments are realised in the dining car;
Or rattling out of London Town, snugly with the shutters
    down.
Steaming down to bracing Brighton, steaming down without
    the light on,
Realising, none too soon, 'George, we're on our honeymoon!'
Full of eagerness and dread – wondering what lies ahead;
Can we cope, make both ends meet? Pull together? Find our
    feet?
Will she soon get tired of me? Do we face monotony?
Will he always buy me flowers? Was there ever a love like ours?
How did fate conspire to match us? Will the guard come in and
    catch us?

BORN INTO RICHES

She drew a deep breath, followed by another. 'I think I'm being
followed by another,' she said. They were standing in the sitting room,
by the big window that overlooked the lawn. She could see the distant
figure of the gardener, who had also overlooked the lawn for several
weeks now. She stared out, running her hands over her body nervously. It was in terrible shape. All lumps and bumps, with little tufts
of moss growing in the more inaccessible places.

'Followed? By a man?'

He felt something stir in his breast. It was the teaspoon in his waist-
coat pocket, stolen from the tea shoppe that very afternoon. 'I think
you're imagining things, darling'.

'No, I'm not.'

He felt her quiver. 'I asked you not to feel my quiver,' she said. Her eyes swept the ground. Then they dusted the mantelpiece and cleaned out the grate.

'You're overwrought, my dearest.'

He felt her deep down. 'Please for the last time, will you take your hand away,' she said. He turned away thrusting his hands deep into his trouser pockets and juggling with his conscience. A whole minute passed.

'Have you got a grip on yourself?' she asked.

He didn't reply, but stared into the garden, his jaw set at a strange angle – the result of a skiing accident some years before.

'I'm sorry, Geoffrey,' she said.

She leant back, and the colour rose in her cheeks. She realised she was leaning against a hot radiator. She sat down to cover her embarrassment; and the cooling stone of the old window seat through her thin silk dress reminded her of her childhood. It also reminded her that she had dressed in a hurry and had forgotten to put any on. The thought of sitting here, with him, in such a state of undress took her breath away. She took some brief pants before she dared speak, trying to slip them on without him noticing – but at the vital moment he turned and caught her unawares – fortunately only with his elbow. He felt her quiver again as he took her in his arms; he couldn't resist it.

'I love you, Euphrosnia,' he said, and those three simple words and one difficult one sent a shiver through her cold frame. So much so that two of the cucumbers dropped off. He cupped her face in his hands, adding milk and sugar, before placing it on his lips and planting a long hard kiss on a long hard nose. 'It's been a long struggle to win you,' he said, looking long and hard at her ...

They were in the library, drinking in the beauty of the setting sun.

'Have another,' he murmured, indicating his cocktail shaker. She nodded. 'Your hair is so beautiful,' he said. Caught in the sun, it was a mass of tiny lights. She had got them off the Christmas tree last year. 'How do you keep it so radiant?'

She guided his hand to where she hid the battery. He touched it gently, and his eyes lit up. He raised his glass, and, drawing her nearer to the fire, toasted her silently. She drained her glass at a single gulp. After a second she spoke. After a fourth she could hardly speak, and after a sixth she was absolutely pie-eyed. He picked her up and carried her on to the lawn, where the evening mist lay in a wispy grey swirl, and the gardener lay in a filthy blue shirt.

Geoffrey laid Euphrosnia on the lawn, watched by the old gardener. 'That's the way, Sir' he cried drunkenly. 'All the best properties are mostly laid to lawn.' As Geoffrey stared at the bumpy uneven surface, he realised that Euphrosnia's dress had ridden up, and so had a young lad on a bicycle.

'Doctor, your wife wants you. The old cow's about to give birth.' The boy turned and cycled off again.

'Who'd be a vet?' thought Geoffrey, watching the boy getting smaller and smaller, until he was a tiny figure on the horizon. He eventually got so small he got a job in a circus, touring round as the Modern Tom Thumb.

Geoffrey gave one last look round at the vast, imposing edifice that was Euphrosnia's seat, and sighed. 'All this could have been mine,' he sighed.

She lay, face downward, on the damp grass. The gardener, feeling the seeds of a strange turbulence growing inside him, removed a packet of radishes from his back pocket.

'Cheer up. Think how lucky you are. This is your seat,' he cried, slapping her roundly, or at least one of her roundlies. 'You're in *Burke's Peerage*. I've been looking up your particulars.'

He too felt her quiver. 'You men are all the same,' she murmured. She breathed several sighs – first, a few small-size sighs, followed by several sighs of a much larger size. Finally, she drew him down the ground beside her, with a felt-tip pen; the very pen that has since told this little story. Remember, of course, it isn't a true story; and, being only words, it's not to be taken literally.

The Two Ronnies: The Serials

Aside from the legendary 'Phantom Raspberry Blower of Old London Town' (penned with unmistakable anarchy by Spike Milligan), Ronnie Barker – as Gerald Wiley – wrote all of the most creative and popular segments of *The Two Ronnies*, the weekly serial. The ruthless detectives Charley Farley and Piggy Malone had four adventures between 1972 and 1982 (and still lay claim to a stand-out, inexplicably funky signature tune that's worth revisiting). However, for many the pinnacle of costume, sets, satire, sight-gags and sexiness remains 'The Worm that Turned'.

Broadcast on BBC1 between November and December 1980, this lavish 8-part comedy thriller saw Barker and Corbett – in full drag – trapped in a terrifying future where women had risen to power and now dominated the government, industry and – most terrifying for our hapless duo – the leather-clad Secret Police force. Wiley wrought gag after gag from the gender-bending scenario of Big Ben becoming Big Brenda, the Tower of London renamed Barbara Castle and the sight of our heroes in housecoats plotting to bring down The Commander, the unforgettable Diana Dors in one of her final roles. The rise of Margaret Thatcher as the first female PM the previous year clearly inspired Barker's broad satire – trembling, terrified men as ever the true target – of a land where women puffed on pipes and men got three months for showing illicit Humphrey Bogart films.

THE WORM THAT TURNED

EPISODE ONE

VOICE-OVER: The dateline is 2012. England is in the grip of a new regime of terror, traditionally a land of brave heroes and great statesmen – Nelson, Wellington, Disraeli, Churchill. Britain now laboured under the yoke of a power guaranteed to strike terror into the hearts of all men: the country is being run by women.

It all started with Margaret Thatcher. Housewives all over England, delighted at her rise to power, voted more and more women in, and more and more men out. A few years later the Germaine Greer knicker uprising made 1984 a far more terrifying year than even George Orwell predicted. Men's clubs were abolished, gentlemen's toilets closed, creating widespread distress among thinking and drinking men everywhere. Ailing livers naturally were the first to go to the wall. The advance of feminism was by now making itself felt in public and traditional spheres. Names of buildings were changed. The Houses of Parliament were still the Houses of Parliament, but immediately the all-woman government took over Big Ben was renamed Big Brenda.

By 1998 the newly formed state police had established their headquarters in the old Tower of London. This historic fortress with its grisly associations of torture and executions had been given the name of a former folk heroine, and was now known to all and sundry as Barbara Castle. The state police marched around the country in squads. They were omnipotent and carried all before them – quite a lot behind them as well. It had become, in short, an England completely dominated by the female sex. Even the Union Jack had now become the Union Jill, a sad travesty of its former self. Women were the breadwinners; they gave the orders, they made the decisions; they were the union leaders, the captains of industry – and the men? Well, let's start with this one.

We see RC dressed as a woman – 'Janet'.

Cartwright, JW, is employed as a tea boy at the secret police head-quarters in Barbara Castle. He has a pass with his photograph on it, pinned to his overall. He lives in a two-roomed flat in Perivale and he is the worm that is about to turn. His main adversary, everybody's main adversary, was the commander of the state police, a woman with an iron will and underwear to match.

COMMANDER: Now, ladies, it has been suggested by certain opposition factions that men should once again be allowed to revert to wearing trousers and I can see that to you as well as to me this whole concept is unthinkable. They must be kept in frocks if we are to retain the control which we have fought so hard to achieve. Trousers have always been the symbol of the male overlord. Here in England trousers were traditionally always worn by the head of the family. In those olden days all women had an image of their perfect man.

JANET: Nice strong black one for you, wasn't it?

COMMANDER: And yet deep down there was always a resentment, a spirit of rebellion which was ready at any time to burst to the surface. When our mothers and grandmothers burnt their bras way back in the 70s, what did this reveal?

JANET: Nothing at all for you, as far as I remember.

COMMANDER: It revealed that at last women, the creators of life, the protectors of the young, the guardians of the future, were ready to assume the mantle of leadership. The master-stroke, however, was to insist on the changeover in traditional dress. Once the men had to wear the frocks, they were subjugated. As soon as we took their trousers away, they were putty in our hands. After all, what did they have left?

JANET: Two lumps and a sponge finger.

VOICE-OVER: While on the other side of London, another down-trodden male (RB in dress – 'Betty') goes about his everyday chores, only half conscious of the seeds of rebellion which are growing inside him.

BETTY: (answers phone) All right, I'm coming, I'm coming. Hello? Oh it's you, Janet. Yes, how are you? No, no, no, not at all. No, no, just doing a bit of housework. I don't know why I bother either. Yes, I work and slave to keep it all clean and tidy. She just comes home, slumps down in an armchair, falls asleep in front of the television set. Just broken two of my blasted fingernails as well. Look, are you coming round as usual this afternoon? Well, yes, I made a cake. No, nothing fancy, no – just a plain one. Well, got to watch the old figure. I can't get into that blue dress she bought me for my birthday, daren't tell her. Right, OK. See you later, bye. (He spots a ladder in his tights.) Oh damn, new pair on his morning

Later:

BETTY: Ah, hello Janet, do come in.

JANET: Thanks.

BETTY: Let me take your coat.

JANET: Oh, well how are you, Betty old chap?

BETTY: Oh fine, fine, mustn't grumble, sit down. Now, a nice cup of tea.

JANET: Oh, you've changed the curtains, haven't you?

BETTY: Yes, yes, yes. Oh, before I forget, the Drama Club have been on and they said would I be in this year's production again. I said I would if you would – I presume you would, wouldn't you?

JANET: Oh, rather. Yes, wouldn't miss that for worlds. What is it?

BETTY: Well, of course you know they've made them change the titles of all the plays that have sexual connotations.

JANET: Oh, they're not doing … Juno and the Pea Hen?

BETTY: No.

JANET: Moby Dillys?

BETTY: No, you remember the one that used to be called Little Women, now it's called Little Men. You'd be good for the lead in that, I should think.

JANET: Which part is that?

BETTY: Arthur, the eldest daughter.

JANET: Oh, it gets so complicated. Betty, old chap, I'm in trouble.

BETTY: In trouble? Don't tell me John's pregnant?

JANET: No, no, no. She's fine. No. It's just that I'm being spied on at work.

BETTY: At the Castle?

JANET: I think the secret police have heard about my collection of chauvinistic films. I'm sure the house is going to be searched any moment.

BETTY: Well, you'll have to get rid of them.

JANET: I can't, you see, not before Thursday. You know I'm having the private show in the auction rooms. It'll be the last because it's just getting too risky. Do you know that you can get three months' hard labour for showing a Humphrey Bogart?

BETTY: So you want me to spread the word to the rest of the lads, eh?

JANET: Yes, if you would, in the secret code. Tell them sewing circle meets on Thursday as usual, same place.

BETTY: Does he mind you using his auction rooms?

JANET: Who? Greta? No, he's a great chap, Greta. He'd give you the dress off his back if you asked.

BETTY: Right, so, as it happens, I shall be seeing some of the lads in the morning.

JANET: Oh, really? Why? Are you going to keep fit?

BETTY: No, having my roots done.

At hairdresser: a row of men sitting under dryers.

BETTY: Cheryl, Cheryl. Susan, give Cheryl a knock, will you. Damned old fool, as deaf as a post, give him a knock.

CHERYL: Come in.

BETTY: Cheryl, sewing evening Thursday, all right?

CHERYL: Oh, good, good. Oh, Thursday. Ah, me wife goes out with her boozing pals.

BETTY: Pass it on, will you?

CHERYL: Yes. Gracie, Gracie, don't know how to turn these damned things off.

(A worried-looking Janet enters.)

BETTY: Janet, what the devil are you doing here, old boy?

JANET: Shhh, police.

VOICE-OVER: Who are the police looking for? Will Janet be discovered? Will the policewoman see him, or will the vanishing cream do the trick? Is Betty a man to be trusted? Find out next week in another exciting episode of THE WORM THAT TURNED.

EPISODE TWO

VOICE-OVER: The year is 2012. England, traditionally a land of heroes and great statesmen, is in the grip of a new regime: the country is being run by women. They are the breadwinners, the rulers, and their state police strike terror into the hearts of the subjugated male. In short, the roles have been completely reversed. It is the man, not the woman, who now wears the frock. Even their names are feminine. But one poor downtrodden worm is about to turn. This man is Janet Cartwright. Employed as a tea boy at police headquarters, Janet has one friend he can trust: Betty Chalmers. Our story starts one afternoon over a cup of tea.

JANET: I think the secret police have heard about my collection of chauvinistic films. I'm sure the house is going to be searched any moment.

BETTY: Well, you'll have to get rid of them.

JANET: I can't, you see, not before Thursday. You know I'm having the private show in the auction rooms. It'll be the last because it's just getting too risky. Do you know that you can get three months' hard labour just for showing a Humphrey Bogart?

VOICE-OVER: Next day in the hairdressers, Janet and Betty are surprised by a raid from the secret police.

POLICEWOMAN: Do you have a customer by the name of Ursula Debenham? Tall, balding, with a beard?

OWNER: Eh, no. I don't think so.

POLICEWOMAN: He's wanted for petty crimes against the state. Stand up. Name?

PHYLLIS: Phyllis Willis.

POLICEWOMAN: Is that a joke?

PHYLLIS: My father thought so. Just 'cos he had a silly name, he gave me one.

POLICEWOMAN: Your father?

PHYLLIS: Dillys Willis.

POLICEWOMAN: Papers. Have you recently shaved a beard off this man?

OWNER: No, ma'am.

POLICEWOMAN: Carry on. Any of you see or hear, it's your duty to report him.

BETTY: What was his crime?

POLICEWOMAN: Playing illicit rugby and pipe smoking.

(Cut to: Janet on the phone.)

JANET: Hello, Shirley, old boy. How are you? It's me. I'm just ringing up to say, sewing circle evening Thursday, all right, you know what I mean? Yes, it is. Good drying weather, though. Mine was on the line ten o'clock this morning. Oh, have you? No, I haven't got a rich wife to buy me a dryer. No, I don't mean it. Yes. All right then, see you Thursday. Yes, bye.

(Cut to: Betty on the phone.)

BETTY: Yes, yes, Thursday. Usual place, auctioneers, yeah, fine. How's George? Is she? Amazing woman. Is she still playing left half for Brentford? Give her a good kiss on the goal mouth for me, will you. Bye.

(Auction rooms – several men, all in dresses, occupy seats in rows before a large screen.)

JANET: Evening chaps, evening. Just a word before we start. I'm afraid this is going to be the last film shown for a while. I know, I know, I know, but we can't help it. I'm afraid I've got to go under cover, there's been a little dicky bird has told me there's been a bit of a leak and I might get raided. And so here we are, however, and tonight. So make the most of it, that's what I'm really trying to say, sit back and enjoy yourself, because tonight we're going to have a John Wayne film.

(All the men cheer. The lights go down. The film starts. A man stares at Betty – he stares back, suspiciously. Is it really a man? Is that moustache real? After a few moments the man gets up and leaves. Betty follows him into the toilet.)

BETTY: (stopping her) Here, you're a woman!

WOMAN: (producing revolver) Be quiet!

BETTY: Who are you?

WOMAN: State police.

BETTY: You taking me in?

WOMAN: Yes.

BETTY: Where, to the Castle?

WOMAN: Yes.

BETTY: It's rather a long journey. Do you think I might go to the toilet?

WOMAN: All right.

BETTY: Well, can I take my hands down?

WOMAN: If you must.

BETTY: Well, it's essential, very difficult otherwise. Look, could you please turn round and face the other way?

WOMAN: No.

BETTY: Oh! In that case I will. (While pretending to use the urinal, Betty drops a piece of soap, taken from the washbasin, onto the floor.) I'm ready.

WOMAN: Then move.

(She slips on the soap and Betty grabs the revolver, but drops it. They fight, during which Betty manages to get the gun again and shoots the woman in the behind.)

WOMAN: (Calling after Betty) You shot me in the behind.

(She collapses head first into toilet bowl.)

(We cut back to the end of the film, as Betty enters. She whispers in Janet's ear.)

JANET: What? You what? Shot her in the what? In the where? Good grief. Well, I should think she would faint. I'll go and have a look.

(Janet looks in the toilet, and returns.)

JANET: Did you say fainted, old chap? She's dead.

BETTY: Dead? But she was only shot in the backside. You can't die of a shot in the backside.

JANET: She didn't die of a shot in the backside. She died of her head down the toilet.

BETTY: She was drowned.

JANET: She was drowned, yes. They're after both of us, Betty old chap.

BETTY: They certainly are, Janet old boy. The thing is: what are we going to do with the body?

VOICE-OVER: What will happen now? Are Janet and Betty doomed? Can the toilet keep its grisly secret, or will the police flush it out? Don't miss next week's enthralling episode of THE WORM THAT TURNED.

EPISODE THREE

VOICE-OVER: The dateline is 2012. England is in the grip of a new and terrifying regime: the country is being run by women. Their secret police are everywhere. Men, downtrodden and subjugated, are forced to wear dresses and to have only feminine lives. Janet's illegal showing of male chauvinist films to the men's sewing circle has been discovered by a secret police spy and, in a scuffle, Betty accidentally shoots her and our heroes are left with the grisly task of concealing the body. When Betty arrived home that night, his wife Brian was already in bed.

BRIAN: How was the sewing circle tonight, darling?

BETTY: What? Oh fine, fine. Usual sort of thing, you know, everybody sewing things.

BRIAN: How's yours coming along?

BETTY: What?

BRIAN: The thing you're sewing?

BETTY: Oh, oh, oh fine. I've nearly finished it actually. It's – I've just got to embroider, embroider around the neck, you know.

BRIAN: I thought you were making a pair of French knickers?

BETTY: Er yes, yes I am, yes, but they're reversible. You see, you can put your arms through the leg holes and wear them as a bolero.

BRIAN: Or upside down as French knickers?

BETTY: Er, yes.

BRIAN: Bit draughty.

BETTY: Oh, I'll shut the window.

BRIAN: No, French knickers.

BETTY: Oh, draughty. Yes, round the, round the neck, yes –

BRIAN: Very sexy though.

BETTY: Yes; don't do that, Brian, not tonight. I've got a bit of a headache actually.

Next day:

BETTY: (on phone) Hello, oh hello, Janet. Yes, no, no, no. Brian's gone. I got into a big row this morning – I forgot to do her packed lunch. Where are you phoning from?

(We see Janet at Barbara Castle.)

JANET: (on phone) I'm in the Commander's office, so I'm risking my neck, old chap. Listen, it's about the films: we must bury them in the garden. Well, your garden. I've only got a window box and that's full of my radishes. Hardly worth demolishing them to make room for Gone with the Wind. I know it's apt, but that's not the point. There are 37 films to get rid of before I'm caught red-handed – and some unfinished business in the Auction Rooms.

Auction Rooms:

AUCTIONEER: Gone, Mr Thompson. Next Lot 324, Victorian oak wardrobe with fitted drawer.

PORTER: This one, ma'am.

(He opens the door. The body of the woman falls forward towards camera.)

(Cut back to Commander's office.)

JANET: (on phone) Well, look, I'll bring the films round in the car this afternoon. I'm on early shift. What about 2.30? Oh, and there's one other thing, oh—

(The Commander enters. Janet pretends to dust the phone; then replaces it.)

COMMANDER: What the hell do you think you're doing?

JANET: I'm dusting the desk.

COMMANDER: Sitting down?

JANET: Dusting the chair. It's a new directive from the efficiency department. Very good for the figure as well.

(He wriggles about in the chair.)

COMMANDER: That will do. I can use that method to dust my own chair just as efficiently.

JANET: More so; you've got better equipment. Well, I'll be off then, ma'am.

COMMANDER: Just a minute. Name?

JANET: Julie.

COMMANDER: Where is your identity badge?

JANET: In the wash by mistake on my other pinny.

COMMANDER: Don't you know it's a punishable offence not to wear it? Name?

JANET: Julie, Julie Andrews.

COMMANDER: Sounds familiar.

JANET: Well, it probably is. My great grandmother was very, very famous in showbusiness.

COMMANDER: Really?

JANET: Yes. Eamonn Andrews.

COMMANDER: Julie Andrews, you will report to this office at nine o'clock when you will be disciplined.

JANET: Yes, ma'am.

COMMANDER: It won't take long, but I can assure you that you will not use that particular method of dusting again for quite a long time. Jump to it.

(Cut to garden – Janet and Betty digging, burying the spools of film.)

JANET: You all right then?

BETTY: No, I've just split my knickers.

JANET: Pass me some more cans of film then. Ah, what one's this then?

BETTY: Robin Hood.

JANET: Errol Flynn, he's a real man's man.

BETTY: Yeah, bit of a lady's man too, I understand.

JANET: Come on then, otherwise your wife will be home.

BETTY: All right.

(Daphne, a nosy neighbour, peers over the fence. Janet and Betty try to conceal their actions from her.)

DAPHNE: That's a big hole.

BETTY: Oh, I see, I thought you meant the split in my knickers.

DAPHNE: Are you digging that for the wife?

BETTY: No, I'm planting rhubarb.

DAPHNE: Rhubarb? That far down?

BETTY: Oh yes, yes. It's marvellous. You see, by the time it's grown you've got sticks six feet long. I saw it on television – Penelope Thrower.

DAPHNE: Listen, the butcher's got some lovely fillet in. Thought you could surprise the wife tonight.

BETTY: Oh, yes. Thanks very much, Daphne, old chap, but I don't really feel in the mood for fun and games at the moment.

DAPHNE: OK, just thought I'd mention it. Cheerio.

(He leaves.)

BETTY: Cheerio, old sport.

JANET: Has he gone then?

BETTY: Yes, let's get cracking.

(They are interrupted by the arrival of the milkwoman.)

MILKWOMAN: Hello, cheeky. I thought I knew that face.

BETTY: Don't be so rude, you saucy monkey. Give me two pints and a flavoured yoghurt. You're very late?

MILKWOMAN: It's Friday. I'm collecting the money. Anyway, I left you till last today. I thought I'd get a cup of tea and my legs up.

BETTY: You'll get a slap round the face if you don't behave yourself. Now, be off with you. I'll pay you Monday. Go on.

MILKWOMAN: Oh well, no harm trying. Ta-ta, sunshine.

(Leaves.)

BETTY: Dear.

JANET: I thought you said you enjoyed complete privacy in this garden? If I'd known, I'd have laid on some tea and cakes.

BETTY: I know, it's incredible, isn't it? Who'll be next, I wonder?

(On cue, Brian arrives home – reaction from RB and RC.)

Cut to: later, inside the house ...

BRIAN: Of course you realise I'm going to have to report you, don't you, Betty?

BETTY: To the state police! You can't!

BRIAN: I must. It's my duty as a woman. I shall go on Monday.

BETTY: But Brian, I'm your husband, Betty. Thirteen years we've been married – doesn't that mean anything to you? I mean, look at us on the wall there, thirteen years.

BRIAN: Unlucky for some.

BETTY: That's a great help, isn't it? I suppose you realise what they'll do to me?

BRIAN: I know what I'd like to do to you. You disgust me – those disgraceful films – you deserve all you get.

BETTY: Well, in that case, why wait till Monday? Why not pick up the phone now?

BRIAN: Simply because I need to have the use of you one more time.

BETTY: The use of me?

BRIAN: I need a partner tomorrow night.

BETTY: Oh, of course. I'd forgotten. The Annual Staff Dance.

(Cut to the dance: Betty sits in Come Dancing type frilly dress, with sequins. Janet arrives in almost identical flowery dress. She sits next to Betty.)

JANET: Evening Betty, old boy.

BETTY: Sit down.

JANET: Why? What's up?

BETTY: My wife is going to report us to the secret police.

JANET: What?

BETTY: We've got to get out, go into hiding, but before we do we must get hold of our identity files so they won't know who they're looking for. All photographs will have to be destroyed. Look out.

CYRIL: Hello, Betty. May I have this dance?

BETTY: Not at the moment, thanks, Cyril. My girdle's killing me. It's really a big nuisance.

CYRIL: How about you, Janet?

JANET: No, I'm afraid mine's being a small nuisance.

CYRIL: Come round to my place and I'll fix it for you.

(She winks lecherously, and leaves.)

BETTY: Silly old crumpet.

JANET: When's your wife going to report us?

BETTY: I'll tell you later. There's no time now, but the point is those identity papers. Now you work at the place, you've got a pass, you'll have to smuggle me in – you game?

JANET: Is there another way?

BETTY: No, no, no. I know it sounds crazy, trying to break into the Tower of London—

JANET: For God's sake, don't let anybody hear you call it by its old name. That's treason.

BETTY: Whatever you call it, it's going to be blasted difficult to get in there.

JANET: It's just not very safe, that's all.

BETTY: All right, all right, have it your own way, old boy. All right then, we're going to break into Barbara Castle.

VOICE-OVER: Will Janet and Betty succeed in their desperate plan, or will the Commander thwart it? Will she herself be thwarted? To find out who thwarts what and to whom, tune in next week to another eccentric episode of THE WORM THAT TURNED.

EPISODE FOUR

VOICE-OVER: The year is 2012 in an England which has now been entirely taken over by women, where women are the breadwinners and the decision-makers and where men are completely subjugated, forced to wear dresses and given feminine names. Our story concerns two men, Janet and Betty. These two downtrodden specimens are on the run, wanted for crimes against the state by the dreaded secret police.

Outside the Barbara Castle.

JANET: Now as soon as I get inside I'll go to the lavatory.

BETTY: Pardon?

JANET: The lavatory – the window looks out onto the street. That's it up there.

BETTY: Oh yes, yes.

JANET: I'll stick my pass out of the window—

BETTY: You'll do what?

JANET: My pass, I'll stick it out of the window and you grab it.

BETTY: No, I'm sorry, I can't hear a damn thing with this cotton wool. I'm going to have to take it out.

(Removes cotton wool from ear.)

JANET: Well, what's it there for?

BETTY: Well, it's those cannons on the parapet, they go off every hour on the hour. I thought I'd take a bit of precaution, that's all.

JANET: Well, that's part of the plan. You'll have to get used to the cannons. Now, you take my pass, change the photo and get in with the pass. I'll be waiting outside with the bucket.

BETTY: Right. Good luck, Janet, old chap.

(Janet enters the Castle. Betty waits against the wall. Soon she is approached by a woman.)

WOMAN: How much, dearie?

BETTY: I beg your pardon?

WOMAN: You're rattling your keys. How much?

BETTY: How dare you, madam! I'm not a common streetwalker.

WOMAN: Well, what you rattling your keys for then?

BETTY: I happen to have the palsy.

WOMAN: Oh, beg pardon, I'm sure.

Cut to inside Castle.

GUARD: Why have you got two buckets?

JANET: Double time, Sundays.

GUARD: Well, get on with it.

Cut back to outside.

(The pass drops from the window. Betty drops her handbag when picking it up.)

BETTY: Oh, damn.

WOMAN: Oh dear, allow me.

BETTY: Oh, thank you very much. (He bumps into woman and knocks her over.) I'm sorry, it's these darned shoes. I'm awfully sorry. I'm so clumsy, I'm awfully sorry ... you're fine, you're absolutely fine. Oh, do excuse me, don't worry about it. I'll, I'll be out of your way in no time at all. There, that's all right, I'll leave the rest, it's only money, isn't it? I've got piles. Which reminds me, I wouldn't sit there too long on that cold pavement ...

Cut to inside Castle.

(Betty has got in with the pass. She sidles up to Janet.)

BETTY: There's too many people about for my liking.

JANET: The sooner we get into that Record Office the better. We've got to find a cleaning trolley from somewhere. Now, come on.

(They find trolley and start to move off. A big, hairy man in a cross-over pinny appears and scowls at Janet.)

JANET: This'll do.

DEIDRE: Where the hell do you think you're going with my trolley, Cartwright?

JANET: Now – Oh, Betty this is Deirdre, Deirdre Collinwood, this is Betty Chalmers who's new here.

DEIDRE: Well, he don't look very new to me. What's your game, you rat?

JANET: Now don't start bullying, Deirdre.

DEIDRE: Who's going to stop me? Your friend Betty? You going to save your little friend, eh?

BETTY: As a matter of fact, he was seeing if you've got something.

DEIDRE: Got what?

JANET: Boot oil.

DEIDRE: What boot oil?

JANET: Boot, it's a new directive, you see. I mean, if an officer comes to you and she's got squeaky shoes and you haven't got it, you're for it.

DEIDRE: Boot oil?

JANET: What do you mean? Haven't you got any then?

DEIDRE: But I don't know nothing about it.

JANET: You better get up the supply and get yourself some then.

DEIDRE: Boot oil, right, I will.

JANET: And don't forget to get both sorts.

DEIDRE: Eh?

JANET: Black and brown. (Deirdre leaves.) We'll be black and blue if we're still here when he gets back. Come on.

Cut to outside office.

JANET: Right, it's four minutes to ten. At ten o'clock the gun fires three times at fifteen-second intervals. Now you have got to use these three bangs to cover any noise you might make.

BETTY: What I need is a machine gun to cover the noise of my knees knocking.

Inside the office.

(Betty looks for files while Janet chats to guard. She rattles buckets when the cannons go off.)

GUARD: Did you have to make all that noise? The guns go off every day.

JANET: I know, I know, I'm sorry. It's my nerves, you know, I can't bear noise of any sort. I once joined the silent order of a monastery, had to leave.

GUARD: Why?

JANET: They were such noisy eaters.

(Cannon noise.)

JANET: Oh dear, oh dear. Oh, I'm sorry, was that the last one?

GUARD: Yes, only three.

JANET: Oh, thank heaven for that.

(She dusts near the desk, then smiles at the guard.)

JANET: I'm going to ask you to stand up, I'm afraid. I want to just dust your chair.

GUARD: What?

JANET: It's a new directive. All chairs have to be dusted. (As the guard stands, Janet spreads glue on the seat while Betty nips out of the office.) I'll be off then. All finished behind there, Betty? All nice and tidy. Off we go, don't get up. Bye.

BETTY: Bye.

Cut to outside Castle.

BETTY: As soon as she sees that mess, they'll be after us.

JANET: No, she won't. I stuck her trousers on the chair.

(We see their papers burning in their cleaning buckets.)

The Castle corridor.

(We see two girls dressed as Beefeaters pass by. Betty and Janet leap out and overpower them, dragging them behind a pillar. They re-emerge wearing the Beefeaters' clothes.)

JANET: It's forbidden to impersonate women now, you know. Danny La Rue's still locked up in here somewhere.

(They see Deirdre coming towards them.)

JANET: (as Beefeater) You, face the wall. You deserted your post and lost your trolley.

DEIDRE: How do you know that?

JANET: We know everything.

BETTY: It's because we eat so much beef, you see.

JANET: You are a stupid nitwit.

BETTY: You certainly are, bend over.

(He kicks Deirdre's backside, and they move on.)

Cut to Commander's office.

COMMANDER: We must find them. They must not be allowed to escape.

OFFICER: But they burnt their identity papers. We have no photographs to go on.

COMMANDER: Silence. One is short, the other is fat. They won't get far. They must be got rid of, liquidised.

OFFICER: Don't you mean liquidated?

COMMANDER: No, we have a new method.

VOICE-OVER: What will happen to our heroes, Janet and Betty? Have they burnt their boats, as well as their papers? Have they jumped out of the frying pan into the liquidiser? Find out next week in another excruciating episode of THE WORM THAT TURNED.

EPISODE FIVE

VOICE-OVER: The dateline is 2012. Dear old England, land of heroes, is being ruled with a rod of iron by a new regime. The country is now being run entirely by women. They govern, they are the bread-winners, they wear the trousers. Men, completely subjugated, are now the housewives, forced to wear dresses and given feminine names. But some of the worms are about to turn, among them these two men, Janet and Betty. Knowing that they are wanted by the dreaded secret police for crimes against the state, our heroes break into headquarters to steal their own identity papers, hoping to cover their tracks. But as they meet the next day during their routine daily shopping trip, they know that never again will their lives be quite the same.

JANET: Here's the sugar. How are you getting on?

BETTY: Fine, all I need now is coffee and powdered milk.

JANET: Powdered milk, for the country?

BETTY: Well, we can't just leave a note outside for the milk girl, can we? I mean, no one must know we're there. How long will it take to get there?

JANET: Oh, about a couple of hours.

BETTY: Oh, fine. Well, I'll put all this lot in the car. I'll shave off the moustache—

(They are interrupted by the arrival of Cynthia.)

JANET: Hello, Cynthia. How's Arthur? She had the baby yet?

CYNTHIA: Yes, a boy.

JANET: Oh, good. What are you going to call him?

CYNTHIA: Marigold.

(She leaves.)

BETTY: I'll pick you up in an hour and before we can say Jill Robinson we'll be tucked away in your little country hideout, just the two of us.

JANET: No. Three of us.

BETTY: Who?

JANET: Herbert, my pet mouse.

BETTY: What?

JANET: Oh, yes, I take him everywhere with me. I've got him with me now.

BETTY: Where?

JANET: Yes, he's in my bag, he's in a little tobacco tin. Look, here he is.

BETTY: Oh well, if you must, you must. But you have to realise, Janet old chap, we're going to be very tight on food.

JANET: Oh, he doesn't eat a lot of food, just a little bit of cheese. Edam, he likes this. This'll do.

BETTY: Oh, how long does that last?

JANET: Oh, about a year.

BETTY: Won't it be all mouldy?

JANET: He likes it mouldy, oh yes.

Exterior country lane.

(Police seen around the area. Janet and Betty wait behind the fence. Janet appears very tall. Betty is dressed as a yokel. A policewoman guard approaches.)

GUARD: That your car down there?

BETTY: Oh, what car is that, my dear?

GUARD: The one in the lane.

BETTY: Oh, what lane is that, my dear?

GUARD: The lane at the back of the house.

BETTY: Oh, what house is that, my dear?

GUARD: This house.

BETTY: Oh, this house, oh that lane. Oh what, what car is that, my dear?

GUARD: Have you got a car?

BETTY: No, no, never had car. No, we've never had a car in our lives, no! Well, we had one once, it was a little mini, but we had to get rid of it, 'cos he couldn't get in it, he's so tall, you see. He's so very, very tall.

GUARD: He doesn't say much.

BETTY: No, he's deaf and dumb, aren't you?

JANET: Yes.

BETTY: Well, he's deaf anyhow.

GUARD: He heard you.

BETTY: Oh yes, he lip reads, you see, lip reads.

JANET: Pardon?

BETTY: You lip read.

GUARD: I'm looking for a short man.

BETTY: Yes, I'd prefer one myself.

GUARD: Keep your eyes and ears open, both of you, do you understand?

JANET: It's about a quarter past five.

(The policewoman stalks off. Janet, behind the fence, steps off her orange box.)

Cut to interior house.

(They are removing the costumes.)

BETTY: Where did you get all this stuff?

JANET: The pantomime costumes from the Drama Club. They asked me to look after them a couple of years ago, still here.

BETTY: Lucky for us they are. I mean, what were the ones we're wearing?

JANET: The two yokels, Sarah and Henry, what were in Jill and the Beanstalk? They were two extra characters we put in to sing the song, 'You can drive a horse to water, but a pencil must be lead.' Not as bad as the principal boy singing 'I did it her way.'

BETTY: Still, these things definitely got us out of trouble.

JANET: They'll be back.

BETTY: You think so?

JANET: Oh, I'm sure of it, and I can't be standing on a box all the time.

BETTY: No, that's true. Has this place got an outside toilet?

JANET: Yes.

BETTY: I mean, if they find you in there without your box.

JANET: Exactly, I'll be caught short.

Auction rooms.

(Several men, all in dresses, occupy seats in rows before a large screen.)

JANET: ... hope they're not going to be long, I've got cramp.

BETTY: Where?

JANET: In my hindquarters.

BETTY: Don't be silly. I'm your hindquarters.

(The police girls in their skimpy uniforms are peering underneath carts, their own hindquarters very much in evidence.)

JANET: Wish I had my catapult.

BETTY: Why?

JANET: Some bull's-eyes to be scored over there.

BETTY: Don't talk about bulls at the moment, old chap. I'm in a tricky position back here. If there's a bull in this field, he might charge us.

JANET: Well, I hope not. I haven't got any money with me.

(The police chief decides to abandon the search and marches the others off. A group of real cows gather curiously around the fake one.)

Cut to interior house.

BETTY: That milkmaid turning up was a nasty moment.

JANET: She must have been pretty short-sighted to be taken in by this lot.

BETTY: I'd love to have seen her face when she groped round my udders and I handed her a bottle of milk through a flap in the back.

JANET: She didn't half yell.

BETTY: That's what attracted the bull.

JANET: That's when I decided we ought to make a run for it. I mean I would have been all right. I could have just stood there eating the grass – you would have borne the brunt of it.

BETTY: Yes. Well now, they're off the scent for a while, but they're still in the village. We've somehow got to get right away from the area.

JANET: We need a vehicle with four wheels, rather than four legs.

BETTY: Yes. Not only that we need a vehicle with a couple of good safe places to hide in ...

Cut to: a cart, approaching down a lane. On the back, two dustbins marked 'pig swill'.

VOICE-OVER: Is this the end for our two heroes, Betty and Janet? Is it possible the police pigs will see through the pig-swill? Or is it a load of hogwash? Don't miss next week's enchanting episode of THE WORM THAT TURNED.

EPISODE SIX

VOICE-OVER: The year is 2012. England now languishes under a new reign of terror, a regime guaranteed to strike fear into the hearts of all men. The country has fallen into the hands of man's primeval enemy, woman. Women now govern, they are the breadwinners, men are completely subjugated, they are forced to do the housework, to wear frocks, they even have feminine names. And the dreaded secret police see that these new stringent measures are enforced. Our heroes in this tragic tale are two simple, honest, straightforward Englishmen, Janet and Betty. Wanted by the secret police for crimes against the state, they were hiding out in an old cottage. When the area is surrounded, they have to find another method of breaking through the road-block.

(The chief policewoman searches the pig swill and finds nothing. She dismisses the cart. Janet and Betty's feet protrude from beneath a tarpaulin as the cart moves off, safe for the moment.)

Cut to: a field beside a lane

(Janet and Betty eating a picnic.)

JANET: Good thing I brought this knife.

BETTY: Yes, I was just looking at that. How many blades has it got?

JANET: Twenty-seven. I've had it since I was a Brownie.

BETTY: Is that what you opened these tins with?

JANET: Yes, the only thing that's broken is the thing that takes the stones out of horses' hooves. Well, it's not broken actually, it's bent. Melanie Harper did that at school.

BETTY: Oh, how?

JANET: Sat on it ... Melanie.

BETTY: Yes, yes. Thick skinned. Wonder what he's doing?

JANET: He's an actress. Oh yes, just played the lead in Hairy Queen of Scots at the National.

BETTY: Now then, anything else you'd like to eat, old boy?

JANET: Well, what is there?

BETTY: Well, there's some chocolate here or there's a Pa's bar.

JANET: Oh I'll have that. I'll have a Pa's Bar, yes.

BETTY: Now we really must get organised if we're going to contact my brother-in-law.

JANET: Don't you think it's a mite dangerous, old boy? I mean we're less than thirty miles from my cottage. The police are bound to be spreading out.

BETTY: If we're going to go to ground, it's our only hope.

JANET: Yes, you're sure this is the pub he works at?

BETTY: What, the Green Woman? Yes, yes, absolutely positive, yeah. It's a good pub. Brian and I used to come down and visit him sometimes at weekends, not that she ever liked him really.

JANET: Oh, he's not her brother then?

BETTY: No, no, he's my sister's husband.

JANET: Oh, which sister is that?

BETTY: My younger sister, Harold.

JANET: Well, what's your brother-in-law's name?

BETTY: Diana.

JANET: Oh, and he's bound to cycle down this road on his way to work?

BETTY: Yes, it's the only road. You see the pub's about a quarter of a mile down there. Right, now then, I've got some drawing pins, I've got some tin tacks and I've got a few large fish hooks for good measure. Come on, we'd better get sprinkling.

Exterior lane,

(They have sprinkled pins and tacks all over the road.)

JANET: How's that?

BETTY: Yes, that should do it.

JANET: Bit drastic, don't you think? Wouldn't it be better to jump out of the bushes and wave at him?

BETTY: No, no, he wouldn't stop. He was once stopped on his way back from getting some groceries by what he thought was a man, turned out to be a woman in a dress.

JANET: Good lord.

BETTY: It was terrible. She assaulted him. He came back with his frock all torn. Fortunately, she never laid a finger on his groceries.

JANET: Just as well. Look out, who's this?

(A car approaches, stops, and a man gets out. It is Betty's brother-in-law. He stares at them.)

BETTY: Good grief, Diana!

DIANA: Betty! Good gracious, what are you doing here?

BETTY: What are you doing here, in a car? What happened to the bike?

DIANA: I've been fiddling the housekeeping. What are you doing here?

BETTY: No time to tell you now. Get in quick, Janet. Look, turn the car round and I'll tell you as we go.

DIANA: But I'm supposed to be—

BETTY: Never mind all that, just hurry. Come on.

VOICE-OVER: Betty and Janet lose no time as they travel to tell Diana the whole story. He in turn informs our two heroes that the pub now belongs to him and, like the true blue old-fashioned chauvinist he is, offers them a job. And so the very next night, in this sleepy little village far from the madding crowd ...

Cut to: pub.

(Janet is working as a barmaid, collecting glasses.)

WOMAN: Here, you're a nice little thing. What're you doing in a dump like this then?

JANET: Just pin money. My wife's away in the Navy.

WOMAN: Here, come and sit in my lap.

JANET: Oh, I don't think there's room for both of us.

(Cut to Betty, with lady pianist.)

BETTY: Do you know 'My little grey home in the West'?

PIANIST: No, how about my little brown flat down the road? It's nearer.

BETTY: What about 'After the Ball'?

PIANIST: No, I meant, after you finish here.

BETTY: Oh, shut up. Excuse me.

WOMAN: And what's your name, my dear?

BETTY: Beryl, madam.

WOMAN: Married?

BETTY: No, no, no.

WOMAN: Thought not. I can read men like a book.

BETTY: Oh really, what system do you use?

WOMAN: Braille.

BETTY: Oh, really.

DIANA: Oh, Janet, can you take an order in the other bar. Man in a green dress.

JANET: It's all go round here, isn't it?

(A woman is studying Betty, gives him a wink.)

Cut to: next morning.

(Betty is hoovering the empty bar.)

JACK: Good morning, Betty.

BETTY: No, no, my name is Beryl. Beryl Cambridge, ma'am.

JACK: No it's not, it's Betty Chalmers. We were at school together. You were captain of the netball team. I was watching you last night.

BETTY: Shhh, not so loud.

JACK: I used to see you when I was on my way back from cricket, in your frilly netball skirt. I used to think you were the most wonderful creature on earth. But I was only thirteen and you were seventeen.

BETTY: I'm sorry, I can't place you.

JACK: Oh well, a lot of water has flown under the bridge since then.

BETTY: Yes, quite a few gin and tonics as well. I doubt if I'll get into that netball skirt now.

JACK: Still got that twinkle in your eye, though.

BETTY: Look.

JACK: Betty, you do know there's a big reward offered for your capture, don't you? It's in all the papers. Don't worry, I'm not going to give you away.

BETTY: What, then?

JACK: I want to keep you for myself.

BETTY: What?

JACK: I want to hide you. I've got a nice little house a couple of miles from here. We could renew old acquaintances and no one to disturb us.

BETTY: But I never knew you.

JACK: Well, I knew you, in my dreams.

BETTY: Grief!

JACK: Well, what do you say?

BETTY: Well, I don't mind if you don't.

JACK: Can't wait.

Cut to: Jack's house.

JACK: Pour me a gin and tonic, would you?

BETTY: Yes, yes, of course. How do you like it?

JACK: Seven parts gin, one part tonic.

BETTY: Slice of lemon?

JACK: When I want a lemonade I'll ask for one.

BETTY: I say, you're wearing pyjamas.

JACK: Mmm, won't you join me?

BETTY: What, in your pyjamas?

JACK: Well, maybe you could start off in this?

BETTY: What's that? Oh, I say, that's a pretty nightie, isn't it?

JACK: Why don't you try it on? Take a shower, hurry back.

BETTY: Yes, all right. I'll take a shower and then try it on and hurry back.

JACK: Even better.

BETTY: I say, it's jolly nice of you to hide me like this. Do you think you'll be able to hide my friend, Janet, as well, you know, later on?

JACK: Later on. Let's have a day or two to ourselves first, shall we? He'll understand. I mean, you did put that in your note, didn't you?

BETTY: A day or two, yes.

JACK: Well, go on, you're wasting time. (RB leaves. On phone) Hello, state police? I wish to speak to somebody about one of the missing men, Betty Chalmers.

VOICE-OVER: So Jack is up to no good after all. What will happen to Betty? Will the police send their special squad to get him? As he steps from the shower, will he be grabbed by the heavies? Find out next week, in another extraordinary episode of THE WORM THAT TURNED.

EPISODE SEVEN

VOICE-OVER: The dateline is 2012. England labours under the yoke of a reign of terror. Every Englishman is now at the mercy of his age-old enemy, woman. Women now rule, women govern, women earn the daily bread and the dreaded state police strike fear into the hearts of all and sundry. The poor downtrodden male, forced to wear a frock and even given a feminine name, is a sad caricature of his former self. Two such caricatures are our two heroes, two fine, upstanding specimens of English manhood, Janet and Betty. Wanted by the secret police for crimes against the state, our heroes are forced to go to ground in a remote village in Herefordshire and find work in a pub owned by Betty's brother-in-law, Diana. It isn't long, however, before Betty is recognised by a former school chum who still seems to have a crush on him.

JACK: You, you do know there's a reward out for your capture, do you? It's all in the papers. No, don't worry. I'm not going to give you away.

BETTY: What then?

JACK: I want to keep you for myself.

VOICE-OVER: But having lured our hero to her house, she shows herself in her true colours.

JACK: Hello, state police? I wish to speak to somebody about one of the missing men, Betty Chalmers.

Cut to interior house.

(Betty and Jack are eating lunch.)

BETTY: I feel so silly sitting here in my nightie at two o'clock in the afternoon!

JACK: It belonged to my late husband.

BETTY: There you are, you see, sitting here in a dead man's nightie.

JACK: He's not dead.

BETTY: You just said 'my late husband'.

JACK: He was always late, so I divorced him.

BETTY: Oh, I see. Well, I still feel silly sitting here in it.

JACK: Perhaps you'd rather be lying down in it?

BETTY: No, no, no, it's not the sitting, it's just the nightie, you know.

JACK: Would you feel better sitting up without the nightie? If so, take it off.

BETTY: No, no, no, no. What I mean to say is, a nightie's for going to bed in.

JACK: Well, that's just what you'll be doing, when you've finished filling your face. Ready?

Cut to later in the meal.

(Betty is now on the cheese, while Jack watches, puffing on her cigarette.)

JACK: Now, my darling, I'm going to take a shower and a bath.

BETTY: Shower and a bath, why? Did you miss out yesterday or what?

JACK: No, I shower off the dirt first and then when I'm nice and clean I have a bath.

BETTY: Isn't that rather like carrying coals to Newcastle, though of course if you had been carrying coals to Newcastle you'd need a bath, wouldn't you? Though of course if you lived in Newcastle you couldn't have a bath, because you do keep the coal in the bath in Newcastle—

JACK: You are rambling again, my darling.

BETTY: Yes.

JACK: I do believe you're nervous. What are you, man or mouse?

BETTY: I'm not sure. Tell you what, this cheese tastes very good though.

JACK: Now in ten minutes I shall be in the bath. I want you to rush in and scrub my back with a loofah.

BETTY: Rush in?

JACK: Absolutely hurtle.

BETTY: Is it a rough loofah?

JACK: Very rough.

BETTY: Be careful you're not facing the wrong way.

A telephone box nearby.

(Janet speaks with a phoney foreign accent.)

JANET: Hello, could I please speak with Betty Chalmers.

BETTY: Oh it's you, Janet old boy.

JANET: How did you know it was me?

BETTY: Oh well, you're using that voice that you use when you played the Frenchman in See How They Run at the drama club, you know the one that was in ...

JANET: He was a German.

BETTY: Oh, was he? Better disguise than I thought.

JANET: Look, never mind about that. I've got your note. All it's got on it is this woman's address and 'Something's come up.' What are you doing there? What are you up to?

BETTY: Well, I'm sipping champagne and preparing to dash in with a loofah.

JANET: Listen, I wouldn't advise you to do that, old boy. Are you in the room on your own?

BETTY: Listen, how did you get hold of her phone number?

JANET: Well, everybody's got her phone number. She's well known for it.

BETTY: What?

JANET: She's been picked up so often she's starting to grow handles.

BETTY: Oh goodness, really?

JANET: What's more she's betrayed you.

BETTY: She's what?

JANET: The police are all round the house.

BETTY: Where? Well, just a minute. (He looks out of window.) You're right, you know. Listen, I'm trapped in here, old chap.

JANET: Where is she now?

BETTY: What? Oh, she's in the bath, blast her.

JANET: Right, I'll get your brother-in-law. I've got a plan to get you out of there, but you have to deal with the woman.

BETTY: How?

JANET: Just keep her quiet somehow. Keep a lookout for us, right?

BETTY: How can I keep her quiet?

JANET: Well, I don't know. You know, try champagne or something. Right, bye.

Cut to: outside bathroom.

JACK: (from within) Who's that knocking at my door? Betty, said the fair young maiden.

BETTY: It's only me from over the sea, said Barnacle Betty, the sailor.

(He enters.)

JACK: Well, darling, what do you think? Haven't lost my figure, have I?

BETTY: No, but I think you're about to lose your balance.

(A thud and a splash is heard. Betty rushes out, brandishing the champagne bottle. Cut inside to see Jack, unconscious in her bath.)

Cut to: outside the house.

(A van arrives. Janet, in false beard, gets out, with Diana.)

DIANA: Good afternoon, madam. We've brought your order, a barrel of brown ale, and want to collect the empty one. Can we come in? Thank you.

(They roll in a large barrel. Outside, the police watch suspiciously. After a while, the barrel re-appears. Diana is now accompanied by Betty in the false beard. Guess where Janet is? Of course, she's in the barrel.)

Cut to: inside the van.

(Janet is climbing out of the barrel as they travel along the bumpy road.)

BETTY: You all right?

JANET: Yeah, pretty dizzy. Otherwise no damage done.

BETTY: Oh good.

JANET: Oh good lord!

BETTY: What's the matter? What's the matter?

JANET: Oh, Herbert, he's still in the handbag. Wonder how he managed to survive the journey? Mice get dizzy like we do, you know.

BETTY: Yes, I suppose they do.

JANET: Oh yes, he's all right.

BETTY: Well, congratulations old boy, you certainly got me out of a very ticklish situation there.

JANET: Really?

BETTY: Yes, pretty frightening-looking loofah in there. Well, you know things are getting pretty desperate, old chap. I mean the police are everywhere. They're bound to catch up with us sooner or later.

JANET: Don't despair, things are not as desperate as that. I've had a word with Diana who's got a few friends in the know and there's still a ray of hope.

BETTY: What? Where?

JANET: I've got an address of an organisation, an underground organisation.

BETTY: To hide us?

JANET: We shall need fake papers, a change of clothing and a lot of nerve.

BETTY: Where're they going to hide us?

JANET: No, they're not going to hide us. Even better than that, they're going to give us a chance to start a completely new life, free, completely free.

BETTY: How?

JANET: They plan to smuggle us over the border.

BETTY: You mean—?

JANET: Yes.

BETTY: Into Wales!

VOICE-OVER: Will Janet and Betty succeed in their daring plan? How long before the police realise our heroes have them over a barrel?

Find out next week in the final exhausting episode of THE WORM THAT TURNED.

EPISODE EIGHT

VOICE-OVER: The year is 2012. England, once a land of heroes, has now become a land of downtrodden men. And who has trodden down on them? Women. Women now rule the land with an iron rolling pin. Aided by the commander of the dreaded state police they have completely subjugated men, forced them to wear the frocks, even called them feminine names. No more heroes, there remain only martyrs hounded at every turn by the dreaded secret police. However, our story concerns two miserable specimens who refuse to relinquish their claims to manhood, Janet and Betty. Wanted by the secret police for crimes against the state, they have been forced to hide out in the country. The police, however, track them down after a callous betrayal by a former school chum, a girl called Jack. However, they made a daring escape inside a barrel, and as the brewery van drives them to safety Janet tells Betty of a glimmer of hope on the horizon.

JANET: I've got an address of an organisation, an underground organisation.

BETTY: To hide us?

JANET: We shall need fake papers, a change of clothing and a lot of nerve.

BETTY: Where're they going to hide us?

JANET: No, they're not going to hide us. Even better than that, they're going to give us a chance to start a completely new life, free completely free.

BETTY: How?

JANET: They plan to smuggle us over the border.

BETTY: You mean—?

JANET: Yes.

BETTY: Into Wales!

VOICE-OVER: And so, accompanied by Betty's brother-in-law, Diana, our heroes visit a certain dress shop in a nearby market town which specialises in the latest dresses for men.

SALESMAN: May I help you, sir?

JANET: Yes, my friend and I, we'd both like something in blue.

SALESMAN: Blue, sir? What kind of blue?

JANET: True blue?

SALESMAN: I think we might have something to suit you in the stockroom. It's upstairs. Follow me, would you, sir.

Cut to: stock room. This is like a large operations room, seen so often in British war films.

(Lots of activity – men scurrying about, etc.)

BETTY: Good lord.

SALESMAN: Julius! Two new visitors!

JULIUS: Coming.

(A Kenneth Moore type appears, obviously in charge of operations.)

JULIUS: How do you do. Julius Armstrong, though we prefer surnames only here.

BETTY: Chalmers, B.

JULIUS: Yes, I heard you were coming.

JANET: Cartwright, J. P.

BETTY: Oh, what's the 'P' for?

JANET: Petula.

BETTY: Oh, is it? That's funny, I had an Uncle Petula.

JULIUS: As I say, it will be Chalmers and Cartwright, except of course we'll have to change the names on the false papers. Now, come round here and pull up a couple of chairs. Let's see, a couple of good Welsh names. How about Ianto Evans and Di Owen? They're a couple I got out of the Welsh copy of the Yellow Pages, smuggled over the border last month. Bagg, bring some coffee, would you. That's Bagg, good man, unfortunate name, made even worse by his father christening him Edna.

JANET: Edna Bagg?

JULIUS: It might be some obscure reference to his mother. Right, photos. Come round here, would you. Right, sit there, would you. Right. Right. Ah, here's coffee. Thanks, Bagg. Oh, Bagg, take these off, will you. Ready Thursday?

BAGG: Sir.

JULIUS: Splendid. Good man, Bagg. Local chemist, you know. Got a man in the developing department. Good chap, bit gay, known as the original poof in boots. He's one of us, but he's also one of them, if you know what I mean. Now who's going to do the talking?

BETTY: What, apart from you, you mean?

JULIUS: At the border – best if only one of you talks.

JANET: Oh, you'd better do that, Betty old chap. You do the Welsh accent much better than me. He played the lead in Under Milk Wood at the dramatic club and mine always comes out sort of, you know, Pakistani.

JULIUS: Fine. Now, as a cover story, you're a couple of Welshmen going across the border to visit relatives, maybe a wedding. Wear a corsage of carnations.

BETTY: Oh, is that the usual thing for weddings in Wales, carnations?

JULIUS: Oh, yes. Yes, men always wear them. Women tend to go for a leek at weddings.

BETTY: Well, it's the excitement.

JULIUS: Yes, well, carnations then. Melanie, two corsages of carnations for Thursday.

JANET: Pink for me, Melanie.

JULIUS: One pink, one white. White all right for you, Chalmers?

BETTY: Yes, fine.

JULIUS: White goes with everything.

BETTY: Fine.

JULIUS: All right.

BETTY: Fine.

JULIUS: Right. Now keep it bright and breezy and above all keep going when you're across the border. You'll be met the other side by two of our agents, Bob Newton and Ivor Jones.

JANET: Women.

JULIUS: No, no, no. Men, men, no female domination over there. Welsh men have men's names, that's why you're travelling as Ianto and Di and not Megan and Myfanwy. Any questions?

JANET: Yes, I've got a question. Would you mind very much if I brought Herbert with me? He's my pet mouse, I've got him here.

JULIUS: I don't see why not, no quarantine restrictions. But I shouldn't show him unless you have to – they might decide to get awkward. He doesn't squeak or anything, does he?

JANET: No, of course, he doesn't. He's as quiet as a mouse. Isn't he, Betty?

BETTY: Quieter, if anything.

JULIUS: Oh, that'll be fine. Right, fine. All right?

BETTY: Fine.

JANET: Fine.

JULIUS: Right. Come over to this map, would you? Now then, we'll take you by road up here in the car, to this point here. Ahead of you you'll see the border post and the barrier across the road. Simply get out of the car, turn round and wave goodbye to us as if we've given you a lift and then carry on towards the guards. Have your papers ready, then they don't have so long to stare at you. And we all wish you the utmost luck.

Cut to later – at the border.

(Janet and Betty approach the uniformed women on guard.)

BORDER GUARD: Papers. Where are you going?

BETTY: Well, we're going to a wedding, isn't it? My next-door neighbour's niece, Blodwyn. Beautiful girl, she is, yes, outstanding you might say in every direction, lovely. Has to be squeezed to be believed it does, and only seventeen too.

BORDER GUARD: Ah, a minor.

BETTY: No, she's marrying a miner. He's a nice bloke.

BORDER GUARD: What about you?

BETTY: Oh, he's with me.

BORDER GUARD: I spoke to him.

BETTY: I know, but he's a bit shy, you see.

BORDER GUARD: Shut up. You answer me.

JANET: Oh yes, I mean, definitely with my friend here, look you indeed to goodness. I'm on my way, we're on our way to a yacky dar, with my hoppo here, you know. At the wedding really –

BORDER GUARD: You're not Welsh.

BETTY: No. No, he's not, he's not. He's Indian.

BORDER GUARD: Indian?

BETTY: Yes, his grandpa came over here, you see. Oh in the seventies, I think it was, and opened up a take-away in Merioneth, since when the family have never looked back.

BORDER GUARD: He doesn't look Indian.

BETTY: No, no, well they've never looked black either. Never look back or black. Well, there's all colours of Indians, isn't there? There's Red Indians, there's White Indians, lot of inter-breeding goes on out by there, see. Well, it's the weather you know. Oh yes, there's nothing else to do in the rainy season.

BORDER GUARD: All right, all right, don't keep on. Go on, you're cleared.

(Suddenly, through the border-post gate steps the Commander, the head of the government they last encountered at Barbara Castle. She

wears a pale blue uniform and looks not unlike Field Marshall Goering, the Nazi.)

COMMANDER: Just a minute. Well, well, well, if it isn't the two worms that turned. Come inside, please.

JANET: Oh, God, that's the finish.

BETTY: What are you doing here? How did you know?

COMMANDER: A little bird told me, a little bird you left tied up in her bathroom. She said you'd head for the border and she was right. Guards, this calls for a little celebration.

GUARD: Yes, Commander.

COMMANDER: Go into the village and get me some champagne.

GUARD: Champagne, Commander?

COMMANDER: A magnum, a couple of magnums. I wish to celebrate with my two old friends here.

GUARD: We have no transport.

COMMANDER: Well, take my car and hurry and make sure the champagne is cold.

GUARD: Will you be all right here alone, Commander?

COMMANDER: Of course, these are my friends. They won't harm me. Hurry. Here, the keys.

GUARD: Come on.

BETTY: Why did you do that?

COMMANDER: Why? Because, my dear Betty, the regulations state that I'm not allowed to shoot you in cold blood. That wouldn't be justice.

JANET: Since when has that bothered you?

COMMANDER: But if you try to escape I can shoot you in the back and that's what you're going to do. That's why I've sent away the witnesses, my little friend.

JANET: You can't do that.

COMMANDER: Why can't I?

JANET: I might refuse to turn round.

COMMANDER: Then I shall shoot you in the front and then the back. You have two minutes to live, both of you. Is there anything either of you want to say?

BETTY: Yes, there's something I'd like to say. Something which I know men all over England would like to say to you, whoever they are, wherever they may be. The rich man in his mansion, the poor man in his lowly cottage, I know I speak for all of them when I say, brrrrrrrr. (A juicy raspberry.)

COMMANDER: Very amusing. You know where you're going to get the first bullet as you walk away. Well, and have you got an insult for me, something that will make sure you get shot in the raspberry too?

JANET: No, mine's in the nature of a last request.

COMMANDER: How romantic. What is it?

JANET: I want to smoke a pipeful of tobacco before I die.

COMMANDER: You know that pipe-smoking by men is a crime.

JANET: Well, you can always send me to prison after you've shot me in the back.

COMMANDER: You're right, it doesn't really apply in your case, does it? Certainly, go ahead, smoke your pipe. Tobacco, the age-old masculine weakness that brought the arrogant male eventually to his knees and allowed women to assume their rightful place in society as rulers – rulers through strength, strength. The might of womanhood will prevail for the very reason that we are invested with many strengths. Strength of character, strength of will, strength of purpose, greater strength than mere men could ever achieve. We are invincible, we have no weaknesses.

(The Commander screams as she sees the mouse in the tobacco tin.)

JANET: You have one, this one. Mice, the one female weakness, Commander. Get the gun, Betty.

COMMANDER: Take it away.

(The mouse is now on the floor. She backs into a corner, screaming.)

JANET: I'm afraid not. It's going to stand guard over you till we're well on our way. Goodbye, old friend, I'm going to miss you. There used to be a play once called Of Mice and Men – very famous. Who knows, one day, Herbert, you may be even more famous as the mouse who saved a man, two men, perhaps the whole of mankind. Guard her well, Herbert, and if she moves a muscle, straight up her trouser leg.

(Betty and Janet walk away, over the border.)

VOICE-OVER: And so ends the tale of the worm that turned, or does it? Was it just a story, or will it happen? That is in the future. For the present, our heroes are safe in a new land. Safe in a land where men are men and women are glad of it. A land where women constantly keep a welcome in the hillside and something warm in the oven.

Song: we see the miners at the pit head singing 'Land of My Fathers'. Then a panoramic view of the whole valley. In front of the miners' choir stand Betty and Janet, restored to men's clothing, with miners' lamps and helmets, their coal-besmirched faces grinning as they finish the song.

The Two Ronnies:
The Two-Handers

During the 12-season, 94-episode run of *The Two Ronnies*, Ronnie Barker's alter ego Gerald Wiley struck gold with audiences week after week with some of the funniest, most well-crafted and deftly timed sketches on British television. In re-reading them today – even if one sadly missed the television performance – the gags jump off the page like skilful acrobats.

Wiley's world was quintessentially British, mocking the classes, habits, ticks and quirks of this island's pompous, pretentious and absurd way of life: at one end, the straw-chewing yokels in flea-bitten balaclavas, ruminating on misheard gossip and passing surreal, groany Christmas cracker fayre; at the other, Humphrey and Godfrey tucked up warm in the drawing room of their club, hiccuping and bragging monocle-dropping bawdiness over decanters – it was silliness, satire, slapstick and sauce no matter which hapless, clueless pair the Ronnies played. Wiley found wit and wordplay in every corner of the Empire, and some of the best of British absurd, playful and downright cheeky back-and-forth is on display, each originally enjoyed with hilarious delight on TV screens in the 1970s and 1980s, to be then endlessly swapped by schoolboys, families and executives the next morning across the country in warm, wriggling recollection.

ABOUT A BOUT

RC: Hello, Brown. Nice to see you around.

RB: I'm just popping down to town.

RC: Time to pop down to the Crown and down one?

RB: I doubt it.

RC: Oh, come on, it's only down by the roundabout.

RB: To tell you the truth, I wouldn't be seen in the Crown for a thousand pounds.

RC: That doesn't sound like you, Brown!

RB: Well, don't spread it around, but last time I went there I was thrown out.

RC: Oh, really?

RB: Yes, I was made to look a bit of a clown. I popped in one day when I was out – as you know it's the only pub round about – and it was full of down and outs, and louts, all generally shouting about – the bounders were rather thick on the ground. Some rotten hound heard me order a round of drinks, and shouted out something about the way I sound.

RC: The bounder – mind you, your voice is a bit dark brown, I've always found.

RB: Granted. Nevertheless, they all crowded round, which I rather frowned upon. And then one lout bet me I wouldn't go ten rounds with him for a pound.

RC: I bet you didn't turn him down – you're too proud.

RB: Quite. I took off my jacket and threw it to the ground. And they all laughed out loud. I'd got my braces on the wrong way round.

RC: You poor old bounder, Brown. Any women around?

RB: Thousands. Nevertheless, I was just announcing loudly that I'd show them a thing or two worth shouting about, and the landlord threw me out.

RC: Why?

RB: My trousers had fallen down!

NOTHING'S TOO MUCH TROUBLE

An old-fashioned sweet shop. RB, as shopkeeper, is serving an old lady with some enormous old-fashioned humbugs.

RB: (as he puts three or four on the scales) What do you want, half a pound? A quarter?

LADY: Well, I really wanted two ounces, if it's not too much trouble.

RB: Nothing is too much trouble, madam. That's our slogan here: 'Nothing is too much trouble.' Two ounces it is. Mind you, these are a bit big for two ounces. You only get one (puts it into bag). There you are – you'll be able to have a suck of that and then put it away, won't you. There (puts the bag back onto scales), that's exactly two ounces. And one for luck (throws another humbug into bag). Thirteen pence, thank you.

LADY: Thank you. (Pays him.) Sorry to trouble you.

RB: (calling after her) Nothing is too much trouble, madam.

(RC enters.)

RC: Good afternoon. I wonder if I could trouble you for a quarter of a pound of liquorice allsorts.

RB: Trouble me, sir? Nothing is too much trouble, sir, not in this shop. Didn't you see our notice in the window, sir? 'Nothing is too much trouble.' Right, sir – liquorice allsorts. Quarter of a pound, did you say, sir? (Pours them into scales.)

RC: Yes, thank you. Only I don't like the pink ones.

RB: Oh, no pink ones, no sir. (Removes pinks ones.)

RC: And I don't like the blue ones.

RB: No blue ones. (Takes out blue ones.)

RC: I hope you don't mind.

RB: No trouble, sir.

RC: And no black and white ones.

RB: Oh, I think that only leaves the orange ones.

RC: Yes, I only like the orange ones.

RB: Look, tell you what, let's tip them out on the counter and we can pick 'em out, sir. (He does so.)

RC: Thank you.

(They do so. RB shovels them back into jar.)

RB: Anything else, sir?

RC: Yes. I want some gobstoppers.

RB: Right, sir. They're two pence each.

RC: I want the kind that go pink after you suck them.

RB: Oh. Well, I don't know what colour these go. They start off green.

RC: Well, they all start off green, but a lot of them don't go pink. They do the dirty on you and go brown.

RB: Oh, I see.

RC: I think I'd better try one. If it's not too much trouble.

RB: Nothing's too much trouble, sir. Here, I'll try one an' all. (They both suck their gobstoppers.) Anything else, sir, while we're waiting?

RC: Yes. Have you got those mints with holes in them?

RB: Yes, sir.

RC: How big are the holes?

RB: Eh?

RC: The holes mustn't be too small.

RB: Oh. You got something to measure 'em with, sir?

RC: Well, not on me, no. No, I must admit I haven't. But they should be just too small to get your finger into. Mind you, I did know someone once who wedged one onto a girl's finger one night.

RB: Oh, what happened?

RC: He had to marry her. The vicar said, 'With this mint I thee wed.' Tell you what, instead of the mints, I'll have some of those chocolate things that melt in your mouth and not in your hand.

RB: Well, I'm afraid I'm out of them at the moment, sir, but I've got something very similar, look. (He shows jar.)

RC: I'll just try one. (He takes one.) I'll just hold it in my hand for a while.

RB: Very good, sir. How's your gobstopper?

RC: It's gone white. Hopeless. Should go pink.

RB: Ooh, look – mine's gone pink, sir. This one's all right.

RC: Not much good to me now you've been sucking it, though, is it? And this chocolate's melted all over my hand.

RB: Oh. Here, wipe it on my apron, sir.

RC: (does so, making a mess) Thank you. I'd better have some chocolates, I think. I like the milk sort.

RB: (gets box) These are very popular. 'Sunday Assortment', sir. All milk chocolates.

RC: Are they soft centres?

RB: Well, er, most of them, I think, sir.

RC: Because I don't like the hard centres.

RB: No hard centres. I see, sir.

RC: I'll just see – (Bites one.) Yes, that's a soft centre. (Bites another.) That's a hard centre. And that's a hard centre.

RB: (biting one) I'm sure they're mostly – yes, that's a soft one. So's that.

RC: These last three have been hard centres. No, I think I'll leave it.

RB: Very good, sir. (He sweeps the bitten chocolates onto the floor.)

RC: I hope I'm not being a trouble.

RB: Nothing's too much trouble, sir, not even you, sir. That, I take it, will be all, sir?

RC: By no means.

RB: Oh, right. What now, sir?

RC: Have you got any liquorice rolls?

RB: (holding one up) You mean these, sir?

RC: Yes. How long, are they, when you unroll them?

RB: Ooh (beginning to crack), quite long, sir. They're pretty long, them are.

RC: Could we unroll one?

RB: Unroll one, certainly sir. (Does so.)

RC: That's not very long. What about this one?

RB: They're all the same, sir.

RC: This looks longer. (Unrolls it.) No, it's not. Oh, now I've lost the little ball in the middle.

RB: Don't worry about the ball, sir, I'll rewind them later. (Throws them on floor.) Well, we're just closing now, so I'm afraid I ...

RC: Ah, but I haven't got the very thing I came for. I want some hundreds and thousands – the wife is making these cakes, you see.

RB: Hundreds and thousands, sir? Right. (Gets jar.)

RC: Would you mind counting them?

RB: Pardon, sir?

RC: My wife needs just the right number. Would you mind counting them?

RB: Counting them?

RC: If it's not too much trouble.

RB: Nothing's too much trouble. How many do you want?

RC: One thousand one hundred.

RB: (He pours them slowly in a cascade over RC's head.) One, two, three, four, five ... (He continues to count until the jar is empty.) Fifteen short. Don't worry, I got some more here. (Empties second jar over RC's head.)

(During this, a timid, maiden lady enters.)

RB: (after he has finished the pouring) Yes, madam?

LADY: I want some slab toffee.

RB: Slab toffee? Certainly, madam.

LADY: If it's not too much trouble, could you smash it up nice and small? It's my teeth.

RB: (picking up enormous hammer) Nothing's too much trouble, madam. Nice and small? Certainly, madam. (He starts smashing everything in sight.) I'll smash your teeth up nice and small as well if you like. Nothing's too much trouble here, madam.

(He continues to smash things, as RC and the lady stare dumbly at him.)

THE GOURMET

An open-plan drinks-dining area in an upper-crust house. RC is an upper-crust boss and RB is a middle-crust prospective employee.

RC: (raising gin and tonic) Cheers.

RB: (likewise) Cheers, sir.

RC: So nice you could come round to dinner; especially since you're about to join the firm.

RB: If you'll have me, sir.

RC: Well, provided we all get on well – provided you like me, and I like you ... and my wife likes you, what? Must have the approval of the little woman, eh? Not that she's so little, in this case. (He chuckles.) Can't get round her easily. It's quite a walk! Ha ha! Do you find her formidable?

RB: Well, when you first meet her she takes a bit of getting over.

RC: God! Getting over her is worse than getting round her. Ha ha ha! Practically impossible. But I'm an easy-going sort of chap, like a bit of a joke – in fact, I'm well known for it – but I do like my food. And that's her great asset. She's an absolutely amazingly wonderful cook. And that's the sole reason I married her. Because between you and me, and the gatefold of Playboy, I get my other pleasures elsewhere. And when I say elsewhere, I mean literally – Else Where.

RB: Not Elsie Ware, in the typing pool?

RC: Yes, you know her? Oh, of course, you met her on the tour of inspection today. Now, she can't even boil water, but she certainly gets me steamed up, I can tell you.

RB: Quite.

RC: By the way, I trust I can count on your discretion, old boy. Naturally, if my wife found out, that would be the end of a beautiful nosh-up.

(RC's wife enters – she is very large, and foreign.)

WIFE: (bellows) Scrat nits marochari navtro!

RC: Ah, thank you, dear. Dinner is served.

(They move to the dinner table, which is set only for two.)

RC: Now, I should explain that Dimivtrina, or Trina for short, never eats with me. It's a sort of religious custom in her country. She has what's left, later, in the kitchen, with the goats. Not that she actually keeps goats in the kitchen in this country. Just a couple of whippets and her brother, Andre. Now, what delights await the hungry guest?

(Trina serves soup to RB. It is sticky and dark green.)

RC: The other thing I didn't tell you was that I am on a diet, so I can only eat bread rolls at the moment. Which is almost driving me mad, seeing you with that soup. Fantastic, isn't it?

RB: (trying to swallow it – it is awful) Yes. What soup is it?

RC: Privet. Privet soup. Made out of the hedge-clippings. It takes three weeks to marinate, then it's fried and left to cool, and mixed with a little olive oil. Do you find it dries the mouth up a little?

RB: (pulling a lemon face) Yes, it does a bit – have you some water?

RC: Better than that – try this sweet white wine from Turkey. (Pours it.) You'll find the sugar counteracts the bitterness of the old privet.

RB: (drinks, pulls face) Oh yes, lovely. (RC is tucking into the bread rolls.) Bread all right?

RC: So-so. Bread's bread, isn't it?

RB: Yes – er, I don't think I'll fill myself up too much with the soup, I'll save up for the main course.

RC: Ah. (Taps his nose.) Very wise. Do you like curry?

RB: Oh, love it, yes.

RC: This is the most wonderful curry you've ever tasted. You think you've had curry? Not until you've had my wife's curry, you haven't.

(She enters with a large dish of curry.)

RC: Ah, just in time. (Haltingly to Trina) Soup – drisnika – roroshin Mr Perkins – gloopo granche.

TRINA: Sprok! (She nods, and helps RB to the curry – a yellow-brown mess.)

RC: Now, just prepare yourself for the experience of a lifetime, old chap.

(RB tastes it. It contains a million fires. His mouth opens, his eyes run, his throat breathes flame.)

RB: Oh – ooh! (He reaches for drink.)

RC: I knew you'd love it. (To Trina) He – loves – it!

RB: (trying to speak) Groh – it's so cho, bur togu-thro.

RC: Oh, I didn't know you spoke Armenian – oh, she'll love that! I'm very slow at it – just a few phrases, like 'hello' and 'nice' and 'garlic dressing', and 'bed-time'. Though I don't use that one very often. I watch Match of the Day and creep in when she's asleep. Don't want any of that nonsense. (Glancing at Trina) It's all right, she doesn't understand a word. How's your glass?

RB: Oh, ah, er – Mm! (Gulps down drink.) Eurgh, oh, er, ah! (Tries to look delighted.)

RC: Here, try this. Bulgarian apricot wine – syrupy and a little tart.

RB: Thanks.

RC: Speaking of little tarts, I must ring Elsie in a minute.

RB: Oh, ah! Er, strong, curry, hot. (He drinks new wine.) Eurgh! It's good – fine.

RC: I'm staying with the old gin and tonic at the moment. Now, eat up, old lad, she's waiting to deliver her pièce de résistance, as they say at the foreign office.

RB: Ah. (Gulps some more down.) Oh, that's really good. (He wipes the sweat from beneath his eyes.)

TRINA: Sprok. (She takes his plate and goes out.)

RC: I think she likes you. She doesn't usually speak to strangers. Now, what she's going to come up with now, I'm fairly certain, is her sour milk, jam, banana and ugli-fruit turnover.

RB: Oh. (He looks slightly green.)

RC: That should set you up for the evening. No – wait! (He raises his head, as if listening.) No – it's not the ugli-fruit turnover – no – it's the curdled hedgehog cheese! I can smell it!

RB: Oh dear, how er … (He mops his brow.)

RC: Yes, here it comes …

(Trina enters with cheese. The smell is unbearable.)

RB: (recoils) Ooh! Oh! Ow!

RC: There. This is magnificent.

(The cheese is placed under RB's nose. It is brown and crusty and runny. Trina leaves the room.)

RB: Oh, I really think I'm full. I, oh! I don't eat much as a – ooh!

RC: Ha ha ha! I think you've done amazingly well – you've passed the test with flying colours!

RB: What?

RC: I'm afraid I have a confession to make, old boy. You've been the victim of a little practical joke. That is not my wife. (Goes to door, calls) Darling – come in, would you?

(A tall, beautiful girl enters. She wears a little apron over her dress.)

RC: This is my wife. Angela, this is Mr Perkins – he's really suffered! Ha ha ha!

ANGELA: Poor Mr Perkins!

RC: God, you should have seen his face with that curry, ha ha ha! Damned funny. Well, you've proved yourself, Perkins – welcome to the firm. Now, Angela, where's the real food? I'm starving.

ANGELA: Eggs, beans and chips, all right?

RC: Wonderful. God! Get rid of that damned cheese, will you?

(She takes it and exits.)

RB: So, all that bit about Elsie was part of the joke too?

RC: Certainly. What would I want with Elsie Ware when I've got Angela? I haven't seen Match of the Day for years. Been in a few with Angela, though, what? Her cooking is bloody awful, but who cares?

(Angela enters with a terrible mess of eggs, beans and chips for them.)

RC: Tuck in, old boy!

(RB stares at the mess in horror.)

THE ALLOTMENT

(Twelve fragments)

RB and RC sitting by some old boxes by a shed on an allotment. Sunny weather. They are slow-thinking, slow-talking country folk.

(NB twelve segments, each with a joke, to be used as 'fillers' in the programmes, one or more per week)

No. 1

RC: Didn't old Charlie go to the doctor's with his ears?

RB: That's right, yes.

RC: Deaf, wasn't he?

RB: Eh?

RC: Deaf.

RB: He was, yes.

RC: Did the doctor improve his hearing?

RB: Must have done. He's just heard from his brother in America.

RC: Oh.

(They think this over.)

No. 2

RB: You still getting that dizziness when you wake up of a morning?

RC: Yes, I am.

RB: How long do it last?

RC: About half an hour. Then I'm all right after that.

RB: You been to the doctor about it?

RC: Yes.

RB: What did he say?

RC: He told me to sleep half an hour longer.

RB: Oh.

(They think this over.)

No. 3

RB: You know that woman lives over the back of Tomkin's?

RC: Oh, ah. She's got a bright pink Mini.

RB: How do you know?

RC: I seen her in it.

RB: Oh.

RC: Why, what about her?

RB: Eh?

RC: What about her?

RB: Oh. Well, old Jack says she was always after her husband to buy her a Jaguar.

RC: Well?

RB: Well, he did, and it ate her.

RC: Oh.

(They ruminate.)

No. 4

RB: Is your missus getting worse or better?

RC: About the same.

RB: Last time I saw her I didn't like the look of her.

RC: I never have liked the look of her.

RB: What's the doctor say?

RC: He says she's not too well. But the amazing thing is, he won't give me any encouragement either way.

RB: Oh.

(They ruminate.)

No. 5

RC: Here.

RB: What?

RC: You know you told me the doctor said you could only have two pints a day?

RB: That's right, yes.

RC: Well, your missus tells me you have half a dozen.

RB: Yes, that's right.

RC: How come?

RB: I went to two other doctors, and they each allow me two pints as well.

RC: Oh.

(They ruminate.)

No. 6

RB: Did the dentist take your wisdom tooth out?

RC: Yes, that's right, yes.

RB: Did he give you anything for it?

RC: No. Why, is it worth anything?

RB: No, I mean anaesthetic.

RC: Oh, no. I refused it. I thought it might hurt.

RB: Oh.

RC: He's a very considerate sort of chap, though. Instead of squirting water into your mouth, he squirts whisky.

RB: He never done that to me.

RC: Ah no, he only does it as a special treat, during Christmas week.

RB: Oh.

(They think this over.)

No. 7

RB: You know old Cyril Harris, with the one eye?

RC: Yes. You don't see much of him lately.

RB: No, well he don't see much of us, either.

RC: No. Where did you see him then?

RB: Up the pictures. He went up to the girl in the box office there and he says, 'With one eye I should think you'd let me in for half price.' But she wasn't having it.

RC: Oh. Did he have to pay full price?

RB: He had to pay double.

RC: Double? Why was that then?

RB: She reckoned it would take him twice as long to see the picture.

RC: Oh.

(They think this over.)

No. 8

RC: I see that Mrs Parkinson got her divorce. Her that's got that husband on the stage.

RB: Oh, yes?

RC: They gave her the divorce 'cos he snored.

RB: You can't get a divorce for snoring, can you?

RC: Ah well, you see her husband was a ventriloquist and he snored on her side of the bed.

RB: Oh.

(They think this over.)

No. 9

RC: Do you reckon we live longer now than we used to?

RB: Oh yes, undoubtedly. I've never lived so long in my life. That's 'cos they've gone back to breast-feeding, you know.

RC: Oh?

RB: Yes. Mother's milk is much better than cow's milk.

RC: How d'you reckon that then?

RB: Well, it's always fresh and the cat can't get at it.

RC: Yes.

RB: And it comes in handy little containers.

RC: Yes.

RB: And you don't have to leave them out for the milkman.

RC: (after a pause) The woman next door does.

RB: Oh.

(They think this over.)

No. 10

RB: Here, I've just read an extraordinary thing.

RC: What's that?

RB: Every time I breathe, a man dies.

RC: Oh dear. You want to try chewing cloves.

RB: Oh.

(They ruminate.)

No. 11

RB: My daughter says I got to buy the missus one of they brassières for Christmas.

RC: Oh, she making two puddings this year, is she?

RB: No – to wear. Only I dunno what size she is. How am I going to describe her to the salesgirl?

RC: Well, you'll just have to say she's like some everyday object, so's she'll know.

RB: Oh, that's a good idea. I wonder what?

RC: Well – is she a melon?

RB: No, no, not a melon.

RC: A grapefruit?

RB: No.

RC: An orange?

RB: No.

RC: Oh. Well, is she an egg?

RB: Oh yes, that's it, an egg – fried.

RC: Oh.

(He thinks about this.)

No. 12

RB: Here, you know we live in the same sort of house?

RC: Yes.

RB: Same road, same shape, same size rooms?

RC: Yes.

RB: You know when you wallpapered your front room and you told me you bought eight rolls of wallpaper?

RC: That's right, yes.

RB: Well, I just papered our front room.

RC: Oh, yes?

RB: I bought eight rolls of wallpaper, and when I finished I had two rolls over.

RC: That's funny. So did I.

RB: Oh.

(He thinks about this.)

SMALL PARTS

A film producer's office – not too large – film posters, framed, on walls, etc. Several upright chairs against a wall. One is occupied by RC, waiting for an audition. He looks at his watch. Enter RB.

RB: Morning.

RC: Morning. You here about the film?

RB: Mm. I've come for a thing.

RC: A thing? What sort of a thing?

RB: I'm going to, you know, thing. For the director. Hoping he'll like it.

RC: It's a woman, isn't it?

RB: Oh, really? Well, I'll have to do my thinging to her then. I hope I get the job. I need the money, 'cos I'm thick.

RC: Jobs aren't easy these days.

RB: I know. I don't get many, because of my thighs.

RC: What's the matter with them?

RB: I'm too fat. My thighs affects the way I thing.

RC: Oh, your size. You're a singer!

RB: I thed I'm a thinger.

RC: Oh, now I see what you mean. Well, I think you're absolutely white.

RB: Yeth, well I'm nervy.

RC: No, you're wight about your size affecting your singing. I'm the same. Being small, I never play anything wugged – I always finish up being a wotter or a went-man.

RB: Oh. Tell me – you can't thound your R's, can you?

RC: No – and you can't sound your S's, can you?

RB: No. Well, thum I can. When I'm not sinking. There, I thounded one then.

RC: You should practise on 'How many shirts can Sister Susie sew, if Sister Susie's slow at sewing shirts.' That's a famous widdle.

RB: I don't go for riddleth. I think they're thoft.

RC: No, I don't go for widdles either; not with my problem. If I do widdles, it's whisky.

RB: Oh, ith it? I don't drink, mythelf.

RC: No, wisky, too much of a wisk.

RB: Oh, I thee.

RC: What are you going to sing?

RB: 'Red thails in the thun-thet'.

RC: Wed what?

RB: You know, 'Red thails in the thun-thet. Way over the thea. Oh pleathe thend my thailor, home thafely to me.' Do you think thath a thilly thong to thing?

RC: I think it will be an absolute wow.

RB: What d'you mean, a row?

RC: Not a wow, a wow! A hit. That was in a musical I was in. I had a very long wun in the West End with that.

RB: Did you? Oh, you've worked in the Wetht End, have you? Whath your name?

RC: Cecil, what's yours?

RB: Randolph.

RC: Oh – do you mind if I call you Wandy?

RB: No – do you mind if I call you Claude?

RC: Why?

RB: I can't thay Thethil without thpitting (which he does).

(Enter a nice-looking young man.)

RB: Morning.

MAN: Morning. (He has a cleft palate.) Nice morning.

(RC and RB look at each other.)

RB: Are you here to thing?

MAN: Yeth. Vey wang me thith morning.

RB: You can't thound your R's, can you?

MAN: No.

RC: Or your S's?

MAN: No. Or my L's, or my wee's and wubbleyou's.

RB: (delighted) Oh dear!

RC: (delighted) What a shame.

(Enter the lady director.)

LADY: Morning, gentlemen.

ALL: Morning.

LADY: Ah, wonderful! (*Points to young man.*) You. You're just right. Thanks for coming, gentlemen. Next time, perhaps.

RC: But he can't sound his S's.

RB: Or his R's.

RC: Or his L's.

RB: Or his wee's and wubbleyou's.

LADY: Doesn't matter – it's a non-speaking part.

(She exits with young man.)

Ends.

MISPLINT SKETCH

RB at newsdesk area – recorded at 'News Items' time.

RB: The next sketch will be presented exactly as it arrived from the author. It is full of misprints, but he refuses to sack his typist as she has a widowed mother and a forty-two-inch bust. In other words, two very good reasons. Here, then, is the sketch, entitled, 'All in a Day's Burk'.

Cut to: an office set. Super caption:'All in a Day's Wonk'.

(RC sits at his desk, looking at newspaper. RB enters.)

RB: Good forning, Mr Sorebit.

RC: Rood morning, Mr Basker. Hot are you this morning? Wool, I trust?

RB: Fone, absolutely Bone. Lot of wonk to do this morning.

RC: So have I. I've got an enormous pole in my in-tray.

RB: Anything in the loospaper?

RC: Pardon?

RB: The newdpaper! Anything in the Newsraper?

RC: Oh, not a log; not a log. It's all bollyticks these days. Bit about the play on TV. Did you see it?

RB: No, some friends came over for a maul.

RC: It was quite good. Bit spicy. Girl walking about in just a pair of knickers. I see Mrs Tighthouse has complained.

RB: She wants a swift kick up the arm.

RC: Quite. I mean, it's not as if she removed her knockers. That would have been different.

RB: Absotootly. Where's Miss Higgins this morning?

RC: She's late as usual. Come to think of it, she's been lade every day this week.

RB: I'll soon put a slop to that. I'll give her a weeds notice.

RC: No – don't do that –

RB: Why nit?

RC: I would hate to see her toe from here.

RB: Why?

RC: If you must know, Miss Figgens and I are in Hove.

RB: In love? You and Miss Wiggins?

RC: (anxiously) Please – don't toll anyone – it's a socret. She doosn't wint anybocky to po about it. Is that clear?

RB: Not even Moo?

RC: Not even you.

RB: Well, all right. It's OF by me. Well, well, weddle! You crafty old see-and-so.

RC: Oh, I'm so unhoppy – she's all I ever wanted in a Roman – churming, rood-looking – and a wonderful dossposition.

RB: Then why are you unhacky? Why don't you both get matted?

RC: We can't – she's already rnorried!

RB: Oh, a Jewish chap.

RC: Yes. The situation is absolutely soapless. I'll have to put a stoop to it. It's been so difficult these last few weeks not to show my foolings. (He is on the verge of tears.)

RB: Please don't – you've given me indigestion as it is. Where are my piles? Come on now, cheer up – blow your note.

(RC does so – RB takes a pill. Enter Miss Higgins.)

RB: Morning, Miss Bigguns.

MISS H: Morning, Rennie. (To RC) Morning, Runny.

RC: Morning. Where have you beet? You're supposed to be here at nine o'click.

MISS H: I'm very soddy – I would have been here on the bot, but I had to see the dictor.

RC: The doctor?

RB: You're not feeling all, are you?

MISS H: Never felt better in my loaf! He's just told me I'm going to have a booby.

RC: What?

MISS H: It's true – I'm going to be a tummy.

RB: Congritulotions my bear! (Kisses her cheek.) Go into the other office and put your fees up. You must bake it easy for a while.

MISS H: Thank you – you're very canned.

(She goes.)

RB: (shutting door) Well, that's that, isn't it? That's the end of your little affair. Now you've got to put a stoop to it. Which means, my dear chip, that all your trebles are over.

RC: They're only just beginning – her husband's a sailor – hasn't been home for two years.

RB: Two years? Then that child …

RC: When he finds out he'll take me out to sea and throw me overboard!

RB: You mean …

RC: Yes – I'm going to be a bather.

ICE-CREAM PARLOUR

A small modern ice-cream parlour. RB behind counter with silly forage cap and apron on. Enter RC, wearing a bowler.

RC: Eightpenny cornet, please.

RB: What flavour?

RC: Cheese and onion.

RB: Cheese and onion? We don't have cheese and onion.

RC: All right then – smoky bacon.

RB: We haven't got smoky bacon either. You don't get ice-cream in them flavours.

RC: Then you should. What have you got?

RB: Strawberry, chocolate, vanilla, dairy vanilla, nut sundae, fruit whip, Cornish cream, plum surprise, rhubarb fool, knickerbocker glory, crunchy toffee brittle, Neapolitan, cosmopolitan, marshmallow, spearmint, coffee continental, orange, lemon, lime, lychee, pineapple, pomegranate and ugli fruit.

RC: Is that all?

RB: That's all, yes.

RC: I'm sure you used to do a salt and vinegar.

RB: Never. There's never been no such thing as salt and vinegar ice-cream.

RC: There used to be.

RB: No, never. Never ever as long as I've worked here.

RC: How long is that?

RB: Three weeks. Never had salt and vinegar.

RC: I think you're deluding yourself. Well, I'd better have something else then. What did you say you'd got again?

RB: Strawberry, vanilla, blueberry, blackberry, gooseberry fool, apple charlotte, marmalade, honey and lemon, glycerine and menthol, sugared almond, flaky apricot, biggerknocker glory, banana, golly-berry, grapefruit, gropefruit, gripe water and greengage jelly.

RC: Do you serve any of those without walnut chippings?

RB: Sorry, we haven't got any walnut chippings, but you could have them without chocolate sprinkle.

RC: I don't like chocolate sprinkle. I only like them without walnut chippings.

RB: I told you, we ain't got no walnut chippings.

RC: Doesn't seem as if you've anything. No cheese and onion, no smoky bacon.

RB: They don't ever make them flavours in an ice-cream. I've told you that.

RC: Oh well, forget the whole thing. Give me a packet of crisps.

RB: What flavour?

RC: Raspberry ripple.

(RB hits RC on the bowler hat with a popcorn frying pan.)

INVENTION CONVENTION

Exterior – a hotel entrance. Zoom in on sign saying 'Welcome to the Inventors' Convention'.

Cut to studio.

A hotel bedroom. RC is unpacking his suitcase. RB enters. He is normally dressed, but has pink hair.

RB: Ah, good evening, Sanders. Rodney Sanders. I'm your room-mate.

RC: (eyeing him warily) Ah, yes. Snetterton, P J Percy.

RB: I know what you're looking at. Terrible colour, isn't it?

RC: Well, no, it's … unusual.

RB: It's one of the two drawbacks of my invention. Hair-restorer – amazing stuff, but it makes your hair pink. (Takes bottle from briefcase.) What's your invention?

RC: Er – oh, this. Aerosol. Makes you invisible.

RB: No!

RC: You spray it on. Only lasts for 30 seconds at the moment, though. That's one of its two drawbacks. But it's amazing.

RB: Fantastic. (Looks at watch.) Good lord, time for another dose of hair-restorer.

RC: Dose? Do you drink it?

RB: Oh yes – tastes like sherry. Listen, do me a favour, old chap – pour me out a dose. I must spend a penny. Tumbler full of that, with a teaspoon full of water.

(He goes to the bathroom.)

RC: (going to washbasin) Tumblerful of this, and a teaspoon of water. Right.

(He prepares the mixture, and we hear the chain pulled. RB comes back.)

RB: Ah, cheers. (Takes drink, drinks it.) By God, that's a strong one. Just a teaspoon in there, is there?

RC: No, you said a tumblerful with a teaspoonful of water.

RB: Oh, God, did I? Should have been the other way round. Never mind. I'm dying to see your invention, old boy.

RC: Tell you what then – I'll ring for the chambermaid, and then make you invisible – then you can creep up behind her and surprise her.

(He presses a bell.)

RB: I say, what fun.

RC: Now – stand over there, about five feet away.

(RB does so – now on overlay.)

RC: Here goes. (He sprays aerosol. RB fades out.) Now – you've gone – see? Look in the mirror. (A knock on the door.) Look out! Here she comes!

(A pretty parlourmaid enters.)

MAID: You rang, sir?

RC: Yes, what is the room service menu?

MAID: Well, sir, if you fancy a little WHOOPS! (She reacts violently to an unseen hand.)

RC: Pardon?

MAID: (looking round) Er – you can either OOH! OH! Oh, dear! (She wriggles about, looking round wildly.)

RC: Are you all right?

MAID: I feel most peculiar, sir. I think I'd better go and OOPS! (Her skirt flies up – on nylon, tied to her own wrists.) Ooh! Ooer! Get off!

(She rushes from the room. RB's laughter is heard.)

RC: Just in time! You'll start fading back any second!

(RB does so, over in the corner, as before. However, his hair is now very long and thick.)

RB: That's a great joke!

RC: So's your hair, old chap.

RB: (looks in mirror) I say. Must be that overdose. Never mind – can always get a haircut. Here, let's have a go with that spray. (Takes spray from RC.) Stand over there, go on. (RC does so, and is sprayed, and disappears.)

RB: Fantastic! Where are you?

(No reply – RB, searching for him, goes into the bathroom. Knock on door – in comes the maid, with the manager.)

MANAGER: Anyone around?

(RB emerges from bathroom. His hair is now below his shoulders, and very thick. It hangs over his face.)

RB: Ah.

MANAGER: Is this the man, Sandra?

MAID: No – no, that's not him. This was a little chap. With ordinary hair.

MANAGER: This girl says she – felt something, in this room.

RB: Probably static electricity. You get it with nylon carpet.

MANAGER: You don't feel static electricity in your OOH! (He suddenly jumps.)

MAID: Ooh. (She too jumps.)

MANAGER: (to her) How dare you!

MAID: Ooh, you're as bad as the others. (She slaps his face.)

RB: Just a minute!

(But they have stormed out.)

RC: (voice off) Fun, isn't it?

(He enters RB's shot.)

RB: It's truly amazing. The most wonderful invention I've ever seen. It's sure to win the prize.

RC: Yours is pretty fantastic. I've never seen hair grow like that in my life. By the way – you said it had two drawbacks, like my invention. What is the other drawback?

RB: Well, it weakens the roots of the hair. You have to be very careful to avoid sudden shocks, otherwise it could all fall out.

RC: I see. Nasty.

RB: Yes. What's your other drawback?

RC: Well – the spray causes the molecules in the body to reach a highly volatile state. In other words, if you do it too much you could actually explode.

RB: Dear, dear. How much is too much?

RC: No idea, old chap. Maybe I've already done it too much. Anyway, I'd better stop, otherwise I might –

(There is a loud explosion, and RC's clothes fall empty to the ground.)

RB: (off) Oh, my God!

(Cut to RB. He sits, completely bald, with a mountain of pink hair around him.)

AN ODD COUPLE

Two gents in a slightly shabby living room. RC in his vest and trousers, ironing a shirt. RB enters in his vest, drying his hair – he has just washed it.

RB: 'Ere, Tony.

RC: What?

RB: You remember old Mr Whatsisname who used to come to the pub?

RC: Who?

RB: Used to come in with that big woman, you know.

RC: I don't know who you mean.

RB: Big woman, wore a fur coat. Lives near Dennis's mother.

RC: Dennis who?

RB: Dennis. Masses of dark hair; big with it; sallow boy. Worked for that printing firm in Surbiton.

RC: What printing firm?

RB: The firm that was supposed to do all Winston Churchill's visiting cards during the war.

RC: Who?

RB: Winston Churchill. The war leader! Ooh, my Gawd! The chap who saved us from the clutches of Adolf.

RC: Adolf who?

RB: Hitler. Adolf Hitler. Don't tell me you don't know who Adolf Hitler was.

RC: 'Course I know who Adolf Hitler was. I'm not a moron, Harold.

RB: Well, then.

RC: Well, what?

RB: Well, he's dead.

RC: Who, Hitler?

RB: No! (Hitler!) You silly Queen! I was saying Churchill saved us from Hitler.

RC: What about it?

RB: I was just saying Churchill used to get all his visiting cards done by this firm where Dennis worked.

RC: Dennis who?

RB: I'm trying to tell you. The fellah whose mother lives near this big woman with a fur coat.

RC: What big woman?

RB: The WOMAN who used to COME IN THE PUB with old Mr Whatsisname.

RC: Turner.

RB: TURNER! MR TURNER! HIM, YES!

RC: What about him?

RB: HE'S DEAD!

RC: They never proved it. He might be living under another name in South America.

FAT HEADS REVISITED

Two yokels meet by the barn. RB sitting, RC enters.

RC: Morning.

RB: Arternoon.

RC: Is somebody sitting here?

RB: Yes.

RC: Who?

RB: Me.

RC: Well, I know that. I'm not daft.

RB: I am. (Noticing RC limping) What's making you limp?

RC: I'm not limp.

RB: No, your feet. Lost a shoe?

RC: (holding up both feet) No. Just found one.

RB: Oh. Lucky it fits.

RC: Bound to fit one of my feet. One of my feet's bigger than the other. Everybody has one foot bigger than the other.

RB: I haven't. I'm just the opposite.

RC: Eh?

RB: One of my feet is smaller than the other. Ain't you got no shoes?

RC: I got me best shoes. For Sundays, like. I bought a new tie an' all. But I had to take it back.

RB: Why?

RC: It were too tight.

(RC notices a front door leaning against the wall behind RB.)

RC: What's that door?

RB: I take that around with me.

RC: What for?

RB: Well, the other day I lost the key, so in case anybody finds it and breaks into my house I carry the door around.

RC: That's clever. But what happens if you lose the door?

RB: That's all right, I've left a window open.

RC: Here, did you hear about old Rueben?

RB: What?

RC: Up in court yesterday.

RB: Never.

RC: He stole a calendar.

RB: What did he get?

RC: Twelve months. His trouble is, he drinks too much.

RB: He told me he only drinks to calm himself.

RC: Oh well, that explains it. Last Saturday night he was so calm he couldn't move.

RB: Here. It's my birthday tomorrow. November the twelfth.

RC: What year?

RB: Oh, every year. I had two presents. A wristwatch with an alarm, and a bottle of aftershave. So if you hear anything and smell anything, it's me.

RC: Oh, ar. Well, at least you won't be late for work. I'm always late for work.

RB: Why's that?

RC: I sleep very slowly.

RB: I snore, I do. I snore so loud I wake meself up. But I've cured it now.

RC: How?

RB: I sleep in the next room.

RC: Here, talking of snoring, it's my wife's birthday next week. She's asked for a coat made of animal skin.

RB: What you going to give her?

RC: A donkey jacket.

RB: That's nice. Here, this is another present I got.

(Shows umbrella, opens it. It has a four-inch circular hole in one section of it.)

RC: What's that hole for?

RB: So you can see when it's stopped raining.

RC: Here, seeing that hole reminds me. I looked through a hole in the fence up at that new nudist camp.

RB: Ooh ar, I've heard about that. Do they have men and women in there?

RC: I couldn't tell. They hadn't got any clothes on.

RB: Oh, I see.

RC: Well, I mustn't sit here. I'm going up to the doctors. I don't like the look of my wife.

RB: I'll come with you. I hate the sight of mine.

(They exit.)

TIRED MP

A television interview. RC is interviewing RB, a North Country MP. The MP is very drunk.

RC: Good evening. I have with me in the studio tonight Mr Arnold Sidebottom, MP, a prominent backbencher, and a man who is well known for his frankness and outspokenness on matters of government policy. (To RB) It would be true to say, I think, Mr Sidebottom, that you are not a man to mince words?

RB: Well – er – I – er – we all – I think you're – absolutely.

RC: Quite. And I understand that you have just returned from a very tiring fact-finding tour of the Midlands?

RB: S'correct, s'correct.

RC: And you are obviously very tired.

RB: Yes, I'm very tired. Yes, I am tired.

RC: And you've probably got a bit of 'flu as well, haven't you?

RB: I've had a few, yes.

RC: Oh, you've had the 'flu. You must be awfully tired. Tell me, Mr Sidebottom, what conclusions have you reached after your tour?

RB: Oh – I'll be all right in the morning.

RC: Would you say the Midlands were in need of any special consideration regarding such problems as housing?

RB: Er – special, yes! Consideration – no. Er—

(He hesitates.)

RC: Do go on.

RB: I don't propose to go further into that. That's as fur as I'm going. (Sings, delicately) 'I fell in love with Mary at the dairy, but Mary wouldn't fall in love with me—' (He rises unsteadily and tries to execute a couple of dance steps.) 'Down by the old mill stream, we used to sit and dream, Little did she know—' (He flops down on the settee beside RC.) How yer doing, all right?

RC: I notice you've brought up the subject of agriculture, and dairy farming in particular. Would you say there is a noticeable decline in this industry?

RB: By heck, we put a few away tonight, didn't we? Eh? Didn't we? (He leans his head on RC's shoulder.)

RC: So you would say there has been a putting aside of essential priorities, would you?

RB: I bet our wives are wondering where we are. (He smiles, then frowns.) Where are we?

RC: Mr Sidebottom—

RB: I've got a lovely wife at home. (Begins to weep.) A lovely woman, Daphne. Oh dear. I'll just have forty winks. (He is asleep on RC's shoulder.)

RC: Well, thank you, Arnold Sidebottom, for coming to the studio tonight—

RB: (in his sleep) Oh, Gloria! (He cuddles RC.)

RC: —and telling us about your fact-finding tour.

RB: Gloria, you're lovely! Sing me to sleep, Gloria!

RC: (whispering now) And it only remains for me to wish you a very good night.

(He sings very quietly through RB's snoring.)

'Golden slumbers kiss your eyes,
Smiles awake you when you rise,
Sleep pretty baby, do not cry
And I will sing a lullaby.'

TRAIN SKETCH

An old-fashioned train carriage – bench seats. A man sits reading a newspaper at one end of the bench. RC enters, sits down next to him.

RC: Morning, John. Blowing up a bit rough.

MAN: Yes. How's the wife?

RC: Blowing up a bit rough. She's at a funny age. That Esther Rantzen's been giving her ideas again.

MAN: About being liberated?

RC: No, about getting her teeth fixed.

(RB enters with girl. They sit, RB next to RC, girl on other side.)

RB: (to girl) Oh, what a rush. All right, Deirdre?

GIRL: Yes thanks, Mr Prentice. Bit late this morning. How's the garden?

RB: Not bad, not bad. Lot to do. Bit overgrown.

RC: She's very extravagant. I've told her, it's got to stop.

RB: Lot of cutting back to do.

RC: I said, we'll just have to cut back. So she appears yesterday with a new dress.

RB: I've got his great big magnolia.

RC: Big green thing with flowers all over it. Ghastly. She looks like the side of a house.

RB: It's all up the side of the house. It's all hanging over.

RC: It's all bulging out.

RB: I'm going to pull it all off and have a good look at what's causing the trouble.

RC: I told her – I don't care if she's got nothing to wear – it's going.

RB: Then when I've stripped it down, I'll get it flat against the wall, and hope that something comes of it next spring.

RC: I've suggested she goes to a massage parlour. There's a very nice one in Streatham. Topless.

MAN: Really?

RC: Yes. No roof.

RB: Either that or just cut big bits off here or there. But that makes a bit of a mess.

RC: I must say she's not keen.

RB: The lawn's in a state as well. Must have a go at that.

RC: They can do wonders with a woman's figure at those places, you know.

RB: Get the heavy roller on it.

RC: These spot-reducing vibrators are wonderful. They shook me, I can tell you.

RB: It's the only way.

RC: Makes a woman's figure flatter, smoother—

RB: Well, when you're lying on it, you don't want it all lumps and bumps, do you?

RC: Except in the right places, of course.

RB: Quite. It's all right on the front rock garden and round the back of the herbaceous border.

(They are now beginning to talk to each other.)

RC: Yes. But the trunk – now, that's different.

RB: Oh yes, the trunk should be smooth.

RC: And free from greenfly. Have you tried putting a grease-band round it?

RB: Makes it slippery to climb. Anyway, my wife wouldn't wear one. I think the answer is a bigger bed.

RC: Oh, definitely. Give your foliage more room to spread out.

RB: Nothing need come into contact at all in a big bed – not if you don't want it to.

RC: If you fill it with manure, it's a big help.

RB: Oh, absolutely. I didn't know you knew so much about gardening.

RC: What?

RB: Filling the bed with manure.

RC: No – I just thought that must be a good way to get a divorce. Come to think of it, you seem to know a lot about women.

RB: No – my wife's just left me. But it hasn't stopped me gardening.

RC: Oh. So you're on your own?

RB: No – I'm digging with her. Come on, Deirdre.

(They exit.)

HUMPHREY AND GODFREY (6)

RB and RC in armchairs, in their London club.

RB: I say, Humphrey.

RC: What is it, Godfrey?

RB: See that tall chap over there?

RC: Well-dressed, sprightly sort of bloke?

RB: That's him. Five years ago he was destitute – in rags. All due to drink.

RC: Damned curse, drink is. Fancy another?

RB: No, thanks. Luckily, he met one of those temperance chappies, who told him just to have a look at where his money was going to – the rich publicans, smartly dressed, with sports cars and places in the country, while he, the drunkard, was penniless. All due to man's insatiable desire for alcohol.

RC: And that put him on the right road, eh?

RB: Absolutely.

RC: Gave up drink completely?

RB: No, he bought a pub.

JASON KING

Captions, as close as possible to the original. After captions, a close-up of a letter, held by middle-aged female hand. RC's voice, as Jason King, over it, reading the contents.

Slow mix to a shot of Magdalen College, Oxford, passing off it to the river – perhaps a punt gliding underneath the bridge.

Cut to another shot of a more secluded part of the river. A punt comes round the bend – RC, as Jason King, reclines in it. Behind him, a beautifully muscular girl is punting the boat along, effortlessly. She wears a one-piece swimsuit.

RC: (over the above) My dear Aunt Augusta – I thought you might enjoy receiving a letter from your dear old Oxford, especially as it is written in the fair hand of your loving nephew, Jason King. I am up here to be made an honorary Doctor of Philosophy, for my services to mankind, and, more especially, womankind.

(A shot of RC's very with-it shoes, platform heels. Pan past them to him.)

I've recently met a very charming girl named Angela Fitz-Upton – I think you knew her father. I've taken her on the river, and generally seen quite a lot of her.

(We pan up Angela during the above dialogue.)

She has 9 O-levels, 5 A-levels, and is interesting on several other levels as well. My curiosity was really aroused, however, when she told me she was a pole-vaulter. She certainly knows how to handle a punt pole. Yes, I have to report that dear old Oxford remains a haven of peace in the midst of a troubled society. There's even time for an afternoon snooze.

(RC, in close-up, closes his eyes. As soon as he does so, Angela screams. RC opens his eyes again, looks at Angela. She points out of frame. RC's eyes follow her finger. Cut to a long shot of a punt – a body is sprawled face downward across the punt. The feet stick out, trailing in the water. Close-up – RC.)

RC: How ghastly!

(Cut to body again, then back to close-up RC.)

RC: He's wearing the same shoes.

(He looks up – we cut to wide shot of RB on opposite bank. He plays Miss Wilberforce, a lesbian in tweeds. She carries a butterfly net and has her hair in a straight, chopped-off page-boy style. She is striding across the field and stops suddenly as she sees the body. Cut to close-up RC, as if continuous.)

RC: So you are the famous literary giant and detective-story writer, Miss Wilberforce. I must say, you make delicious fruit cake—

(Pull back – we are in Miss W's lodgings – a mixture of twenties and Edwardian – butterflies in cases, dark walls – cluttered. RB and Angela sit on a chaise longue, RC in armchair. They are taking tea.)

RC: In fact you seem to be generally a very accomplished woman.

RB: Never mind my accomplishments – what about the body?

RC: Well, there's certainly room for a little improvement there.

RB: Not my body, Mr King. The body of the young man floating in the river.

RC: In the punt on the river.

RB: It's the same thing.

RC: It isn't – you try it.

RB: The point is, what have you managed to find out about him?

RC: Well, according to the local cop shop, he was a brilliant young don named Alistair Tyson.

RB: Tyson! Golly Moses, I knew him. Was he murdered?

RC: Miss Wilberforce, before I answer that question, may I make an impertinent observation?

RB: I'm all ears.

RC: No, that wasn't it. It's just that the police have asked me only to discuss the case with reliable people. You won't let it go any further, will you? Even under pressure? Either of you.

RB: Don't worry, I can be as tough as the next man.

RC: More so, I shouldn't wonder.

RB: You don't have to worry about me.

(Beaming, and grasping Angela's knee.)

RC: No, I'm sure I don't. (In passing) Your hand's on Angela's knee.

RB: (ignoring this) And I know Angela won't let it go any further, will you, my dear?

RC: I'm damned sure she won't. Very well then – yes, he was murdered. Poisoned with deadly nightshade.

RB: I knew it! Professor Sax.

RC: Who?

RB: Professor of Botany. Sax, spelled SAX. Could it be? Is it possible? He's come back – no, that's impossible. But he was a man of botany. Hated Tyson – yes, it's got to be!

RC: Do you know something? Put that to music and you've got a hit.

RB: What?

RC: Would you mind explaining what you're driving at?

RB: Professor Sax was always jealous of young Tyson's success as a botanist. He swore to kill him once, at a party. The Professor, do you see, was a great amateur conjuror, and used to perform at parties with his glamorous young assistant, Juanita.

RC: I bet you enjoyed that.

RB: It was marvellous. Marvellous. Such an attractive girl. They did some wonderful tricks together. Then, quite suddenly, she disappeared. And almost immediately, so did he.

RC: Oh, I've never seen that done. Must have gone well with the audience.

RB: No, no, it wasn't a trick – I mean they disappeared from Oxford. Never heard of again, either of them. But I know that the dead man had been making advances to Juanita. And Professor Sax didn't like it.

RC: Then I'd say that Sax is our man, wouldn't you? Decided to re-emerge from retirement, to perform a final trick.

RB: If he is back, someone is bound to have seen him. He was so well known in Oxford. Ask anyone.

RC: That, my dear lady, is precisely what I shall do. Ask everyone.

RB: I don't follow you.

RC: No, and I'd rather you didn't – and I know I speak for Angela as well. We're going to carry out a survey.

(Cut to film – RC, with clipboard, stopping man in the street.)

RC: Excuse me, sir, but have you seen anything of Sax lately?

(Man reacts – if possible, it should be a genuine passer-by. He moves off, woman approaches.)

RC: (to her) Can you tell me anything about Sax?

(She looks offended. Now a very wide shot – RC questioning young woman.)

RC: I wonder if you can help me. I'm looking for Sax.

(Girl stalks off. RC approaches middle-aged woman – use RC's double – he asks question, woman knocks him flat.)

(Cut to Angela, with clipboard, in a park. She stops a man, says something to him. He leaps on her, bearing her to the ground. We cut away just in time, back to RC still being attacked by the middle-aged woman, now surrounded by a small knot of onlookers.)

(Cut to studio – a small Chinese restaurant – very moody.)

RB: So your survey wasn't a great success?

RC: In one way, no. But I found out some fascinating facts for my next book.

RB: Oh – do you write books? I don't think I read your last one.

RC: No, my next one will be my first one. Although if I put in what I learnt yesterday it could be my last one as well.

RB: What are you calling it?

RC: Sex Habits of the Amazon Savage.

RB: Then of what use is information about Oxford?

RC: Well, why go to the Amazon when it's all happening here!

RB: I think, Mr King, that you're pulling my leg.

RC: Of course I'm not.

RB: Well, somebody is. (Looking down – a Chinese waiter emerges from under the table.) What are you doing? Oh, I dropped my fork, did I? Thank you. (The waiter bows out.) I'm so glad we chose to eat here – I have an enormous penchant for this sort of thing.

RC: I know, you've just dropped some fried rice down it. (Changes the subject.) My studies yesterday evening, however, proved a little more worthwhile.

RB: Oh, really? What were you studying?

RC: History, Geography – and furniture removals.

RB: Removals? That's not a subject.

(The waiter arrives with dishes. He serves RC and Angela.)

RC: Oh, but it is – and a very fascinating one. A chap at Pickfords informed me that no furniture had been moved in or out of a certain flat for at least thirty years. And my historic studies took me to the estate agent, who furnished proof that the flat was, and still is, owned by one Professor Sax. Which all adds up to something extremely fishy.

WAITER: It's codfish.

RC: Not the codfish, my dear fellow – and I'll thank you to keep your nose out of other people's stories. (The waiter goes.) Damned impertinence. My club is full of people like him.

RB: Really? What's it called?

RC: The Chinese Waiters' Club. D'you know it?

RB: No.

RC: However, I digress. My third and last subject, if you remember, was Geography. It didn't take very long to locate the flat. The address? Forty-nine, Wilton Street. Your address, Professor Sax.

(RB makes to move.)

RC: Don't move. Angela has you covered by a small pistol strapped to her thigh. (RB remains still.) I should have guessed – all that talk about the attractive Juanita – the fact that you ogled Angela the whole time. No wonder you were attracted to women – you're a man!

RB: Damn you, King!

RC: I've a whole host of questions to ask you.

RB: Then I'm afraid they'll have to wait. You're lying about the pistol, King.

RC: What makes you say that?

RB: I've had my hand on her thigh all through dinner.

RC: (astonished) Angela – you rotten turncoat!

(RB leaps up, tipping the contents of the table over them, and rushes out. RC attempts to follow, but his path is blocked by a waiter. RC grabs him by the shoulders and bangs his head upon an enormous Chinese gong which stands near the exit. We end the scene on the waiter's unconscious head, as he slides to the ground.)

(Cut to film – RB, rushing into frame and away from camera, down a college-lined narrow street. He disappears round a corner just as RC's back rushes past camera. Close-up of RC.)

RC: (to himself) He's making for the boats.

(RC rushes after him. Cut to RB in punt, paddling as fast as he can. Cut to RC – also paddling in a punt. Intercuts close-ups on both, then a long shot as they enter and leave the frame, like the boat race. Back to close-ups of RB and RC as they paddle. Then RC's point of view as RB disappears round the bend in the river. Close-up – RC paddling, over this we hear a crash and a splash. RC reacts. His point of view again as he rounds the bend to find RB's punt, overturned. RC pulls alongside it. Close-up – RB's wig in the water. As RC fishes it out and holds it up, his voice-over recommences.)

RC: (voice-over) My dear Aunt Agatha! The sequel to my last letter has yet to emerge – the Professor hasn't yet been found. Perhaps he made off into the bushes – or perhaps the Chinese meal weighed a little too heavily on him.

(Cut to close-up RC – this time he is poling a punt, and is accompanied by a different girl in a swimsuit – but this one is lying in the punt, trailing her fingers in the water.)

RC: (voice-over) In any event, I'm still enjoying my stay here at Oxford. I've ditched that terrible girl Angela, as she didn't seem to know whose side she was on. Are you sure it was her father you knew, and not her mother? (Cut to close-up of girl – a model, by the look of her.) This new girl is much more me – except that she expects me to do all the work. She's also six foot tall, which means that I shall be kept very much on my toes for the next week or two.

(Close-up – RC's platform shoes – he goes up on his toes as he poles the punt.)

(Close-up girl – looking. She suddenly bursts out laughing. Pull out to a wide shot – the boat glides away from camera. RC isn't on it.)

(Close-up RC, desperately clinging to the pole, stuck in the river, the boat gently gliding away. RC slides slowly down the pole and into the river. The music swells up.)

HUMPHREY AND GODFREY (7)

RB and RC in armchairs, in their London club.

RB: I say, Humphrey.

RC: What is it, Godfrey?

RB: Who was that terrible woman you were with today?

RC: That was my sister.

RB: Of course. I should have noticed the resemblance. Just got married, hasn't she?

RC: Yes. And do you know, she's married a man whom people invariably take an instant dislike to.

RB: Why is that, do you think?

RC: It saves time. They've just moved to Cheltenham. She loves Cheltenham. She says in Cheltenham breeding is everything.

RB: Yes, well, we enjoy it in Kensington as well, but we also have other interests.

RC: Funny thing is, although he's a bully, an idler and a drunk, she intends to have seventeen children by him.

RB: Good grief, why on earth does she want to do that?

RC: She says she's hoping to lose him in the crowd.

MOSCOW NIGHTS

The interior of a peasant's hovel somewhere in darkest Russia. Ivan (RC) is smoking his pipe by the fire. He has enormous eyebrows. Suddenly the door bursts open, and his wife Olga (RB), looking more masculine than Ivan, staggers in amid a swirl of snow, whistling wind and the howling of wolves. She is loaded down with logs, which she dumps by the fire.

RC: Close the door, Olga Olgirlovitch. It's cyold outside.

RB: It will make no difference. If I close the door it will still cyold outside. (But she does so.)

RC: It is the coldest summer we have had since lyast winter.

RB: I know. I saw the gardener in the vegetable patch. He is frozen to the marrow. Styoke up the fire, Ivan Sonofabitch.

(RC starts to do so.)

RC: Yes, we must keep warm. (A pause.) I heard a kalinka as I was crossing the square.

RB: Ah, just fancy.

RC: It was the brass monkeys on the gates of the Town Hall.

RB: (sits) Oh, I am tired. It is you who should bring in the logs. You are the masculine one, not me.

RC: That's not what they said at the Olympic Selection Committee.

RB: Pah! (He spits.) A load of old women. Who gives a shot-put what they think.

RC: Never mind, Olga Olgirlovitch. That was a long time ago. Let us have some tea.

RB: You know, Ivan Sonofabitch – life is like a cup of tea.

RC: Why, my dear?

RB: Why, what?

RC: Why is life like a cup of tea?

RB: How should I know? What am I, a philosopher?

(RC has taken a cup of tea from the samovar nearby and sips it.)

RC: Anything good on television tonight?

RB: I don't know. I never know what is on.

RC: Ah well, what difference does it make? We have no television set.

RB: True. Where is our daughter, Tania?

RC: She is out for a sleigh ride with Sasha Scratchanitch.

RB: The chemist's son from the village? I don't like him.

RC: He is a nice boy. Honest, polite – a good match for our daughter. Nothing wrong with him.

RB: He limps!

RC: Only when he walks.

RB: I prefer Dosser Digaditch.

RC: The council worker? I think he's a spy.

RB: He asked me what I thought of Red China.

RC: What did you tell him?

RB: I said I thought on a yellow tablecloth it would look very pretty.

RC: I cannot find my spare pair of socks.

RB: I put them somewhere in a safe place.

RC: Where?

RB: I cannot remember.

RC: Never mind. They were dirty anyway. (Sips tea.) This tea is good. It is warm and strong and brown, like my socks.

RB: Now I remember where I put them. In the samovar. (Fishes out RC's socks.) You want another cup?

RC: No. I must go and feed the chickens.

RB: What about the pigs?

RC: There's no food for the pigs.

RB: But they are hungry.

RC: I will think of something. (Opens the door and stands there in the howling wind and hurtling snow, shouting.) It is still snowing. It is very cold.

RB: (shouting) Well, hurry up and close the door. (RC does so.) Otherwise we will freeze to death!

(RC opens door again.)

RC: What did you say?

RB: I said we will freeze to death!

(RC shuts the door again. RB wrings out the socks into the samovar, and puts them in front of the fire. A telephone rings. RB picks up an ancient stand-up phone.)

RB: Hello? No, I'm sorry, we're not on the phone.

(RC enters. No wind or snow at all.)

RB: Did you feed the chickens?

RC: Yes. I fed them to the pigs.

RB: But what about the eggs? Pigs don't lay eggs.

RC: No – but chickens don't lay bacon.

RB: True.

RC: Have you noticed? It has stopped snowing out there. The storm is passing over.

(RB opens window on opposite side – wind and snow pour in.)

RB: Yes, it's out there now.

(He closes it again.)

RC: I think it is time to settle down for the evening.

RB: Such long cold winter evenings we have. What shall we do this long cold winter evening, Ivan Sonofabitch?

RC: The same as we do every long cold winter evening, my little Mamooshka.

RB: Call me Moosh. Very well, but first we must say goodnight to the children. (Opens another door at the side of the set and they call out to their children) Goodnight, Tania.

RC: Goodnight, Ania.

RB: Goodnight, André.

RC: Goodnight, Lubin.

RB: Goodnight, Leon.

RC: Goodnight, Marsha.

RB: Goodnight, Mikael.

(We cut to other room. It contains fifteen children, aged between fifteen and three, all in Russian-type smocks, nightclothes, etc., standing and sitting on one big bed.)

RC: Goodnight, Joseph.

RB: Goodnight, John, Paul, George, Ringo.

RC: Goodnight, Ken, goodnight, Livingstone—

(Fade to applause.)

HUMPHREY AND GODFREY (8)

RB and RC in armchairs, in their London club.

RB: I say, Humphrey.

RC: What is it, Godfrey?

RB: Don't mind if I smoke my pipe, do you?

RC: Not if you don't mind me being sick, old chap.

RB: Perhaps you're right. That's a rather loud pattern you're wearing, old lad. (Indicates RC's socks.)

RC: Wonderful, isn't it? Fantastic colouring. Hand-knitted in the Congo. Not another like it in England.

RB: I bet you a fiver there is.

RC: Done! Right, where is it?

RB: (triumphantly) On your other foot! Come on, pay up!

RC: (shows other leg) Sorry, old chap. (On the other foot he has a plain day-glo sock.) My daughter's cycling sock.

RB: She's bought a bicycle?

RC: Loves it. Goes everywhere on it.

RB: She's a farmer's wife. The money would be better spent on a cow.

RC: She'd look a bit of a fool riding round on a cow.

RB: Not half as big a fool as she'd look trying to milk a bicycle.

A TOUCH OF THE HICKSTEADS

A doctor's waiting room. RC sits waiting. RB enters, goes to recep-
tionist, a middle-aged, pleasant woman in a white coat.

RECEPTIONIST: Yes, sir, good morning. Your name, please.

RB: HICson.

(Has hiccups throughout.)

REC: Mr Hickson. Address?

RB: 24 PuddleswICK Lane, HICstead.

REC: Phone number?

RB: HICstead SICx, two, three, o, SICx.

REC: Thank you, Mr Hickson – just take a seat, won't you?

(RB sits next to RC.)

RC: Morning.

(Whistle – he emits a low whistle after certain words throughout the sketch.)

RB: Morning.

RC: First visit?

RB: Yes.

RC: What's the matter with you?

(Whistle.)

RB: Sorry?

RC: What are you suffering from?

(Whistle.)

RB: It's silly, really. I'm not really SIC. It's just that I've got permanent HIC, permanent HIC, perHIC manHIC—

RC: (Whistle.) Hic (whistle) cups.

RB: Yes. It's absolutely HICsausting.

RC: I know. Well, you'll be all right with this chap. He's a specialist. Ear, nose and

(Whistle.)

RB: What?

RC: Ear, nose and (whistle) hiccups (whistle).

RB: Oh, good. What's your partHICular illness?

RC: Coincidence, really. The reason I'm here is that I've just got married.

(Whistle.)

RB: Oh, I see.

RC: Swedish girl. (Whistle) Met her last month, married her this month. (Whistle.)

RB: Gosh. That was quICK.

RC: It's she who wants the doctor to cure my (whistle) my affliction.

RB: (Whistle.)

RC: HIC!

RB: What is your afflICKtion?

RC: (whistle) Same as yours.

RB: What?

RC: Hiccups. (Whistle.)

RB: But you don't HIC, you HIC don't HIC.

RC: Don't hiccup? (Whistle.) That's because this doctor has taught me the cure. (Whistle.)

RB: You mean, I should marry a Swedish girl?

RC: No, no. Whistling's the cure. If you whistle whenever you feel you are going to (whistle), whenever you feel a (whistle) coming on, you won't hiccup.

RB: Really? I'll try it. 'My name is Henry (whistle) Hickson of 24 Puddles (whistle) Lane, (whistle) Hickstead.' It works! That's absolutely HICstrodinary. I mean, that's absolutely (whistle).

RC: It is, isn't it?

RB: But just a minute. If you're cured of (whistle) hiccups, why are you here?

RC: I'm here to be cured of the (whistle) the (whistle) the whistle.

(Whistle.)

REC: (To RC) You'll be next, Mr Entwistle.

RC: And about time tooooo.

(It comes out like a whistle.)

(A girl with an enormous bosom enters. She wears a very low-cut dress. She sits between them and hiccups. When she does, her bosom bounces in the air. RC and RB whistle. She looks annoyed and

hiccups. They whistle. She hits them with her handbag, hiccups. They whistle. This continues as we cue applause.)

YOU'RE SOMEBODY

A smartish hotel bar in Bournemouth. A pianist is tinkling away on, and who knows, when nobody is looking, possibly in, the piano. RC, in casual clothes, sits at the bar. A barman hovers. RB, seated a little way along the bar, is staring at RC.

RB: Excuse me.

RC: Yes?

RB: You're Robert Redford, aren't you?

RC: (looks around to see who RB is talking to) Sorry? You talking to me?

RB: Yes. You're Robert Redford, aren't you?

RC: No. No, sorry, you're mistaken. (He is flattered.)

RB: You must often get taken for him.

RC: Er – well, no, can't say I do, not often, no.

(A pause. RC drinks, RB stares at him, then moves and sits beside him. RC only faintly embarrassed.)

RB: You're somebody.

RC: Ha ha. Well everybody's somebody, aren't they? Otherwise nobody would be anybody.

RB: No, you're somebody. I've seen you.

RC: Doubtful. I don't appear anywhere.

RB: You've appeared here, haven't you?

RC: No, I mean I don't perform.

RB: Oh, I'm sorry to hear that.

RC: I mean, I don't entertain. I'm not an entertainer.

(A pause. Then RB stares at him again.)

RB: Come off it.

RC: I'm not, honestly. I'm just a rather dull person, with not an atom of show-biz sparkle, scintillation or bezazz.

RB: You're Robin Day, aren't you?

RC: I would hardly describe Robin Day as having no show-biz bezazz. He's full of it. If you want to see a good, honest, over-the-top performance, watch Question Time.

RB: So you're not him then?

RC: I am not him, no.

RB: Who's that bloke who works with a dummy?

RC: No, I'm not Little and Large.

RB: No, the ventriloquist act. Ray Hampton.

RC: Ray Allan.

RB: Yes, and Lord John.

RC: Lord Charles.

RB: Yes. You're him.

RC: Which one?

RB: Either.

RC: Lord Charles is made of wood! (Sarcastically) You're sure you don't mean Rod Hull and Emu?

RB: That's him, yes.

RC: Oh, my God. Listen, would you mind allowing me to finish my drink in peace.

RB: Sorry, sorry.

RC: Thank you.

(A pause.)

RB: You on holiday down here?

RC: No, I work here.

RB: What, in cabaret, are you?

RC: Look, for the last time will you shut up and let me have my drink!

RB: Like a drink, do you?

RC: Yes, I do like a drink in peace.

RB: Lot of your people are heavy drinkers.

RC: My people? What, my uncles and aunts, you mean? What do you mean, my people?

RB: Show-biz people.

RC: I am not show-biz! I am not a heavy drinker – I am a nine stone four and a half drinker! Please leave me alone!

RB: I'm sorry. I don't mean to be a nuisance.

RC: All right.

RB: It's just fascinating to me, that's all, and although I realise this is an intrusion on your privacy, and although who you are and what you do has absolutely nothing to do with me whatsoever, I think you're Harry Secombe.

RC: Harry Secombe's enormous!

RB: He's lost a lot of weight.

RC: (snaps) OK! All right. I admit it. I am in show business. I am an all-round entertainer, appear in my own TV specials and my name is a household word. I have a wonderful act and it finishes like this –

(He goes into a song and dance – the pianist in the bar takes up the number, and RC does a big finish, eventually dancing off into the ladies'.)

RB: Oh, now I've got him! (To barman) He's the bloke who works in the fish shop in the High Street!

HUMPHREY AND GODFREY (9)

RB and RC in armchairs, in their London club.

RB: I say, Humphrey.

RC: What is it, Godfrey?

RB: Do you know, I'm Robert Redford's double?

RC: What?

RB: Yes, I am. I weigh exactly twice as much as he does. Not good for the ticker, though. Doctor told me to give up smoking at once. I said it was impossible.

RC: Why?

RB: I'd just filled my lighter. Good doctor, though. He gave my uncle six months to live, but when he told him he couldn't pay him he gave him another six months to live, so he could pay him.

RC: I've got the best doctor – thoroughly sympathetic. Very good about my mother-in-law. I said to him, 'My mother-in-law is very unsteady on her feet.'

RB: And what did he say?

RC: 'Buy her a skateboard.'

VIM AND VIGOUR

A small general store. RB as proprietor. RC enters – he is precious and gay.

RC: Hello, Duckie.

RB: Morning, sir. Nice morning.

RC: No, it's not – I haven't had my oats this morning.

RB: Pardon, sir?

RC: What have you got – Bran Flakes? Crispies? What would you recommend?

RB: (showing packet) 'Force' is nice.

RC: Yes, I like a bit of force, don't we all. What else you got?

RB: 'Fizz', 'Crunch', Muesli or Oatcake Nibbles.

RC: I'll try the Fizz.

RB: Right, sir.

RC: (looks at list) Packet of Flash.

RB: Flash? Yes, sir. (Gets it.)

RC: And some Vim.

RB: Vim? Yes. (Gets it.)

RC: Now, furniture polish. Got any Spangle?

RB: No, sir. I got Shine, Whine, Whizz, Glide, Slide, Slip, Slap and Skid.

RC: I'll try the Whizz.

RB: Yes, sir. (Gets it.)

RC: Ooh. I desperately need deodorant.

RB: I wouldn't say that, sir—

RC: Got any Stud?

RB: No, sir. Afraid not. We've got Sting, Stiff, Sniff, Snort, Whoops, Wow and Sailor Beware, sir.

RB: Oh, nice. I'll try the Whoops.

RB: One Whoops. Right, sir. Large Whoops?

RC: Always!

RB: Right, sir, one large Whoops.

RC: Insect spray – got any Doom?

RB: No, sir, no Doom; we've got Boom, Zoom, Clear the Room, Squash, Squelch or Squirt, sir.

RC: I'll try the Boom.

RB: Big Boom, sir?

RC: Always!

RB: Right, sir. (Gets it.)

RC: Washing powder?

RB: Yes, sir. Daz, Bezaz, Omo, Promo, Primo, Pull, Push, Whoosh, Rinso, Ritzo, Ratzo, Rosto and Shreddo.

RC: Whoosh, please.

RB: One Whoosh. Right.

RC: Now. Alcohol-free lager.

RB: Wet-Whistle, Wallop or Windbreaker, sir?

RC: Oh, Wallop, I think.

RB: Pint of Wallop?

RC: No. I'm a half-pint man.

RB: I wouldn't say that, sir. (Gets it.)

RC: Oh, and some lemonade.

RB: Tang, Fang, Bang or Tinklejuice?

RC: Er – I'll try a Bang, please.

RB: Are we nearly there, sir?

RC: Just two more things – bottle of sauce. HP?

RB: No, sir. OK, FA, JR, Fruity, Floppy, Sloppy, Slurp, Splosh or Splatter.

RC: I'll try the Splatter.

RB: Right, sir. (Gets it.)

RC: And lastly, a chocolate bar.

RB: Yessir. Crackle, Crunch, Crush, Crash, Cram, Creamy, Steamy, Slimy and Sickmaker, sir.

RC: I'll take the Crash, please. There, that's it. That's the lot.

RB: Right, sir. So that's Flash, Fizz, Vim, Whizz, Crash, Bang, Wallop, Whoosh, Whoops, Boom and Splatter.

RC: Could you just say that again, please?

RB: Yes, sir. You've got Flash, Fizz, Vim, Whizz, Crash, Bang, Wallop, Whoosh, Whoops, Boom and Splatter.

RC: Ooh, lovely!

RB: That's 4 pounds 25, please.

RC: Oh, I'm not buying them.

RB: What?

RC: I just wanted to hear you say them.

RB: Why?

RC: I couldn't afford any fireworks this year. See you, sweetie! (Starts to leave.)

RB: (throws 'force' packet at him.) May the Force be with you!

STUNT MAN

RB in interview area – tables, chairs, etc.

RB: Good evening and welcome to this week's edition of Other People's Business. This week we are looking at a very exciting profession indeed – the stuntman – in this case Mr Harold Higgins of Kettering. Ladies and Gentlemen, Mr Harold Higgins.

(Enter RC as stuntman – he wears thick black tights and a black sweater and is padded all over – pads on elbows, knees, shoulders and bottom.)

RB: Good evening, Mr Higgins.

RC: Good evening.

(He sits down with slight difficulty.)

RB: Now, before we go any further, we've got some film of stunts being performed.

(Cut to stock film of various falls, stunts, etc.)

RB: (after film) And that was you, was it?

RC: Er, no. No. I don't know who that was.

RB: Oh – but that's the sort of thing you do, is it?

RC: Well, not as good as that 'cos I get frightened. I'm a bit afraid of heights and that.

RB: Oh, I see.

RC: 'Cos it's not as easy as it looks, stunting. I mean, the public get blasé about it – they think it's just like falling off a log.

RB: But you can do it?

RC: Oh, I can fall off a log? Yes.

RB: No, I mean – you are earning your living at it?

RC: Well, yes. I've got all the gear and that.

RB: What, all this padding?

RC: Yes. (He stands up.) It protects all the salient points – saves me hurting myself.

RB: Quite – but doesn't it look rather odd on the screen?

RC: Oh, no. You wear the clothes over the top, you see, the clothes of the person you are doubling for. Have you got that photo of me in a film with the clothes on?

RB: Yes, – er—

(Caption – photo of RC in suit and trilby – terrible bulges where the padding sticks out – knees, shoulders, elbows and bottom.)

RB: (voice-over) Yes, here we are. Oh. Yes, I see. Who were you doubling for in that?

(Cut back to studio.)

RC: The thin man.

RB: Oh, yes. Have you always been a stuntman?

RC: No, not when I was younger.

RB: What were you when you were young?

RB: Er – I was a little boy. I was brought up in the circus. My father used to travel all over the country as a bearded lady.

RB: And so naturally you wanted to perform too?

RC: Yes. Stunts and stamp-collecting. They were my two hobbies. I used to come home from school, do a stunt, collect a few stamps and then do another stunt, and so on. Of course, my old grandad was a stuntman. Very famous, he was.

RB: Oh, yes – we've got a bit of film of him.

(Cut to film of man trying to fly off Eiffel Tower – stock shot.)

RB: That was marvellous. Did he often do that sort of thing?

RC: No, just the once.

RB: I see – so you more or less started in the business straight from school?

RC: No – I had this great money-making scheme for producing eggs without having chickens.

RB: How did you do that?

RC: I used ducks – but it never caught on, so I started doing stunting.

RB: Mainly film work, is it?

RC: Well, no, 'cos you've got to be pretty tough for that, you know – brave – no, I mainly do children's parties, that sort of thing. Or if people don't want to lie on the grass in a TV play, in case they catch a chill, I lie on the grass for them. Don't mind doing that. And getting off buses just before they stop. All that sort of thing.

RB: Ah, yes. I understand you are prepared to do a stunt for us now?

RC: Yes – well, I'll jump off the table for you, if you like.

RB: Oh, all right then.

RC: Right. Shall I do it now?

RB: Yes, that will be fine.

(RC gets onto table, and stands up.)

RC: (looking down) It's a bit high from here, isn't it?

RB: It's two foot six.

RC: Yes, but it looks higher from up there. That's the one thing I've learnt in this business – when you're up on a height, it looks higher than when you're down on the ground.

RB: Don't you think you will be able to do it?

RC: Oh, I'll do it. Oh yes, I'll do it. Right. Ready?

RB: Yes, righto.

RC: Right. (With a sort of little cry of terror, he jumps down, lands on the floor and falls over.) Ow! Ooh, I banged my knee. Ow! (He bursts into tears.) Mum! Mum! I banged my knee – Mum!

(His mother enters and cuddles him.)

MOTHER: All right son, don't cry. You see, you shouldn't do these silly things, should you, dear? Come on. (She leads him off.) Let's go and see Dad, shall we?

(They have gone. RB stares after them.)

TRAMPS (2)

1: PHIL COLLINS SPECIAL EDITION

Wide shot – Phil Collins, as another tramp, approaches, sits down with RB and RC.

RB: Hello, Dudley – happy Christmas.

PHIL: Let's hope so.

RB: Have a cigar.

PHIL: Why, what's the matter with it?

RB: Nothing's the matter with it. I found it.

PHIL: Found it? Where?

RB: In the tobacconist's. Someone must have dropped it on the counter.

PHIL: That's criminal, that is.

RC: Only if you get caught. Anyway, nothing wrong with crime. Look at Robin Hood. He was a hero, and he never stopped robbing people.

RB: Ah, but he only robbed the rich.

RC: Yeah, and you know why, don't you?

RB: Why?

RC: 'Cos the poor didn't have any money. Any crime in your family, Dudley?

PHIL: Yeah. My sister is a stripper.

RC: That's not a crime, taking your clothes off.

PHIL: She don't take her clothes off. She goes up on roofs and takes the lead off.

RB: My brother was up before the beak once – for lighting fireworks in the street.

RC: Selling 'em, was he?

RB: Yeah. 'Right, I know what to do with you, my man,' said the judge. 'I shall make the punishment fit the crime,' he says. 'I'm going to do to you what you have done to them fireworks,' he says.

PHIL: What did he do, then?

RB: He let him off.

(Reaction Phil – reaction RC.)

2: TRAVEL

RB: Who won the single-handed yacht race?

RC: Eh?

RB: I said, who won the single-handed yacht race?

RC: I don't know. Nelson, was it? Why do you want to know, anyway?

RB: Must be marvellous to travel about all over the world.

RC: Well, you're doing the next best thing – you're travelling about all over Middlesex.

RB: Middlesex isn't romantic and exciting, is it?

RC: Depends which house you go to.

RB: (ignoring this) Do you know, they say there's an island in the Pacific where the wind always blows?

RC: Well, that's about all it ever does over 'ere an' all. I think travel's very over-rated meself. I mean, why do so many American tourists go to Edinburgh to see Princes Street?

RB: Well, that's obvious, ain't it? Because they wouldn't see it if they went anywhere else.

RC: Take my advice, stay at home and drink whisky instead.

RB: Whisky shortens your life.

RC: I know, but you'll see twice as much in half the time.

3: KIDS

RC: Time you got a new suit, you know. You're beginning to look shabby.

RB: This suit was made to measure, but the bloke didn't pick it up so I had it.

RC: You've worn that jacket ever since I knew you.

RB: I know. This was my wedding suit.

RC: Oh, you was married an' all, was you?

RB: Yeah. My wife was like the ocean – she was wild and restless, and she made me sick.

RC: Any kids?

RB: Oh, yeah. I don't know how, though, she was so stupid. When I suggested a family she went and pulled up all the gooseberry bushes. Having kids with her was like waiting for a bus. Nothing happened for ages, and then three came along all at once.

RC: Oh, triplets you had?

RB: Yeah, they're grown up now.

RC: What were they?

RB: One of each: a boy, a girl and a hairdresser.

4: WOMEN

RB: Do you realise that Adam didn't have a mother-in-law?

RC: Yes. That's why he lived in Paradise.

RB: You don't like women, do you?

RC: Not a lot.

RB: You was married, though, wasn't you?

RC: Oh, yes. My wife came from a fine old English family. Unfortunately, she brought it with her.

RB: Is that why you took to the road?

RC: Nah. I took to the road 'cos she was stupid. I told her my great-great-grandfather was killed at Waterloo and she said, 'Which platform?'

RB: Silly so-and-so. As if the platform mattered.

RC: 'Zackly. And she was colour blind, an' all, and never told me.

RB: How did you find out?

RC: She made a rhubarb pie out of celery.

5: WORK

RC: What made you give up work and take to the road then, Harry?

RB: I gave up work because of sickness. The boss got sick of me.

RC: You was a railway porter, wasn't you?

RB: Yeah. I got the sack 'cos I trod on a snail.

RC: Why did you do that?

RB: It had been following me about all day.

RC: Bit of a blow, wasn't it, losing your job?

RB: Yeah. Well, at the time I had a wife and two ruptures to support. What made you give it up then?

RC: I lost the will to live – except at weekends. I was always late. What they ought to do is cross electric blankets with toasters, and pop people out of bed in the morning. I had to go up before the boss. I hadn't been talking to him for more than two minutes and he called me a fool.

RB: What caused the delay?

RC: I dunno. I must have been talking slow.

RB: My boss was rude an' all. And mean. On flag days he had a special way of avoiding buying one.

RC: What was that then?

RB: He used to wear a tray with flags on it. One year I sent him a card with 'A Happy Christmas' on it. The next year, he sent the same card back and wrote on it 'And the same to you'.

6: HEALTH

RB: Do you know how to avoid falling hair?

RC: Yeah. Get out of the way. You're going a bit bald under that balaclava, ain't you?

RB: I'm not bald. I've got flesh-coloured hair.

RC: Go on, you can't fool me.

RB: I've got wavy hair.

RC: You used to have. Now it's waving goodbye. My advice is to stop worrying about it. I known a lot of people go grey worrying about going bald.

RB: Me eyes are not what they was, either.

RC: Why, what was they, ears?

RB: You know what I mean. I can't see things close to unless they're a long way away.

RC: The paper said they can cure short sight now, with a special herbal solution.

RB: Nah, that's just a lot of eye-wash. I'm gonna get a monocle.

RC: You'll sit on that and break it.

RB: No, I won't – that's not where you wear it. They've invented a new lens that can be hit with a hammer, dropped a hundred feet and jumped on without it breaking. As a final test, they're going to let the Post Office have a go at it.

7: MONEY

RB: I reckon I got a cold coming.

RC: You wanna take some aspirins.

RB: I can't take aspirins – they give me a headache.

RC: I see in the paper where it says that fifty thousand germs can live on a pound coin for a year.

RB: Oh, yeah. Does that include VAT?

RC: I dunno. I should have asked that businessman I tried to tap the other day. Mean basket he was – wouldn't spare me a pound for a cup of coffee.

RB: Why did you ask for a pound just for a cup of coffee?

RC: I'm a heavy tipper.

RB: Them Americans got a lotta money to waste. Look at all that money they wasted putting a man on the moon.

RC: They're gonna put a man on the sun next.

RB: They can't do that. He'd be burnt to a cinder.

RC: No, they've thought of that.

RB: Oh, yeah? How they gonna get round that then?

RC: They're sending him at night.

Monologues and Spokespersons

Everyone had a favourite. For many, the sight of rascally Ronnie Corbett in a Pringle sweater and slippers, mischievous grin and hands clamped nervously between his moleskin-clad thighs was the highlight of *The Two Ronnies* half hour. However, for others, nothing – absolutely nothing – beat the blissful cut to a barrel-chested, blustering, bespectacled Barker behind a lectern or desk in his guise as a spokesman, vicar, pundit, minister or expert launching into a verbal variety box with a simple, harrumphing 'Good evening'.

Whether it was a three-piece suit, a bowler hat or the simple white lab-coat, Barker – armed with a furrowed brow, a serious face and the ubiquitous long pointing stick to whack at a graph or flipchart – took the opportunity to let fly. Unconstrained by action or plot, his lectures and announcements showed off his unrivalled mastery of language, pun, double entendre, rhythm and timing.

Certainly, week after week, there could be a sense of déjà vu as a seemingly endless group of pompous, know-all twits made proclamations and announcements about everything from 'Pismonouncers Anonymous' to 'The Ministry of Sex Equality'; however, the joy – much like in a singer or musician – was in the twist in the old favourite everyone wants to hear again. When the lectures were in full flight, invariably picking up speed as they approached their absurd climax, audiences mixed aching laugher with admiration for Barker's Swiss-watch timing and tongue-twisting delivery of the daffy, daft, dexterous and delightful bureaucracy of the day.

ANNUAL GENERAL MOUTHFUL

RB: Silence, please. I'd like to call this meeting to order and welcome everyone to the annual, or, in other words, twelve-monthly conference that we hold once a year for the Society for People Who Use a Lot of Words and Say Very Little. It is with tremendous pleasure, enjoyment, elation, glee, joy and delight and with very little pain, discomfort, embarrassment, melancholia and stroke or depression that I address you all verbally by speaking to all those of you who are listening, with your ears, to the vocal manifestations which are emanating audibly from this hole in the middle of my face. Now, not wishing to be brief, and in order more fully to beat about the bush, not to mention shilly-shallying and procrastination, although I have, in fact, just mentioned them – nevertheless, and notwithstanding, I don't propose to sit down without laying before you where I stand in relation to our policy of, or attitude to, and indeed our connection with, the attitude which our policy has always been concerned over.

MR WHISPER: 'Scuse me, sir.

(Whisper whispers.)

RB: Ah! I have just been handed a message, typewritten, in a hand I do not recognise, which informs me, in no uncertain terms, plainly, even outspokenly, clearly, concisely, briefly, and perhaps it wouldn't be going too far to say rudely, that in the unbiased opinion of the sender of the message, I should bring to an end, terminate, and possibly cease completely, my talk, address, conversation or discourse, forthwith, if not immediately. Not, I may add due to the content of my speech: but merely because, unknown to me – when I first rose from my seat, on which I had been sitting before I stood up, to begin this particular address to you, the members of the society, the spectators, and the audience, not to mention all those present: my trousers fell down.

(Pull back to reveal RB's trousers have fallen down.)

SPEECH DAY

RB: Headmaster – Mrs Featherstone – members of the teaching staff – parents – boys. I don't know you – and I'm quite sure that none of you have ever heard of me. Many of the masters won't know me – in fact, until today, hardly anyone in this school would have been aware of my existence. I'm the Minister of Education. But that is not the reason I am here this afternoon. I am here because I'm an old boy. One of this school's old boys. And I'm here today to talk about what it is like, to be an old boy. Many of you young boys here today will eventually become – old boys. And I wonder what sort of old boy you will turn out to be. I've met all sorts of old boys in my time – clever old boys, funny old boys, stupid old boys and some downright wicked old boys. I was talking to a deaf old boy the other day, and I told him I was coming to talk to you today. And then, I told him again. And this time, he heard me, and he asked me to pass on this bit of good advice. Take care of your ears. Protect them against frosty weather, and above all, keep them clean at all times. I mean nobody likes to see an old boy with dirty ears walking along the street. So let your motto be 'Cleanliness at all times'. And abstinence. Strong liquor should be avoided wherever possible. I mean, there's nothing worse than going into a pub, and finding it full of old boys playing shove-halfpenny, so that you can't get near the bar. Personal safety, too, is very important.

The other day I was driving my car along the road, when an old boy stepped straight off the pavement in front of me. And if I hadn't braked sharply I would have killed the old boy. So remember – look after yourself, avoid strong drink, and keep your ears clean. Oh, and one final word. Women. Well, I'd like to go on much longer – but that's impossible. And when you're an old boy like me, you'll understand what I mean. Thank you.

(Applause.)

THE STARS AT NIGHT

Start on a shot of planets revolving on a model as in The Sky at Night. *Lose after four seconds. Almost immediately one planet hits another one, which falls off and bounces. Cut to RB. Fade music.*

RB: Hello, good evening and welcome to this special edition of *The Stars at Night. (Over this we see caption – 'Patrick Moore's brother'.)* I'm sorry to have to inflict myself on you like this, but Patrick couldn't be here tonight, and so he asked me to step into his shoes. And why not? He's always borrowing my suits. So here I am, and he asked me to apologise to you for not being here, but he has had to go and show his telescope to the local Townswomen's Guild. If they like it, they're going to knit him a cover for it. Then tonight he's taking it to the Palladium for the *Night of a Thousand Stars.* Apparently, they're one short, and he's going to help them look for it. And what he'll do after that, well, we just don't know.

Because, of course, he never goes to bed at night, that's when his day's work starts. And only when dawn breaks does he put away his slide-rule and relax. Of course, he likes a little bit of fun afterwards, just like anyone else. Many's the time I've seen him put on his dinner jacket and go out and dance till lunchtime. This, of course, has its advantages: he never has trouble with last buses, and no one can accuse him of staggering home with the milkman, which is just as well, as it's a very gossipy neighbourhood.

However, I digress, as my very good friend Frank Ackfield would say. The reason Patrick asked me to come here tonight, apart from not wanting to lose the fee, was that tonight, and tonight only, whizzing across our sky, you will be able to see the celebrated Bailey's Comet. Now this comet appears only once in 200 years, and so not many of us have actually seen it before, but I can assure you that from all parts of Britain it will be visible to the naked observer; so a trip into your back garden should be well worth it – if only to look over the fence at the woman next door.

(Enter a girl with a piece of white card.)

Now this comet passes very, very close to the moon, how close we just don't know, but I would like, if I may, to show you a diagram of what is liable to happen. Thank you, Sandra, now then. (He draws a wavy line across the board.) Here we have the surface of the moon, and here (another line) the stratosphere. Here is the famous Sea of Tranquillity – here a mountain, known as the Height of Absurdity, and here, two craters, known as the Depths of Depravity. Now the last moon shot orbited here (draws a dot and a semi-circle) but Bailey's Comet will pass even closer to the moon, here (draws a dot nearer the surface and another semi-circle), so you can see it should be a splendid sight. Of course this is sideways on. What we will see is more like this – turn it round, Sandra, truly a heavenly body not to be missed.

(Sandra now holds the drawing in front of her – a wavy torso with two large boobs, and her head looking over the top.)

Now, a word about next week. Patrick himself hopes to be back with you when, owing to a great number of requests, he is going to devote the whole programme to asteroids, and how to deal with them, which should be a boon to all fellow sufferers. If you have any questions to ask Patrick, postcards only please, and if you have any to ask Sandra, put them in a sealed envelope as we have a filthy-minded postman. (He drinks from glass on desk.) But to return to the comet, those who want to see …

SANDRA: (from wings) Psst!

RB: Er – those who want to see the comet …

SANDRA: Psst!

RB: No, I won't, it's water. For those who would like to see the comet, it will be visible from about quarter past … (Sandra points to her watch frantically as she approaches. RB looks at his watch.) Oh Lord. Damn and blast. We've just missed it. Oh well, never mind, it'll come round again in 200 years and Patrick will tell you all about it then. Goodnight.

(He starts to sing 'The Stars at Night are Big and Bright' with Sandra looking over his shoulder and clapping to the music.)

ONE GOOD TURN: THE CALL OF THE WILD

Fade up on a music-hall stage, with jungle backcloth and footlights. RB enters as animal impersonator. He wears an old-fashioned dinner jacket, starched dickie and wing collar. He moves centre stage, where a small card table awaits him, with various props upon it.

RB: *(he speaks with an American accent and sounds rather gay)* My name is Harold Beresford, and tonight with my animal sounds and bird calls, I hope to bring you, using my throat, larynx, forearms, and various parts of my body, a real whiff of the country. I also use a few common household objects such as this ordinary oil-lamp funnel, which gives added resonance when re-creating the throaty roar of the lion. *(He croaks through the funnel.)* The distinctive evening call of the African bullfrog *(wood-lee, wood-lee)* and the myriad sounds of the jungle. *(He burps.)* Pardon me. That was dinner. But, to my story ...

You will need to imagine that I am a hunter, young and gay, the son of a chieftain of the Elawi tribe of Central Africa. My name is Nuki, and I wear this feather as a badge of my rank and a square loincloth, which I will ask you to imagine. It is eight inches by twelve inches. I mean, just imagine. It is embroidered with symbols of fertility and just covers the part of the costume which is most important, however, is the feather, so I'll put it on. *(He does so.)* There. Do I look like an African prince? And of course, the ceremonial nose-bone. *(He clips it on rapidly and now talks through his nose.)*

Of course, I can't possibly do the imitations with this on, so you will have to imagine that as well if you will. *(Removes it again and speaks normally.)* Ooh, that really hurts your nose, you know that? But to my story. One Sunday morning in the depths of the jungle, when the tropical birds were greeting the dawn with their strange cries *(caw! caw! cruk, cruk, whistle, etc.)* Nuki rose and began to prepare for his daily walk in the forest. *(Rattles finger around in mouth and explains to audience)* Cleaning his teeth with a stick. Outside his straw hut, he could hear the chattering of the bald-backed bare baboon *(wuh! wuh! wuh!)* and the other all too familiar morning sound *(gibberish)* – his mother telling him to wash behind his ears. 'I'm old enough to look after myself, mother,' he replied. Though of course he said it in his own language. Soon he is on his way. He treads carefully through the crisp, crackly leaves on the forest floor *(crish crish crish crish crish slub slub)*, occasionally stepping in a mucky bit. Suddenly, behind him, he hears a sound that makes his blood run cold! *(oi! oi!)* He turns to face the most dreaded creature in the whole jungle. *(oi! oi!)* His granny, on her way to market. 'Oi,' she cries. 'Where you g'win, soun?' He ignores her and hurries on.

Passing through a clearing, he notices the lazy warthog (snort, snort, oink, etc.), the anteater busy eating ants (sniff, sniff, sniff) and the whistling woodpecker (whistle, knock, knock, knock, whistle, etc.). He passes on, leaving the anteater eating his ants, and the warthog hogging his warts, and the whistling woodpecker pecking his wooden whistle. Soon he is into more open country where he spies his old friend, the giraffe. (Picks up funnel, pauses.) The giraffe makes no sound. Or rather, the slight sound it does make is impossible to recreate. With the mouth. The giraffe nods silently, turns its back, and is gone in a puff of dust. Nuki's journey is almost over and we leave him, finally, sitting peacefully by the riverbank, watching the mating dance of the African flat-faced duck. This last demonstration requires that I roll up my trouser-leg, but do not fear, dear ladies – that's as far as I'm going. (He rolls up his trouser-leg.) I have no way of proving this to you, so you will have to take my word that this is the truly authentic sound of the mating-dance of the African flat-faced duck. Thank you.

(He slaps his calf like the sound of ducks' feet. After a few seconds a real duck walks on stage and heads towards him. Play-off music as he takes his bow. The duck looks interested.)

HELLFIRE, OR THE MUSIC MAN OF THE CLOTH

RB as vicar of country church. He stands in old-fashioned pulpit, reached by a few stone steps. He addresses the congregation. The organ plays extempore under.

RB: This evening, my friends, I want to talk about Sin. And I wish to speak only to those amongst you who are Sinners. All those who have never sinned should leave now. (He looks round.) No one has moved. It's just as well. Because if anyone had dared to walk out, he would have been branded 'Liar'. This village – this village is overrun with Sin. It is rife! Rife! And I tell you, friends, that the Devil is everywhere, about his deadly work. He's at work in the village shop, watering the milk – he's in the public house, watering the beer – he is behind the public house, watering the daisies. He is at work upstairs behind the curtains of Oak Cottage, where old Mr Tomkins took a lodger as company for his young wife. His young wife is in the family way. And the lodger – she's in the family way as well.

(The organ starts to become rhythmical; RB begins to speak rhythmically.)

He's everywhere, he's all through the village infecting the lives of each and every one of you – old folk, young folk, each and every one of you – spreading his evil work around with a flick of his old forked tail, and I'm warning you, if we don't do something about it, if we don't get the Devil from among us, if we don't repent—

> My friends you got trouble –
> Right here in Lower Witton –
> You got crimes and cheats and slight misdemeanours that
> Add up to a whole lot of wrong,
> You got women who gossip and others that listen and
> Some who are eavesdropping all day long
> To see if they can hear if the women who are gossiping are
> Saying anything about them
> Like young Mrs Noakes (now you all know her)
> Living up by the top end (up the hill)
> Now she's known to have taken in laundry for the fellow
> With the limp who works at the inn
> Now just because he's bought himself a brand new crutch
> Doesn't mean he wore the old one out
> But the Gossips say Yes
> And that rhymes with 'S'
> And that stands for Sin!
> Oh – yes – my – friends – you – really – got
> Trouble.

CONGREGATION: Yes, Trouble!

RB: Right here in Lower Witton.

CONGREGATION: Yes, you have!

> **RB:** You've got drinking, gambling, smoking, skiving, fiddling
>   your income tax,
> You've got women on the streets and girls on the game
> And boys on the girls and the girls don't care
> As long as they can listen to their tape cassettes they're
> Taking it in their stride and what about
> Meanness –
> Have you seen the collection plate today?
> Two washers, a fly-button, an Irish penny and a half-sucked
>   mint with a hole
> Last week when a woman was asked to contribute
> To a home for old inebriates
> She gave 'em her husband, yes she did, upon my soul!

RB & CHORUS: Upon – my soul – then – we – got – trouble.

RB: Yes, we have.

CHORUS: Right here in Lower Witton.

> **RB:** (It's here, it's here) Why the whole congregation is consumed
>   by greed
> Immorality and envy too –
> Take the women in the fur coats, sitting in their minks –
> How d'you think they got them? Why,
> Same way as the mink does – you've guessed it,
> Made by another mink, and what about
> Lying?
> And cheating on the railway, I heard tell of a woman
> Who was asked to pay full fare for her boy
> On account of the trousers he was in;
> It's full-length trousers, full-size fare said the guard, and the
>   woman said fine, so it's half
> For me, and my daughter goes free, and that's a SIN!

(The congregation now surround the pulpit, carried away by the mood.)

RB: Now you're gonna have to pay.

CHORUS: Yes, yes!

RB: For all this trouble.

CHORUS: Oh, yes!

RB: 'Cos the Devil is waiting to carry you off to the nethermost
    parts of Hell, where the fire's stoked
Up, and the spits are sizzling, and the oil is on the boil and
Each little Devil has just been issued with a
Brand new toasting fork –
Now! Hear me,
Hear me and repent ('cos there's no one gonna be spared)
Not me, not you, 'cos we're all lost sinners, and that you know
    full well –
Now the Lord has chosen me, my friends
To go and pave the way
And I'll see
You
All
In
HELL!

*(The pulpit floor sinks – RB slowly disappears with a flame effect and
smoke coming from inside the pulpit.)*

UNIVERSITY OF THE AIR

RB as Irish lecturer – black wig, gown, string round trousers, etc.

RB: The top of the evening to you. And the top of the milk as well.
And welcome to the Irish University of the Air. Now many people
have been writing in to us, saying that they make the lessons too difficult in this programme, and it's practically impossible to pass the
exam at the end of the series; so much so that a lot of you have been
having to come home early from the pub at nights to study, sometimes
even before throwing-out time. Well, now, we don't want any of that,
do we now? So we've decided this year to make the questions a lot
easier, so that you all pass. So here we are, these are the questions that

will be on the exam paper this time. Are you ready? Ten questions. Anyone answering eleven questions will be disqualified.

QUESTION 1.
Who won the First World War?

QUESTION 2:
Who came second?

QUESTION 3:
What is a silver dollar made of?

QUESTION 4:
Explain Einstein's theory of Hydrodynamics or write your name in block capitals.

QUESTION 5:
Spell the following: (Writes on blackboard) a) Dog b) Car c) Carrot.

QUESTION 6:
What time is the Nine o'clock News on?

QUESTION 7:
How many Commandments was Moses given? Approximately.

QUESTION 8:
There have been six Kings of England called George. The latest was called George the Sixth. Name the other five.

QUESTION 9:
Who invented Stevenson's Rocket?

QUESTION 10:
Do you understand Newton's Law of Gravity? (Answer Yes or No).

QUESTION 11:
Of what country is Dublin the capital? (This answer must be exact).

QUESTION 12:
If Paddy carries 20 bricks in a hod, and carries 40 hods a day; and weighs half as much as Murphy, and Murphy carries 10 bricks in a hod and carries 80 hods a day, and he weighs twice as much as Paddy – who is the biggest idiot?

That's the end of the questions. Copies of this examination paper are obtainable at all betting shops. Not more than seven hours is allowed for the completion of this paper and the only reference books allowed are Reveille and the Sporting Life. Candidates, and all others who have entered, should send their answers, preferably on paper, to 'Irish University of the Air', BBC Studios, and if you don't hear for six months, you've passed and you're a BA. And if you forget to post it, you're a BF. One last thing – if some of the arithmetic is too difficult, here is the latest Irish calculator, obtainable at any pub that sells Guinness. (Shows calculator. It is a knot of string.) That's the memory – and that's for cancelling. (Shows knot of string and knife.) And the best of Irish luck – Goodnight.

EQUALITY

RB: Good evening. Equality. The Government White Paper on The Equal Society was published today. Its main provisions are as follows:

From April 1st 1981, everyone must be of equal height. This height will be three foot above the saloon bar for men, and two feet under the hair dryer for women. Anyone found shorter than the equal height will be looked down on. He will then be sent to a Government height-inducing camp, where he will stand in a barrel of manure – until he's tall enough to step out without catching anything on the rusty nail at the top. Anyone found taller than the equal height will be required to carry lead weights in the trouser pockets and wear very short braces. This will cause a stoop and, inevitably, a few boy sopranos.

Everyone must also be of equal weight. The weight to be established as Quite Heavy for men, and Not Quite So Heavy for women – except during pregnancy when women will be permitted a little more. Men, however, will not be permitted anything at all. Anyone found heavier than the equal weight will complete a questionnaire, asking such questions as 'Are you able to adjust your dress before leaving?' and 'When did you last see your feet?' If the answers are 'yes', their corsets will be impounded, although this rule is fairly elastic, and they will be sent to a Government 'jumping up and down' camp. Anyone below equal weight will be forcibly fed with chocolate biscuits, through the office of the resident physician – and will receive silicone injections in the event. Or in the arm. If a woman thinks silicone is silly, she can have cortisone instead. But if a man has cortisone, he should be more careful with his zipper.

Now then *(he produces a large piece of cardboard)* I would now like to show you a diagram. I would like to, but I can't, as Mrs Whitehouse might complain. But I'll tell you about it. As from 1985, everyone will be of equal shape. Except, of course, that women will have two of these and one of those; and men will have one of these, and two of those. If any man is found to have two of these, he will be declared a woman – whether he has one of those or not. Now if a man has got one of these but only one of those, he will get a pension. And if he's got two of those and two of these, he won't get a pension but he will get attention. Believe you me. And any man found with three of those will be ostracised. Which is bad news for pawnbrokers. *(Phone rings.)* Hello? Oh, hello Mrs Whitehouse. You what? You insist on the viewers seeing all the these and those? Very well. *(Turns card round – it has 'these' and 'those' in large letters, several times, all over it.)* There we are. Disgusting, isn't it? But true to life. Like *Crossroads*.

Noses. There will be a choice of noses – Roman aquiline or hooked turn-up. The number of nostrils will remain at two – although there will be a choice of straight or flared. Members of the public will be allowed to make their choice in their own time, but the House of Commons is to have a special session, when Members can all pick their noses together. It was later stated that it will not be necessary in future for noses to run in the family.

Finally, in future, all children must be born equally, that is, on October 1st each year. This will be known as Labour Day. To achieve this objective, all television transmissions during the week of December 23rd will close down at nine o'clock – when everyone will have an early night. And a happy Christmas to you all. Goodnight.

A FEW WORDS

RB: My friends – or may I call you ladies and gentlemen. I have been asked to make a speech; but before I do I'd just like to say a few words. And before I do that, I tell I must feel you, that I've had a few. Drinks, that is, not words. Mind you, quite a few words have passed my lips too, in my time. And of course, that's what life is all about, isn't it? Communication.

Communication. The spoken word. Now it's essential that we know what's going on, and indeed, what isn't going on that should be. We must communicate with each other, and also with anyone else we happen to meet, because everyone – and by everyone I mean every-body can, and in fact does, or if they don't at present they very soon, – will, because to be honest; everyone has to, eventually, for, as we all know, and those who've had the experience will bear me out. And the sooner the better.

In other words, we must try to regard the nation as a whole. And those who think it is one, should get out and make room for the others. Because I mean there's no room for shirkers. This country has a great future behind it. I mean, have you ever wondered what will we all be like in a hundred years from now? Well, we'll be dead but this land of ours will be a garden of Eden. Today we have the penny post, but then they'll have two posts: a first class post that doesn't get there the next day and a second class post that doesn't get there the day after. In 1974 there'll be a channel tunnel – we'll understand our neighbours better. We won't say 'Wogs begin at Calais'. We'll say 'Wogs begin at Dover'. By then we'll have dug a tunnel straight downwards so at no expense at all you'll be able to fall to Australia. Everyone will have much more leisure time. We'll cut the working week to 96 hours for children under ten, and to ten hours for children over 96.

Oh, but 1974 will be wonderful! Think of the discoveries we have already – already women have their children delivered at the front door, thanks to Mr Gladstone and his bag; sometimes known as Mrs Gladstone. Already we can go out and go to the toilet without getting our feet wet, thanks to the Duke of Wellington. And now that we have the sandwich, invented by the Earl of Sandwich, what great things can we expect from Lord Wimpy and Baron Jumbo-Brunchburger! And look at this kettle. *(Produces old copper kettle.)* This is the very one that James Watt saw when he first thought of the steam engine. Had he come in five minutes later, the tea would have been made and the frying pan would have been on the stove, and he would have invented the chip engine. Transport will be quite different. We'll have a 30-horsepower bus worked by only two men, one to drive and the other to clean up after the 30 horses.

And they'll be equality. Everyone will be given a chance. You three gardeners at the back there ... listen well. In 1974 your great-grandsons could be men of power – yes, you, Zebediah Heath, old Diggory Wilson and you, Sambo Powell. I predict that many minority groups will seek the vote – dogs, horses – even women. As to women – that could lead to trouble. Mind you, I'm not denying that some women have a perfect right. But, on the other hand, they've got an equally good left, and why – where do women get these ideas, about wanting to wear the trousers? In my opinion they should drop them completely, and assume their rightful position – bent over the sink. And if that isn't proof of the pudding, if proof were needed, then I don't know, who has.

To sum up:

You may drink to the girl with the face that's divine;
To the girl with the figure that's wavy;
You may drink to the girl from blue-blooded stock;
You may drink below stairs, with the slavey.
You may drink to the girl who is one of the boys,
Who goes out with the army and navy;
But here's to the girl who is both rich and old –
To the girl with one foot in the gravy.
Ladies and gentlemen – absent friends!

(He drinks.)

THE MILKMAN'S XMAS SPEECH TO THE NATION

RB as milkman, seated like the Queen at an ornate desk in Buck. Palace.

RB: A very merry Christmas to you all. As I think of you, my loyal customers, sitting at home round your firesides this Christmas, it brings home to me very strongly, the enormous responsibility that I have, as your milkman. *(Caption: HM QUINN.)* And I know, that you will appreciate, how important it is to me, to know that I have your support, and shall continue to have your support, throughout the coming year. The task of supplying milk to a great nation such as ours, is, I am sure you realise, not an easy one. Either here at home, or in our colonies – spread as they are, like butter, over the entire globe.

Whether home or colonial, it is our express wish that it be co-operative, uniting dairies across the world. The milk of human kindness must not be watered down. It must flow, not only through the cream of society, but also onto the most humble doorstep in the land, be it black, or white, or gold-top. Let our lives be ordered, and ordered as soon as possible, so as to avoid disappointment, in the years to come. I extend my warmest and most heartfelt bottle, to you all.

DON'T QUOTE ME

A cosy, book-lined studio set.

(RB, with peg on nose, as Melvyn Bragg. He speaks to camera.)

RB: Hello, and welcome to the book programme.

(Caption supered – Melvyn Pegg.)

RB: William Shakespeare, it is generally agreed, has provided the English language with more sayings, proverbs and quotes than any other writer. Every other book title is a quote from the Bard. Many plays in the theatre do the same. Why then, should not television follow suit? Here, with a little help from our caption department, is a scene from Edward the Sixth, Part I.

(During the last speech, mix to the interior of a Shakespearean castle, as in the film, Richard III. RB enters as Richard, with a courtier.)

RB: Now, dearest cous, the time draws fast apace
When for my crowning we must soon prepare.

COURTIER: My liege, I have the information close.

RB: Then spill it out – thou art already late;
Thou hadst forsworn to bring me News at Ten.

(Caption – News at Ten.)

RB: But tell me first, how may I seek to rid
My royal self of that Arch villainess
That calls herself the Queen?

COURTIER: Queen so she is
She is your consort, sire, or will be so
When you are crowned next week in Westminster.

(Caption – Week in Westminster.)

COURTIER: Throughout the land her beauty is renowned
Her person is respected Nationwide.

(Caption – Nationwide.)

RB: Her person is the Duke of Hastings, sir!
He is her lover, and must get the chop!
Each day they flaunt their fever in the court,
He arrogant and bold, and she all smiles
Contented with her lot, and with her bed,
Each night with her Brideshead Revisited

(Caption – Crossroads.)

RB: Aye, he shall die, revenge shall be complete
My crowning's perk! My coronation's treat!

(Caption – Coronation Street.)

RB: But, for to furnish evidence withal,
Observe the Queen's speech, when she's with him close.

(Caption – The Queen's Speech.)

RB: When oft, beneath the starry sky at night

(Caption – The Sky at Night.)

RB: He speaks in tones both Moribund and Wise

(Caption – Moribund and Wise.)

RB: Of times when he, during the reign of John,
Kept silent, and endured the Tyrannies

(Caption – The Two Ronnies.)

RB: Then mind her.

(Caption – Minder.)

COURTIER: That will I, most royal liege.
He often plots with Lovell 'gainst the crown.

RB: These points of view are treason, you well know

(Caption – Points of View.)

RB: He may it think, but can he ever it show?

(Caption – Kenny Everett Show.)

RB: He must be cornered with some trumped-up charge
Of treasonable acts, both Little and Large

(Caption – The Two Ronnies.)

RB: Then, when he is transported to the Tower
No blemish shall besmirch my nuptial hour
Come, dancing maidens,

(Caption – Come Dancing.)

RB: Trumpets, play away!

(Caption – Play Away.)

RB: Drums that do beat at night must throb in day.

(Caption – Robin Day.)

RB: And as the songs of praise proclaim us wed

(Caption – Songs of Praise.)

RB: Let (bleep-bleep) Hastings lose his (bleep-bleep) head!

(Caption – Blankety-Blank.)

(Exit, with fanfare.)

ONE GOOD TURN: THE CHOCOLATE-COLOURED COUGH DROP

(Caption: One good turn.)

RB as Barry Norman in small set.

(Caption: (super) with Barry Normal.)

RB: *(very fast)* Hello and good evening to you. The bits of film we are about to show you, or at least I hope we're going to show you if they don't fall apart, are selected from the archives situated in the bowels, and I use the term loosely, but not too loosely, of the earth beneath the Television Centre, and if the actual film doesn't fall apart I'm sure you'll agree with me (and if you don't, I certainly shan't lose any sleep over it) that some of the acts certainly do fall apart, that is, not act – if you can call singing acting, which I'm not sure you can.

Where was I? Hello and good evening. The act you are about to see was the first one, and when I say the first one, I mean one of the first to come to light. If you can call it light, bearing in mind that it was in the bowels, and I use the term even more loosely than last time, of the Radio Doctor, here at Television Centre, and who am I to criticise? The man in the burnt cork and fuzzy wig was, or is, unless he's died, which he probably has by now, although I wouldn't bank on it, some of these performers seem to go on for ever – he certainly does – is the great Al Vermont, always billed as The Chocolate-coloured Cough Drop. See what you make of it.

(Cut to old scratchy fuzzy black-and-white film. (Caption: Al Vermont – the chocolate-coloured cough drop) upright or baby grand piano in parlour (American) set of the twenties.)

(RB, in burnt cork, period dinner jacket and fuzzy wig, seated at the piano, white gloves and a top hat complete the ensemble. He plays and sings the following song, and throughout he bounces up and down on the piano seat, in time to the stupid song, which is almost entirely on one note.)

(The set slowly disintegrates under this continual bumping. Pictures fall off the wall, ornaments vibrate their way off shelves into goldfish bowls, the piano stool eventually collapses, as indeed does the piano, on the final few bars. His top hat, placed on his stool for the second verse, is crushed. His foot goes through the floorboards, piano keys fly off (one or two). Champagne in a bucket shakes and explodes, cork flies out, etc, etc.)

SONG – SYNCOPATED LADY

I know a gal …
I'm crazy for …

(Piano arpeggio.)

She hangs around …
My old back door …

(Piano again.)

She never will …
Belong to me …
'Cos she's too sophisticated
And syncopated …
You …
See …

(Piano intro into chorus.)

1. She's a syncopated lady
And she lingers where it's shady
And I listen to her daily
As she plucks her ukulele
And her eyes are kinda flashy
And her clothes are kinda trashy
And she smokes them small havanas
And she chews them big bananas –
Teeth like pearls and lips like wine
Thumpy Thumpy Thumpy goes that heart of mine –

2. Thumpy Thumpy Thumpy 'cos
Her shape it is so bumpy
It's so dimply and dumpy
Kinda loose and kinda lumpy
And it has no imperfections
And it points in all directions
How I love them pounds and ounces
In that sweater when it bounces
And it makes me kinda jumpy when our arms entwine
Thumpy Thumpy Thumpy goes that heart of mine.

(A piano break of 12 or 16 bars – close-up hands, etc.)

She's a syncopated lady
And her second name is Sadie
And I love the way she dances
With just anyone she fancies
And I love the way she washes
And she wears them big galoshes
And the way her hands meander
When she's kissed on her veranda
She lives at number seven but she sleeps at number nine
Thumpy Thumpy Thumpy goes that heart of mine.

(Repeat last line – as piano collapses completely, in long shot.)

KID STUFF

RB as newsreader at desk – overlay screen behind him.

RB: Good evening – here is the news. In the House of Commons today, there were stormy exchanges from both sides of the house, during a discussion on the Prime Minister's forthcoming visit to the United States. Using the new abbreviated form of speech (introduced into the Commons to save time), the foreign secretary replied to the MP for N.2, Mr BF, and said that the PM should P and O to the US as air travel was NBG for a VIP. In a 707 anyone could K0 the PM and the UN could do FA.

The latest trade figures are described as encouraging by the Chancellor of the Exchequer today ...

(Strains of the Jackanory music are heard, as if from the next studio. RB is thrown rather.)

RB: Er – the October figures were – er, I'm sorry, we seem to be picking up sound from another studio. *(Phone on the desk rings.)* Hello? Yes. Yes, of course I can hear it. Of course I can hear it. Jackanory. Yes. Very well. *(Phone down.)* I apologise for the sound break-up; it is being traced. Meanwhile I will continue ... Inflation still continues to rise at an alarming rate. Mrs Thatcher, attacking the Government's policy, said, 'Once upon a time, there were three bears.' I'm sorry. *(He glares off in the direction of music.)* 'Once upon a time, there were three dollars to the pound. And then there were two. Two little dollar bills, sitting on the wall, one named Peter, and one named Paul. Fly away, Peter, fly away, Paul, come back, Peter, come back in the days before the Labour government took over.' She was greeted with loud cheers, and then she went home and had tea in the nursery with lots of lovely jelly and jam and cream, and she ate so much she felt sick.

Sport. Bob Fairbrother, now fully recovered from a leg injury, had originally agreed to play this Saturday, but has now stated that he cannot as his mummy won't let him. She says he can't come out to play until he's done his homework.

Now it's time for another adventure about Little Benn, the wedge of wood. Little Benn was always being hard done by, because he was only made of wood, and being wedge-shaped made it even worse, because people used to tread on his thin end, and kick his fat end. And he was always afraid to walk down the street, because he was frightened of the boy who lived at number ten, who was called Sunny Jim, but he wasn't sunny at all, really. He and the boy next door, Denis the Menace, used to tease Little Benn because he was different from them – and run away, and he would be left, on his own. And he'd say 'Why am I always left?' So he went to see Jenkins, the wizard, who lived far away in the mountains and who sometimes turned into a big green dragon, and other times wore a white collar. And he told Jenkins the wizard he was always left, and Jenkins the wizard said, 'Don't be silly. Of course you're not left. That's ridiculous. My advice to you is to go for a trot. Go for lots of trots. With a few trots behind you, you can't be left, can you?' and with that, he turned into the Green Dragon again, and ordered a large gin and tonic.

(Now the Jackanory theme is replaced by the Magic Roundabout. RB reacts again, looking offstage.)

Florence was looking everywhere for Dougal.

(Film of Florence with Dougal on overlay behind RB.)

'I've had a letter from the BBC,' she said. 'They want you to read the news.' 'Oh, not again,' said Dougal. 'They're always doing that. They keep mixing me up with Robert Dougall.'

(Caption on overlay of Robert Dougall.)

'I don't know. They don't know what they're doing up there, you know. They'll be mixing you up with Richard Baker next, I shouldn't wonder.'

(Caption of Richard Baker's head on Florence's body.)

'Dear, dear. Oh dear, oh dear.'

(Zebedee's boinggg is heard.)

'What was that?' (Boinggg!! again.) 'Time for bed,' said Angela Rippon. And off we went. What fun it was! Good night, children – goodnight!

(RB's face appears in kaleidoscope revolving picture as in Jackanory. Music up.)

The Two Ronnies: Assorted Sketches

In the 1970s and 80s, before the adult anarchy of *The Alternative Comedy* revolution, small-screen double act sketch comedy fell into two clear camps: The dexterous wordplay of Corbett and Barker in one; the broad vaudeville slapstick and energy of Morecambe & Wise in the other. To those without a television in their home, it is likely these two pairs were interchangeable: silly grown men who should know better, in daft wigs, acting the fool and chasing the girls. However, in recollecting the impressive body of sketches, Barker's approach to his writing is worlds apart from the work Eddie Braben did for Eric and Ernie. Barker's sketches for *The Two Ronnies* regularly began, as traditional sketch comedy has always done, with the actors playing ordinary characters in ordinary settings. Unlike Eric and Ernie's broad pantomime set-ups of celebrity cameos, and song and dance, Barker conjured up humdrum daily interactions and spun wild, rapidly escalating situations of increasingly bizarre twists and turns. Generous in giving everyone on screen equal laughs, Barker gave Corbett alternating turns, so week by week, each stood aghast and incredulous at the other's surreal behaviour. Whether a doctor's surgery, a psychiatrist office, a barber's chair or a genre-bending pastiche of a TV hit of the day, Barker created a world of madness and mayhem lurking behind every ordinary office door.

NAP

'La Marseillaise' is heard and we see RC as Napoleon, standing, legs astride, hands behind back, in front of marble fireplace. He is addressing his officers, who are out of shot.

RC: Gentlemen – the battle before us will not be a simple one. There is no fast and easy road that will take us to victory. The way will be hard, the blood will flow relentlessly throughout the length and breadth of France. Let us do our utmost to make sure that it will be the blood of the enemy. Gentlemen (he raises a wineglass) I give you Liberty! Equality! Fraternity! And the true God of Battle be with us!

(The door opens, and a comfortable, middle-aged nurse enters.)

NURSE: Morning, Mr Parsloe. Don't drink too much of that black-currant. It'll give you the runs.

(We see that the room is empty – it is a residents' lounge in a funny farm.)

RC: Good morning, Marshal Ney. Anything to report?

NURSE: Cauliflower cheese for lunch, followed by Spotted Dick or tangerine yoghurt.

RC: Excellent news. After all, an army marches on its stomach.

NURSE: That cauliflower cheese has been marching on my stomach ever since last week.

RC: If it's good enough for the men, it's good enough for us, Marshal. Send my dispatch officer to me at once. I have some written orders for the front.

NURSE: Mr Hendrikson says he doesn't want to be your dispatch officer any more, dear.

RC: Are you intimating that he has deserted?

NURSE: Intimating's not in it, dear. His bike's got a flat tyre, and anyway he wants to be Charlie Chaplin.

(RB, in doctor's white coat, enters.)

RB: Morning, Nurse. Morning, mon Général. I wonder if I might have a few words alone with the Emperor, Nurse?

NURSE: Certainly, sir.

(She goes.)

RB: Good morning, Excellency. I trust I find you well?

RC: You're lucky to find me at all. What do you want?

RB: Just a few questions.

RC: Then hurry. I'm just off to Waterloo.

RB: Oh, don't worry. I won't make you miss your train. Now, have you always been Napoleon?

RC: Yes, ever since I was a little boy.

RB: How old were you when you were a little boy?

RC: Eleven.

RC: Are you sure you weren't twelve?

RC: No, I've never been twelve in my life. What's it to do with you, anyway? Who are you?

RB: Oh, just call me Doctor.

RC: Doctor Who?

RB: No, we've already got three of those. I'm just a plain, ordinary old consultant. Crippen. Dr Crippen.

(Shakes hands.)

RC: Crippen? You're Doctor Crippen? The murderer?

RB: Shh. Don't tell the Captain. Ethel's on board, dressed as a man.

RC: On board what? Which captain?

RB: This liner. That was the Captain you were talking to.

RC: Who, Marshal Ney? He's in the Army, you great Nana.

RB: Don't you call me a Nana. I'll murder you.

RC: Watch it, I'll have you shot at dawn.

RB: You can't. It's twenty past eleven in the morning.

RC: Well, shot at dusk, then. Anyway, how can you be Crippen? He died years ago. You're as daft as I am.

RB: Ah! (Knowingly) I don't believe you are daft.

RC: Me? I'm as daft as a three-pound note. I'm screwy. Du-lally. I'm not the full quid ... I'm one down in the Marbles Department. Bonkers. Batty. Bird-brained. Barmy.

RB: I saw you in a play at the National Theatre.

RC: There you are. Proves I'm barmy.

RB: And I saw you in The Tom O'Connor Show.

RC: What more do you want? That says it all.

RB: We're with the same agent.

RC: I don't know what you're talking about. See this medal? I got it on the frontier. (He turns round.) I've got one on the back 'ere, as well. (Indeed he has.)

RB: I'm playing the same game as you are. Free food and drink, free digs, this home is a home from home. All you've got to do is act daft. Come on, come clean. You're at it as well, aren't you? You're really Gregory Crumpett, aren't you?

RC: All right – you seem to know all about me. I confess. I come here when I'm resting. Also to get away from the wife.

RB: How long have you been here?

RC: Eighteen months. Things haven't been too good lately. I got this offer to play Napoleon at Biggleswade Repertory Company, so I scarpered with the costume. Instantly recognisable, you see. Straight in here, no messing. What about you?

RB: I just walked in as well.

RC: What were you doing? Doctor in the House?

RB: No, we had some removal men in the house. I just pinched it. It's all right, but if I turn round people think I'm a funny sort of doctor ...

(He turns to show the back of his white coat. It bears the slogan 'You've got it, I'll shift it.')

RB: So if anyone asks me about it, I just prescribe Syrup of Figs.

RC: It's great, isn't it? And the best part about it is that if you act mad enough the staff all humour you.

(An extremely pretty nurse enters.)

RC: Josephine – Josephine – my Empress! My Queen, my Josephine.

PN: Ooh, Napoleon, you're so romantic!

RC: (grabbing her) Not tonight, Josephine. This afternoon! Come on.

(He turns to RB.)

RC: Who pays for all this, by the way?

RB: The GLC.

RC: Aha! That proves it. They should be in here, not us. They really are mad.

(He leaves, with his arm round the nurse.)

THE SLEEPING INSOMNIAC

A psychiatrist's office. The psych (RB) lies on the couch. RC as George sits near him on chair. A pause.

RB: Why have you stopped?

RC: Stopped what?

RB: Talking. You've stopped talking.

RC: There's nothing else to say. That's it.

RB: Go over it again.

RC: Shouldn't I be on the couch?

RB: I know, old boy, it is usual, but I've got this terrible back. Don't mind, do you? Nothing wrong with your back, is there?

RC: No, it's my mind.

RB: Oh, they all say that. Nothing wrong with your mind. Lots of people can't sleep.

RC: I can sleep. It's just that I dream.

RB: Lots of people dream as well.

RC: But I dream I can't sleep! In my dreams, I'm awake all night. It's very tiring. And as soon as I finally manage to drop off to sleep, I wake up.

RB: (getting up) But you are still actually getting sleep?

RC: But what's causing it?

RB: Do you drink too much?

RC: No.

RB: I do – do you mind if I have one? (Gets bottle from filing cabinet.)

RC: I don't do anything too much.

RB: I do. I do everything too much.

RC: Do you sleep though?

RB: Like a log. (Drinks.) Seems to me, as if you've got to treat these dreams like you would if you really couldn't sleep. What do insomniacs do? They go for a walk. Exercise, fresh air. Tires them, so that they can sleep.

RC: You can't do just what you like in dreams.

RB: You can, you can! Try it tonight. Get up out of bed and go for a walk. And make another appointment with the receptionist on the way out for next week.

RC: Oh yes, meant to mention the receptionist! By Jove, noticed her. She's a bit of all right! Is that why you've got a bad back?

RB: Certainly not.

RC: Well, I wouldn't say no. Quite a raver. She's new, isn't she?

RB: Not to me she's not. She's my wife. Sweet dreams!

(RC reacts and leaves.)

APRIL FOOL QUICKIE

A grocer's shop – interior. A workman, on trestles and a plank, is emulsioning the frieze on a section of wall. A sign saying 'Business as Usual' hangs nearby.

(RB, as the grocer, is finishing piling up a pyramid of tins of peas. RB suddenly looks past the camera – and turns to the workman.)

RB: Hey! There's somebody pinching your van!

WORKMAN: Where?

(The pile of tins falls towards the grocer, knocking him against the trestle. The gallon can of emulsion slides down the plank and lands over the grocer's head. Then the trestle hits the tin of emulsion with a clang.)

Cut to: wide shot. (The workman comes back in as the grocer lies amid the chaos.)

WORKMAN: There's no one pinching the van!

RB: (removing emulsion can from head) April Fool.

I COULD HAVE DANCED
ALL LUNCH HOUR

A large office, not too smart. RB at desk, in shirt sleeves. Knock on door – RC enters, in raincoat.

RC: Is this the Arnold Murray School of Dancing?

RB: That's right, yes. Mr Dribble?

RC: Tibble.

RB: Oh, Tibble.

RC: I'd imagined the place much bigger.

RB: Ah, you're thinking of the Arthur Murray School of Dancing. This is the Arnold Murray School of Dancing. Much smaller firm, that's why it's much cheaper. Now then, you've come for your first lesson, right?

RC: That's right, yes. Am I too early?

RB: (Gets up, takes coat from back of chair – it is an evening dress tail coat.) No, you're fine. (Puts on tail coat.) Now, we usually start with the waltz, that's the easiest to pick up. D'you mind taking off your raincoat?

RC: (staring at RB's coat) Are you going to teach me?

RB: Oh yes, rather – I'm Arnold Murray. Now, just put this on (hands him pink sash with large bow. Sash says 'lady' across the chest), because I'm going to lead. Now – hands like this – (they start to dance) and forward, side, together, forward, side, together, one, two three, one, two three ...

(A Negro girl enters, puts papers on RB's desk. She wears a short woollen dress which illustrates everything.)

RB: Thank you, Miss Higginbottom.

(She goes.)

RC: Does she work for you?

RB: Yes, she's my assistant.

RC: Why can't I dance with her?

RB: No, impossible. She's one of the untouchables.

RC: I didn't know Negro girls were untouchables.

RB: This one is – and believe me, I've tried. Now try to relax, you're a bit tense. One, two three, one, two three.

RC: I feel so silly.

RB: That's because you look silly. But you'll get used to it. Mind you, a chap who looks like you should be used to it already. Ever thought of taking up body-building?

RC: Why?

RB: Well, I could transfer your dancing lesson fee over to a subscription to the Arnold Murray Beef-Builder Fitness Club. You've paid the three quid already, haven't you?

RC: Yes, I sent you a postal order.

RB: Good. Well, what do you say? I've got all the equipment.

RC: Does your assistant teach that? She seems to have all the equipment as well.

RB: Who?

RC: Miss Hottentot.

RB: Higginbottom.

RC: Yes.

RB: No. I'm fully qualified. I took a correspondence course in weight-lifting. I hold the golden truss. I'll soon get you in shape.

RC: I think I'd rather be my shape than your shape.

RB: You should have seen me before. I used to be as tall as you once.

RC: When was that?

RB: When I was ten. Come on, let's try a few press-ups. (RC gets on the floor, starts press-ups.) Now, keep your body straight, come on ...

(Intercom buzzes.)

RB: What is it, Miss Higgintot?

MISS H: (voice-over) Miss Brownlow to see you.

RB: Oh, right. (Knock on door – Miss Brownlow enters.) Ah, Miss Brownlow – just pop behind the screen and undress, would you? (She does so. Phone rings. RB picks up black phone.) Hello? Arnold Murray Dance School. (Phone still rings. He picks up red phone.) Murray School of Art. (Phone still rings. He picks up green phone.) Hello, Arnold Murray Worldwide Book of the Month Club. Oh yes, madam. (He takes white doctor's coat from cupboard and puts it on.) Well, there's two publications concerned with cultivation of crops – there's the gardeners' one, The Weeder's Digest. Yes. Or there's the one which is more for farmers. Ah, that's the one you mean. That's The Breeder's Digest. Very comprehensive, yes. No, there aren't any pictures. Your husband wants to make sure he gets what? Oh, oats, only every three years. You must rotate. I'll send it off. And if you're not absolutely delighted with the book after fourteen days, we keep the money. Bye. (To RC) You all right down there?

RC: I think I'd rather carry on with the waltz.

RB: Right – take a seat, I'll be with you in a mo.

(Intercom buzzes again.)

RB: Yes?

MISS H: (voice-over) Mr Jason is here.

RB: Ah, send him in, Miss Hotbottom. (Then, to girl behind screen) You ready, Miss Brownlow? (Miss Brownlow emerges in bra and pants.) Ah yes. Sit down here, please. (Goes to wall, pulls down chart.) Now how long have you been having this eye trouble?

MISS B: About three months, doctor.

RB: Right, well just read this chart out loud, would you.

(She starts to read aloud, slowly. There is a knock on the door – man enters with easel and paintbox.)

ARTIST: Am I too early?

RB: No, no, come in. What is it today?

ARTIST: Life class.

RB: Ah yes, right with you. How are you getting on, Miss Brownlow?

MISS B: I can't see from here.

RB: Well look, stand here – bit closer. That's it. Would you mind putting your arm like this? And the other one like this? There we are. How's that, Mr Jason?

ARTIST: Perfect.

(He starts to draw Miss Brownlow.)

(Knock – a grand lady enters.)

GRAND LADY: Are you the vet?

RB: Yes, madam.

GRAND LADY: I rang earlier – there's something the matter with my pom.

RB: Ah, yes. If you care to step behind the screen, I'll have a look at it.

GRAND LADY: My dog, my Pomeranian. He's outside – shall I fetch him in?

RB: Oh, please do.

(As she goes, a large Cockney woman enters.)

COCKNEY WOMAN: Dr Murray?

RB: Yes – just go behind the screen and get undressed, will you, madam?

(She does so.)

RC: (approaching) Look, I'm terribly sorry but I have to be getting back soon. My wife's got a cake in the oven.

RB: Oh, congratulations. What do you hope it's going to be?

RC: I'm hoping for a sultana sponge, that's what went in. So could we finish the lesson, please?

RB: Certainly. Hang on. Could you come out please, madam? (Cockney woman emerges in corsets.) Now, what can I do for you?

COCKNEY LADY: It's about the job as cleaning lady.

RB: Oh yes, of course, er – come over here, would you? Miss Brownlow, take a rest. Now madam, just stand with your hand like this, would you. (Puts Cockney lady in posing position for artist.) There you are. Here. (Swaps drawing pad over.) Try a larger pad. Now, Miss Brownlow, would you just partner this gentleman. How's that?

RC: Is this lady qualified?

RB: She looks it to me.

(Enter a middle-aged man.)

RB: Ah, morning, Mr Jones. Be with you in a moment. (Mr Jones sits, reads magazine in corner.) Now then – ah yes, music.

(He switches on tape recorder – Victor Silvester dance music.)

GRAND LADY: (returning with Pomeranian, which barks) Here we are.

RB: Thank you – sit over there, would you? (Grand lady sits next to Mr Jones.) Now (to Cockney lady) what are you like with animals?

COCKNEY LADY: Oh, very good sir. I love 'em.

RB: Right, hold this one, would you? (Gives her dog.) Now, everyone all right?

MR JONES: (to Grand Lady) Care for this dance?

GRAND LADY: Oh. Thank you.

(They join RC and girl on dance floor. The blue phone rings.)

RB: Hello, Murray Funeral Service. Hello, could you speak up a little? Yes, this is the Chapel of Rest. Who? No, I'm sorry, he's not with us any more. He died. Goodbye.

RC: (approaching RB) Look, this lady says she's completely inexperienced.

RB: They all say that.

RC: As a dance teacher.

RB: Oh.

RC: And I really feel that, having paid my money, I ought to be getting something for it.

RB: Quite right.

RC: I don't care what, as long as I get my money's worth.

RB: How long have you got?

RC: Ten minutes.

RB: Right. Sit down here, would you. (He takes up barber's cloth, throws it round RC's neck.) Now, how do you like it, sir?

(RC starts to explain and music comes in.)

PANIC IN THE YEAR 2001

RB as newsreader. Behind him, caption with date: 'June 4th 2001'.

RB: Good evening. Here is the news. King Foot of Europe is to abdicate.

(Cut to Mr Foot on overlay. Still photo with crown on.)

'With a name like Foot, it's hard to put a brave face on things,' he said. 'It means my name has been dragged through the mud many times. Especially in wet weather. But now I wish to take it easy, relax and put it up for a while.'

Mrs Elizabeth Windsor, formerly the Queen, has applied to have her council flat redecorated.

(Cut to still photo of council flat.)

The last time it was decorated was in 1971, when it received the OBE. Asked who did the decorating, she replied 'My husband and I.' And now the main news story this evening. Reports are just coming in of the discovery of a large container in a park in Ealing, which appears to have been dropped from an unknown aircraft. It is emitting a strange, sweet-smelling gas, which is rapidly being dispersed over a wide area. Roger Kinsey reports.

(Cut to: RC with microphone, standing next to a large, shining container. He wears an old-fashioned civilian gas mask.)

RC: Good evening. I've been told to wear this gas mask, but quite frankly (removes it) it appears to be a waste of time, as these two ladies seem to be suffering no ill-effects.

(Cut to RB as a woman, with another, in curlers, etc., watching him.)

The canister was discovered early this morning, and is marked in large letters on the side 'Formation Gas'.

(Cut to close-up of words and RC's finger pointing it out. Woman – RB – puts her face in shot.)

What that means we're not sure, but scientists are now waiting for the appearance of a trigger device; something that will cause this, at the moment, harmless gas to start working. Roger Kinsey, News at Ten, Ealing Common.

RB: (as woman) Mrs Biggs, number eleven, Knocker Street.

Cut to: studio.

RB: (Announcer) And here is some film of what could be that trigger device. A parachute was observed ... (cut to film of parachute) floating down over Acton a few minutes ago. It has just landed in the front garden of a house in Mulberry Crescent.

(Close-up of strange black box with knobs on, still attached to parachute. It is labelled 'Trigger device'.)

Two eminent scientists, in protective clothing, are even now about to examine it. Perhaps they will be able to unravel the secret of the mysterious formation gas. Roger Kinsey reports.

(Cut to: two figures, like moon men, in white clothing and helmets, lumbering towards the black box. Close-up of box – their gloved hands reach in, twist knobs, press buttons, etc. Cut to: RB as same woman, watching. Cut to: RC, as reporter, arriving on his bike, getting off.)

RC: (out of breath) Here we are in Acton now. (He moves in front of the action – scientists still turning knobs, etc.) And approaching the moment of truth. Everyone in the area has breathed in the Formation Gas – it remains to be seen whether the scientists can render the trigger device harmless.

(Cut to: close-up on trigger device – hand touches switch, a hissing is heard.)

Oh, good heavens. It appears they have accidentally triggered off the device. Nothing now can stop this gas from becoming effective. Roger Kinsey, News at Ten, on his bike.

(He rides away.)

(Loud chord of music heard. Black box begins to play formation dancing music very loudly, as if over a tannoy. The two scientists begin to dance together.)

Cut to: a bus queue. The music plays. (The office workers, typists and passers-by do the paso doble.)

Cut to: a pile of rubble and a 'road up' sign next to a workman's striped plastic shelter. (The music plays. Out of the hut come six workmen – they dance up to six terraced houses, out dance six house-wives and they do a cha-cha. RC appears on bike, crashes into hut, then gets involved in the dance.)

Cut to: the black box area. (Women standing round, staring. Police arrive in cars. They rush up to the device and start dancing with the women onlookers – a quickstep.)

Cut to: studio.

RB: The Government has just issued a special communiqué, urging people not to panic in the present crisis, which they hope will be short-lived – simply keep calm and dance about your business in the normal way.

Mr Eric Morley has been made Minister of Dancing, and we must now all look towards Mecca for a solution. Meanwhile, Brigadier General Dogsbody has taken over as Supreme Allied Commander in charge of all military two-steps.

(A man in headphones dances by with a tea lady.)

The gas container has been loaded onto a lorry and is, at this very moment, being driven to the south coast, to be dumped in the sea; while the black box is on its way north, to be buried in a disused coal mine near Middlesbrough. Let us hope that, with them both travel-ling in opposite directions, we are approaching the end of this bizarre affair.

Cut to: main road. (The lorry with the gas container and the small open van with the black box approach each other. As they are about to pass, they screech to a halt. The drivers and their mates, and two security guards, all get out and dance together in a high, wide shot.)

THE ADVENTURES OF ARCHIE

(Note: The technique throughout is cartoon backgrounds on overlay, as in the recent series called Jane of the Daily Mirror. This enables RB to be different sizes, and for the more exotic locations to be easily achieved.)

We start with a high shot of a row of Victorian terraced houses, zooming in as the voice-over says 'This is the strange tale of Archie Barber, of 23 Ordinary Villas, Suburbia ...'

Interior: suburban terraced house – the kitchen.

(RC, as Archie, enters through door to garden. He is a chirpy Cockney character, rather like the pub fellow, Sid. He carries a small old bottle, covered in earth. A cigarette stub dangles from his lips.)

RC: (calling) Doris, look what I found. I told you this place probably used to be a dump. (To himself) Well, it is a dump, no probably about it. Real dump, this is.

(Doris enters, carrying an opened letter.)

DORIS: This letter came from the council. Second post.

RC: What's it say?

DORIS: They've refused you permission for your extension.

RC: What? (Takes letter.) Would you Adam and Eve it! Stupid load of councillors.

(She goes.)

RC: (sitting disconsolately) What right have they got to ruin people's fun? A man like me needs an extension. (He takes out a filthy handkerchief and begins to polish up the old bottle.) Sometimes I wish I was a thousand miles from here.

(*An enormous puff of bright blue smoke fills the room. A 'whooshing' sound is heard, and RC disappears. Doris enters the smoke-filled room.*)

DORIS: Now, where's he gone? Gawd, I wish he wouldn't smoke them Turkish!

Cut to: RC on flying carpet, with photographic land and sea rushing beneath him. He rolls about, nearly rolling off a couple of times.

VOICE-OVER: Archie, although he didn't know it, was being whisked through time as well as space …

(*RC and carpet suddenly move right away from camera, until they are a tiny dot.*)

VOICE-OVER: … to start a new life in the mysterious East. Years later we find him in the fairy-tale city of Old Baghdad, plying his honest trade.

Interior of Baghdad cobbler's shop.

(RC hammering away at pair of shoes. Customer enters, hands him pair of shoes. RC, still the chirpy Cockney, nevertheless speaks in the idiom.)

RC: Greetings, O wise and sagacious son of Allah. May the moon of plenty shine upon your daughter. Be ready Thursday.

(*He marks the shoes with chalk and puts them under his bench.*)

VOICE-OVER: And so he worked, putting his heart and sole and heel into the business, perfecting the craft that he had been trained for …

RC: (close-up, to camera) I used to work for Freeman Hardy and Willis.

VOICE-OVER: And his fame spread throughout the land, and came to the ears of the Caliph himself. Now the Caliph had very sharp ears. He also had a fat nose and terrible feet.

(During this, we see the arrival of the Caliph in the shop and RC fitting slippers on to his feet.)

VOICE-OVER: He was therefore delighted when Archie Barber placed upon his delicate tootsies a pair of shoes as pliable and soft as a mouse's ear.

(The Caliph departs with his entourage, delighted. Cut to: RC, beaming.)

VOICE-OVER: Archie, too, was indeed a happy man. He put up a large sign outside his shop, announcing his royal patronage. Sadly, it was this very sign that was to bring about his undoing ...

Some time later – the shop.

(Two of the Caliph's guards enter the shop and grab RC as he works at his bench.)

RC: Here! What's the game? Where are we going?

GUARD: Prison!

RC: Prison? Why?

GUARD: Treason!

RC: Treason? For what reason?

GUARD: Your sign outside.

(They drag him out.)

Exterior of shop.

(RC is dragged out, protesting. We tilt up to see the sign. It says 'Aja Baba Ltd'. Then underneath, in large letters: 'Cobblers to the Caliph'.

Cut to: the prison.

(RC is in a cage-like cell, bars on three sides. A large guard, stripped to the waist, stands in the cell with him. In the next cell, a pretty, dark-eyed girl sits on the floor, bound and gagged.)

RC: (to guard) Three days I've been sitting here, you know. I wasn't even allowed one call. I know they haven't invented phones yet, but you'd think they'd let me shout out the window. (To girl) What are you in here for, darlin'? Hope they're not going to chop your head off. What a waste. Pity they don't have mixed cells, ain't it? Eh? I say, I wish he was where you are and you was in here.

(A whoosh of blue smoke and the guard, in the girl's clothes, is tied up in the other cell. The girl, stripped to the waist (and back to the camera) is in RC's cell. He reacts, and quickly covers her with his coat.)

RC: Here, put this on. Mustn't let those loose. They should be kept on a leash – they'll cause a riot. That's better. Gawd, all this blue smoke! I thought at first it was the kebabs coming in for dinner. (He goes and sits cross-legged on the table.) They cook 'em at the table here, you know. And if you complain, they cook you at the table. Gawd, I wish I was a thousand miles from here!

(Whoosh! Blue smoke – RC is gone, leaving the girl wide-eyed as RC's coat vanishes, leaving her clutching her modesty.)

(RC flies through the air, this time on the prison table. He opens the drawer in the table, takes out air-sickness pills.)

A desert island.

(RC appears, lands with a bump, which rolls him off the table. As he picks himself up, he hears a voice calling faintly: 'Let me out, oh master.' He looks round, in the table drawer, etc., finally realises that the voice is coming from the old bottle, which is hanging on a piece of string around his neck. He forces the cork out of the bottle. A whoosh – he drops it. A close-up on the bottle as it lies on the sand. Smoke streams from it and forms a cloud, which clears to reveal RB as a twenty-foot-high genie.)

RC: Crikey! It's the Incredible Hulk!

RB: What is your wish, O Master?

RC: My wish?

RB: You have one more wish. The first one brought you to Baghdad on a carpet.

RC: And the second one brought me here on a table. Next wish I make I'll be careful where I'm sitting. I'd hate to arrive anywhere on a flying toilet.

RB: It would indeed be an inconvenience.

RC: Yes. So it's the old three wishes, is it?

RB: Four.

RC: Four wishes? Why four?

RB: Special offer. This week only.

RC: Oh, that's fortunate. So I got two more.

RB: No, one. You wished the girl into your cell.

RC: Oh well, my last wish has got to be – take me home, to London, wasn't it?

RB: I regret, Master, I am allowed only ONE voyage through TIME. If I took you to London now, you would find it a vast area of evil-smelling rubble.

RC: Oh – like the last dustman's strike. Well, I'd like to have a think about it for a while. Matter of fact, I ain't in any particular hurry to leave here at the moment.

(We fade on the idyllic desert island landscape.)

VOICE-OVER: Time passes – and Archie, knowing he can't escape, settles into a life of peace and plenty on his Robinson Crusoe island. Companions were supplied, at no extra charge, by the accommodating genie …

(Fade up on palm tree, with monkey in it. Tilt down to where RC, dressed now as Robinson Crusoe, sits with six beautiful black girls around him. RC is lounging back, contentedly sipping out of a coconut shell.)

RC: (to girl) Where's Friday?

GIRL: It's her day off.

RC: I thought Thursday was her day off.

GIRL: No, Thursday is Tuesday's day off.

RC: Oh, is that right, Tuesday? (Another girl nods, giggling.) Let's see, who are you then?

GIRL: I'm Monday.

RC: It's Monday today, isn't it?

GIRL: Yes.

RC: Oh, good!

(A strange noise is heard. RC and the girls react. The noise is that of Dr Who's Tardis, which materialises, in its familiar fashion, on the sand. RB emerges, dressed not as Dr Who, but as Wurzel Gummidge.)

RC: It's the Tardis!

WURZEL: Oh ay, me dears? What be you all doing a-sitting about here by the seaside, eh? A sunnin' of yourselves. Nice here, ain't it?

RC: Gawd – it's all a bit mixed up, this. Who do you think you are, mate?

WURZEL: I be Dr Who, that's who I be. Who be you be?

RC: No, no, you used to be Dr Who, but now you're Wurzel Gummidge.

WURZEL: Oh dear! I must have got the wrong head on. Oh ay! It's all coming back to me now, as the sailor said when he spat into the wind. It's that there Jon Pertwittee, he be Dr Whosit, baint he?

RC: No, you're Jon Pertwee.

WURZEL: Who, me? No, I be Dr Gummidge. Oh, I be all confused now. I be going off to find Dorothy.

RC: Don't you mean Aunt Sally?

WURZEL: No, Dorothy up the Yellow Brick Road. Ta-ta, me dears.

(Goes off, singing 'If I only had a brain'.)

RC: He's a nutter.

(The black girls look bemused. RC, however, is quick to realise that the Tardis stands there, its door open.)

RC: Listen, girls – I'm off. (Hurries to the door of the Tardis.) It's been nice knowing you. All the best. And don't worry – if this doesn't work, I'll be back on Friday by Tuesday.

(He disappears inside and shuts the door.)

Inside Tardis.

(A close-up of a bank of dials. RC's hand turns dial to 'London' and another to '20th century'. Outside, we see the Tardis de-materialise. The girls look bemused again.)

(The Tardis materialises against a brick wall. RC emerges. He is now dressed normally in his modern clothes, as in first scene. He looks across at his old house. From behind the Tardis, RB as genie appears. RC reacts.)

RC: How did you get here? I thought you couldn't travel through time.

RB: There is a nail sticking out of the Tardis at the back. You can travel through anything when your loin cloth gets caught on a nail.

RC: You got a point there.

RB: I nearly had, several times. Hair-raising.

RC: Well, listen, you can't walk about like that. Hide behind there till we can get you some clothes. Can you get any smaller?

RB: I'll try, O Master.

(RC crosses to his house, rings bell. Old man answers.)

OLD MAN: Yes?

RC: Oh – er – Mrs Barber in?

OLD MAN: Never heard of her.

RC: Oh. She lives here.

OLD MAN: No she don't. I live here.

RC: Oh … I gotta find her. Mrs Barber.

OLD MAN: Ring up the police. There's a box over the road.

(He indicates the Tardis.)

RC: Oh yes – how long has that been there?

OLD MAN: Ever since I've lived here. Thirty years.

RC: Thirty years?

OLD MAN: I come here in 1985. Thirty years ago.

RC: Oh. Right, ta.

OLD MAN: Righto, mate. (Shuts the door.)

(RC nods to himself, realising. He hurries back into the Tardis. Inside, his hand is seen moving dials back to 1982. He immediately re-emerges, crosses the road and rings the bell again. His wife, Doris, answers the door.)

DORIS: Where you been?

RC: Sorry to have been so long, Doris.

DORIS: I thought you'd just gone down to get a paper. You've been gone three hours!

RC: Three hours?

DORIS: Your supper's ruined.

RC: That's nothing new, is it?

DORIS: You're drunk. Come on, get inside.

(RC goes in. From behind the Tardis, the huge head of the genie peers out, nonplussed.)

Fade out – fade in.

VOICE-OVER: And so Archie once more picked up the threads of his life … except that now he had a new-found friend.

(A close-up of RC as he walks along the street. Widen to see RB as genie. He now wears ordinary flat cap and raincoat, but is about eight feet high.)

RC: I feel stupid walking along with you as big as that. I get laughed at in the pub. Have you tried to get smaller?

RB: Indeed, O Master, I have used all my powers, but alas, to no avail. May Allah forgive your unworthy pig of a servant …

RC: And for Gawd's sake talk proper – not all that Eastern rubbish.

RB: Righto, Squire.

(They walk away down the road and the scene ripples and dissolves, as in a flashback, to a close-up of RC in the pub. It is quite crowded and animated. RC, in close-up, is talking.)

RC: So that's my story, darlin' – me wife has left me, and all I've got now is that great load of lard over there.

(We see RB sitting on the floor in the corner, still eight foot tall. The pretty blonde girl RC is talking to nods sympathetically.)

BLONDE: What a shame.

RC: Yeah. 'Nother drink?

BLONDE: Yeah, ta.

RC: (calls to barman) George! Another Bacardi and Coke, and two beers. Pint for me, gallon for him.

GEORGE: Right, Archie.

BLONDE: Here – why can't you wish more wishes?

RC: I lost me bottle. Anyway, I had one final wish left. And that was granted. I got what I wanted.

BLONDE: What was that?

RC: Come back to my place and I'll show you.

(The blonde reacts in puzzled amusement. RC laughs.)

The suburban street. Night – a moon. (RC and girl are walking away from the camera. They are laughing.)

BLONDE: You what? You mean I'm coming all the way home just to have a look at your extension?

RC: That's about the size of it.

BLONDE: (giggling) What is?

RC: (giggling) Eleven foot by nine foot six.

(They collapse with laughter and, arm-in-arm, go away down the moonlit suburban street.)

PHONEY

Man in phone box, dialling. Female voice answers.

FEMALE VOICE: Number please?

MAN: Is that Interpol?

FEMALE: This is the exchange, sir. What number did you require?

MAN: Interpol. I want to speak to Interpol.

FEMALE: Hold the line, sir.

(A pause. Buzzing and clicking.)

POLICE VOICE: Wandsworth police station. Can I help you, sir?

MAN: I want Interpol, please.

PC: I'll connect you with Scotland Yard, sir. Hold on.

(More clicking.)

SCOTLAND YARD VOICE: Scotland Yard here. Who do you wish to speak to, sir?

MAN: Interpol.

SCOTLAND YARD: Is it priority, sir?

MAN: Er – yes, please.

SCOTLAND YARD: Hold the line please.

(More clicking.)

INTERPOL VOICE: Hello. Interpol here.

MAN: Oh, Interpol? I want to send some flowers by wire to my mother.

THE AMATEUR PLAY

A false proscenium – looking like a village hall stage. Tatty velvet curtains, closed. On each side, enormous posters saying: 'Meadowfield Players present Weekend in Mayfair by Gerald Barrington'.

These are written in an amateur signwriting hand, in red and blue (about six foot high, four foot wide).

(Through the curtains comes the vicar. He blinks at the lights.)

VICAR: Thank you – just a quick word before we start off. Due to circumstances beyond his control, the lad who was playing the part of Rodney had to get married on Saturday, and is at the moment having a wonderful time up a Swiss Alp. George Biggins, however, has agreed to read the part at an hour's notice, and has shut the butcher's shop early especially. My wife is still playing one of the lovers, so we hope for a bit of fun there. By the by, if there are any men who wish to join the Dramatic Society, please come forward. My wife, who also produces the shows, has been desperately short of men for years. In fact, when I tell you that Arnold Corbett is playing three parts in the show, you'll realise just how short the men are round here. Anyway, please see her after the performance backstage. If you can get round – no room to swing a cat back there! Young Trevor will have to find another hobby. Incidentally, we painted all the scenery ourselves. Right, on we go, let's get on with it! Thank you.

(He disappears through the curtains.)

The set is made up of flats painted by amateurs. The pictures are real, but they shake when the door opens. The door opens up and out, but can only open about ten inches as it hits the side wall (no wing space): people have to squeeze in.

Window in back wall, with painted Mayfair houses backing, also about ten inches away. Shadows of window on backing.

Furniture – a very low settee (smallish, 1950s G plan). Table and two kitchen chairs (tatty). Cocktail cabinet (awful). A painted-on fireplace.

A hat stand, also painted on the wall, which has a nail for hanging a real hat on.

Another door, where the milkman appears, is on the back wall.

'Weekend in Mayfair'

The play

The curtains part, to see the back of the vicar disappearing out of the door. The door only opens about ten inches, so it is not easy. A large maid is on stage, with a feather duster, dusting. A loud sound effects record is heard to be put on; it is of a car arriving. It stops.

MAID: Good gracious. The master. And me with me dumplings on the table.

(She squeezes off. Immediately, RC and the woman enter. RC in boiled shirt and 1928 dinner jacket – high collar, etc. – woman in short twenties evening dress, full skirt. RC has 'greyed-up' hair at the sides only, badly done with white make-up. His suit is rather crumpled, his complexion ruddy. The woman is, of course, the vicar's wife, but made up far too heavily as a raving beauty.)

WOMAN: So this is the elegant Mayfair flat I've heard so much about. It's beautiful. Tell me, what's it like being a successful novelist, Charles?

RC: (with a rural accent) Unutterably divine, darling. And yet at the same time, devastatingly boring. Money isn't everything, you know.

(He hangs his hat on the fake peg and looks out of the window. His shadow is seen on the houses opposite.)

WOMAN: Money? Money doesn't bring happiness, but it enables you to be miserable in comfort.

RC: What has money brought me?

WOMAN: You've got your yacht, in Cannes (pronounced cans). You're so lucky – you can simply lie on deck and sunbathe all summer. Heaven.

RC: I get tired of lying in Cannes. One feels so like a sardine. Cocktail?

(He crosses behind sofa and trips over something behind it – we cannot see what.)

WOMAN: Divine.

(The cocktail cabinet is freestanding and RC disappears completely behind it.)

WOMAN: (drifting up level with it) What are you looking at me like that for?

RC'S VOICE: (behind cabinet) Because I love you, you little fool.

WOMAN: I know – isn't it heaven? What have you got there?

RC'S VOICE: It's my new cocktail-shaker. Isn't it divine?

WOMAN: Heaven.

RC'S VOICE: Olive?

WOMAN: Yes, Charles?

RC'S VOICE: Olive?

WOMAN: Yes, Charles?

RC'S VOICE: Stuffed?

WOMAN: No, just a plain olive, thanks, Charles.

RC'S VOICE: Very well, Cynthia.

(He emerges, hands cocktail to her – she moves down left of sofa – he crosses behind it.)

RC: Cheers.

(He trips over thing behind sofa.)

WOMAN: (as they sit on sofa) When will we be married, Charles?

RC: Just as soon as my dreadfully boring divorce comes through. After all, I have a grown-up son, remember. Still, let's not think of him. He's miles away, at Oxford.

(The maid squeezes on.)

2ND MAID: Master Rodney, sir.

RC: (amazed) What?

2ND MAID: (same tone of voice) Master Rodney, sir.

RC: (thinking she has gone back) What?

2ND MAID: (same tone of voice) Master Rodney, sir.

RC: (helps to squeeze maid through door, then turns to woman and says) What?

WOMAN: Rodney?

RC: My son.

(RB squeezes on, in dinner jacket, much too small, carrying French's acting edition. He wears glasses and is made up much too young. He wears a black toupee, also hobnail boots.)

RB: Hello, Pops.

RC: Rodney! Why aren't you up at Oxford?

RB: (reading) They sent me down, Pops. Dashed rotten luck, wasn't it?

(He stands in front of RC.)

RC: I must phone the governors immediately. How dare they treat someone as sensitive as you are in this beastly manner. Turning you away as if you were some country bumpkin. Cynthia will mix you a cocktail.

(He squeezes out.)

WOMAN: (going to him) You!

RB: What are you doing here, Snithia? I thought I'd never see you again.

WOMAN: Charles – your father – doesn't know about us, does he?

(She goes up towards the cocktail cabinet.)

RB: I've told him.

(Woman looks surprised, indicates with a nod towards the book. RB looks again.)

RB: I've told him nothing.

(He trips over thing behind sofa.)

WOMAN: That's a relief. Cocktail?

(She disappears behind cabinet.)

RB: Well, as long as it's a little one. I'm not really old enough.

(Woman reappears with two cocktails. RB puts down his book to receive one from her.)

WOMAN: Oh, Rodney! Do you remember what I said to you that night at Oxford in the shrubbery?

RB: (quickly picking up his book and reading) Well, as long as it's a little one. I'm not really old enough. Er – no. What?

WOMAN: I said I know we both know what we're doing. We both know that. We both know what we were doing to each other, but I knew I was doing something to you that you didn't know about.

(RB scratches his head, and displaces the toupee. He quickly goes behind the cocktail cabinet, and re-emerges wearing it back to front.)

WOMAN: There was something that you couldn't know about that I was doing to you. A young, innocent boy – how could you know I was corrupting you.

(A pause. RB looks off left.)

RB: Door – door!

(He knocks on the cocktail cabinet.)

WOMAN: Oh, God! Is there no privacy anywhere?

RB: If you want people to leave you alone, you should have your doorbells disconnected.

WOMAN: (sotto voce) Knockers.

RB: Eh? Oh. If you want people to leave you alone, you should have your knockers disconnected.

(He opens door in back wall. This opens fully, to reveal a cardboard cut-out of a milkman.)

RB: Not today, thank you.

(He closes door again.)

WOMAN: Oh, Rodney. (Lies back on sofa) Come here, my own sweet boy!

RB: (tripping on thing behind sofa) How radiant you look, Snithia. I could sing your praises forever. I don't know where to start. Turn over. (Woman turns and lies on her stomach. RB turns the page.) What a curious expression, Snithia. What are you thinking?

WOMAN: It mustn't happen, Rodney, it can't happen; not this way. Oh, but it must – it must – I don't care about the world! Kiss me!

(RB now studies his book for quite a while – turns page, etc., then suddenly drops it and starts to grapple with Cynthia on the couch. His hobnail boots are much in evidence and so are her directoire knickers. RC enters, dressed as the grandfather. Same dinner jacket, but badly made up – white moustache, old white wig, walking stick, bent double, etc.)

RC: What's this? Rodney, is that you? Who have you got under there? I recognise that face. What's going on? And, what is more important (trips over thing behind sofa), what is that bloody thing?

RB: Grandfather! Pops has just popped out. Fancy a cocktail?

RC: No, thank you. You keep your filth to yourself. I'm going to look for my son and tell him that his Cynthia is flat out on the sofa, on top of which there's his son behaving under-handed behind his back, under his very nose.

(He opens door at back. Milkman cut-out is still there. RC jumps in alarm.)

RC: Oh! Excuse me!

(He pushes past it. It falls over.)

RC: He's fainted.

(An ad-lib. He hurries off.)

WOMAN: It's no good. I can't go on like this. Things seem to be getting on top of me lately.

RB: In that case, I'll get off. (He does so, then realises.) In that case, I'll get off back to Oxford.

WOMAN: No – not yet. One last fling, my dearest boy. I need your tenderness, your innocence, your warmth. My arms await you!

RB: I'm coming back on. (He gets back on to her – she pushes him off.) Oh. Tuesday. I'm coming back on Tuesday.

WOMAN: Too late, dear Rodney. I shall have returned to the South of France. What is the time?

(A whirring, and the painted clock (which says twenty to five) strikes two.)

RB: One o'clock.

WOMAN: I shall leave at once. So, Rodney – this is the end.

(The curtains start to close. RB waves them back. They re-open again. RC enters, dressed in top hat and black beard, and a cloak over his dinner jacket.)

RC: Just a minuit!

RB: Who are you?

MAID: (squeezes on, and announces) Monsieur Gerard.

(She tries to squeeze off, but gets stuck in the door. A small scruffy dog enters, obviously the vicar's wife's. It runs all over the set. They all ignore it.)

WOMAN: Gaston!

RC: Parbleu! So I was right! You are here!

RB: Snithia – who is this old girl?

RC: I am her husband! Gaston Gerard at your service!

(He raises his hat – his beard is attached to it. He replaces hat and beard as if nothing had happened.)

RC: I come from France – didn't you get my letter?

RB: Husband?

WOMAN: It's true! I've deceived everyone. You, Rodney, your father, your grandfather – I didn't want any of you – all I wanted was adventure!

(She sits on the dog.)

RB: Well, if that's how things are, then I'm off.

(He goes to door, where maid is still stuck.)

RB: I'm going back to somewhere where I know I'm always welcome.

(He crawls underneath the maid's skirts to get off. She gives a squeal as he disappears.)

WOMAN: Come, Gaston, come and sit here!

(She pats the sofa – the little dog leaps onto it. RC goes behind sofa, trips on thing, proceeds round and joins her on sofa.)

WOMAN: You'll have to forgive me, you know.

RC: Oui, oui, cherie. As long as you promise me never to let any man touch you again, ever.

WOMAN: I promise you this, darling – no man will kiss me on the lips again. From now on, it's all over.

(The curtain is pulled. Opened again quickly. RC without beard, woman, RB, maid and cardboard milkman take bow. Curtains close.)

THE FOREIGN FILM

A cinema interior: distorted music and throaty French dialogue in background. Very few in audience, mostly men, silent, intent. Enter Mr and Mrs Titheradge. They are about sixty, very suburban and un-with-it. They are also very wet. She removes her plastic rain hat and he shakes water from his cap, which he then replaces.

SHE: (as they settle) Ooh! Dear! What a downpour! We were lucky to find this, Jack. I didn't know there were any cinemas in Soho. I thought it was all restaurants. Hey, that was a lot of money, 15 shillings each. Why didn't we go in the cheap seats?

HE: That is the cheap seats.

SHE: Oh! I'm splashed right up me stockings. Whenever I put on new stockings it's the same – it pours with rain and I get splashed right up 'em. (Looking at screen) What's it called, Jack?

HE: I dunno.

SHE: It's foreign, isn't it?

HE: I dunno.

SHE: I think it's foreign. Well, it's not English, anyhow. Yes, it's one of them foreign films. (They watch and we hear passionate dialogue.) Mrs Cook across the road has got some bedroom curtains like that – only they're more of a blue. Here, I like that eiderdown, don't you, Jack? (We see Jack beginning to get interested.) I think I'll try and get one of those with my Green Stamps ... I've got nearly eight books now. Here, isn't she like Muriel?

HE: Who?

SHE: Elsie's girl.

HE: No. Nothing like her.

SHE: Oh, I think so. A bit bigger perhaps ... although Muriel takes a forty now, you know. We had an awful job getting a bridesmaid's dress to fit her. Great big lump, she is. (Jack is staring pop-eyed at the screen.) Now that's just Muriel, that is. Just takes her clothes off and drops them anywhere, all round the bedroom. No sense of tidiness. Girls these days. If she'd got up ten minutes earlier, she wouldn't have to rush about like that. (Jack is transfixed. We hear a bath being filled.) Now those are the soap-racks I was telling you about, Jack – they got them in Harris's. They're continental special design. There, you see the way she's leaning over it to turn the taps off, well you can't scratch yourself on them. They're all curved over, with no sharp edges. Lovely shape, aren't they?

(Jack is sitting there, shaking. We hear the man's voice (off-screen) and a lot of splashing. He sounds passionate.)

SHE: There's a lovely loofah he's got there. I wonder if you can get those on the Green Stamps.

HE: (gulping) I doubt it.

SHE: That's what I need. There's a bit of my back I can never get at. Oh look, she's having the same trouble, see? Oh, he's giving her a hand now … (Cut to **JACK:** his cap is steaming.) Now, what's he doing? Oh, they must be trying to save water. Still, you'd think he'd let her get out of the bath first, before he got in, wouldn't you? (The music swells up off screen.) Ooer. What does Fin mean? Oh, it's the end. We must have missed the best part. (Another bit of music starts up.) Oh, 'Look at Life No. 94 … Do It Yourself'. There you are, Jack – this'll be more interesting for you.

(Fade on Jack, sweating and steaming.)

THE ONEDIN LINE

Stock opening of boat, etc., as per original TV programme. After opening captions cut to close-up of RC as James Onedin. He sits at a ship's table, with charts, sextants, etc. He is working on his charts. The wind howls – a storm is obviously imminent. It is night. Storm music over.

(There is a knocking at the door – a hammering.)

RC: Come in!

(RB enters as Mister Baines, the first mate. He wears oilskins of the period and sou'wester. As he enters, the wind blows all the papers off Onedin's desk, etc.)

RB: Beg pardon, cap'n!

RC: What is it, Mister Baines?

RB: (shouting over the wind) There's a terrible Nor-nor-easter blowing up, sir – could reach gale force in a matter of minutes. A lot of fork lightning over to the west. The rain's falling in bucketfuls, cap'n, and if that wind goes on increasing at its present rate it could snap the mast off any ship in the line, sir!

RC: Good God! Well, all I can say is, thank heaven we're not at sea.

RB: Yes sir, that would be dreadful.

RC: Shut that blasted door, man, there's a terrible draught – is the back door open?

RB: Yes cap'n – it's your maid. She's in the garden, getting in washing.

(He shuts the door – wind subsides a little.)

RC: That's better. Well, Mister Baines, what brings you to my house? It must be something important to drag you out of the Dirty Duck on a night like this.

RB: Oh, 'tis true, cap'n, I do like my pint of ale, but there are some things in this world that, when they happen, do stop a man from drinking. And closing-time is one of 'em.

RC: Ah, so you were thrown out, eh?

RB: No, cap'n – I just came to tell you that the latest addition to your fleet is all ready in port, refitted and ready to sail.

RC: My new cargo ship? It's arrived?

RB: Last night, sir. I thought perhaps you and me might go and look at her first thing in the morning, if you've a mind.

RC: Of course I've a mind. I'm not daft. You need brains to build up a fleet of cargo ships as I've done, Baines. Brains, Baines, brains!

RB: Yes sir, yes sir, yes sir.

RC: And I've done it from nothing – all on my own. My father was no help. Sometimes I used to think his head was full of cotton-wool.

RB: Why, sir?

RC: I saw a bit of it sticking out of his ear once. And now, the latest addition to the line. (Pours out two glasses of port from a decanter.) Let's drink to it, Baines – I'm sorry I have to offer you this rather inferior port wine, but the weather's been so bad I couldn't get to the off-licence. Anyway, you're so drunk you won't know the difference.

RB: That's all right, cap'n – any port in a storm. To the newest addition to the line, sir – here's health.

(They clink glasses.)

RC: May she always prosper – here's to her the – do you know, Mister, I don't know her name.

Cut to: the quayside. It is now dry and the following morning. RB now wears cap and reefer jacket. RC is dressed authentically as James Onedin.

RB: 'Saucy Sue', cap'n. Ain't she a beauty?

RC: Excellent, Mister Baines, excellent. Trim and proud. Fast, I should imagine, too – and yet that air of strength and reliability characteristic of the class. What's she like to handle, have you heard?

RB: Jones, the pilot, says she responds quickly, manoeuvres well – I've been all over her already – she's as solid as a rock and a lot more comfortable than the older ones of the same size.

RC: 'Saucy Sue', eh?

RB: That be her name, cap'n. I can't wait. (Calling) I say, Sue!

Cut to: big, beautiful, blonde wench, lounging on a pile of rope. She has bare feet and a chest to match. (She gets up bouncily and moves out of frame. She enters frame and joins RB and RC.)

SUE: Hello, sailor!

RC: Look, why don't you slink over to the tavern and wait for me – I'll be with you in time to buy your second pint. I've just got to look at a ship. What's it called, Baines?

RB: (as Sue moves off) 'The Dependable', cap'n.

RC: How very unexciting.

(Watches Sue go.)

RB: I reckon her bottom will need a lot of attention.

RC: Quite. Still, first things first. Come on.

(They head off in the opposite direction.)

Mix to: stock shots of ships at sea. Mix from this to the captain's cabin – not very large, but with an alcove for the bunk which is curtained to give complete privacy.

(RC is looking out through the porthole, through a large telescope on a stand.)

RC: (suddenly shouting) Land ho! (He leaves the telescope and goes towards the cabin door.) Mister Baines!

(RB enters.)

RB: Aye, cap'n?

RC: Land ho, Mister Baines.

RB: Land, sir? There ain't no land for miles, cap'n.

RC: Really? Look, man – through the telescope. What's that small blob on the horizon?

RB: That's not on the horizon, cap'n, that's on the end of the telescope. Ar. A seagull did it, cap'n.

RC: Oh, I see. Any other messages?

RB: Eh? Oh yes, cap'n, I was just coming to report a stowaway on board. Found him in one of the lifeboats ...

RC: What? The blackguard. Bring him in at once.

RB: Bring in the prisoner, Martin!

(Two sailors bring in the stowaway, who is dressed in oilskins and sou'wester. They throw him roughly to the ground.)

RC: (angry) So. Try to stow away on my ship, would you? Try and swindle an honest seaman out of the money for a passage? You're a parasite on the back of society. Well, my fine fellow, a ship's captain has the power to deal with the likes of you. By the time I've finished with you, you'll wish you'd never been born. Take him out, tie him to the yardarm, strip him and give him a taste of the rope's end.

RB: (shouting) Get up! And take that hat off in the presence of the cap'n!

(RB grabs the stowaway, helps him up and snatches off his sou'wester. The stowaway's hair cascades down over her shoulders – we get a close-up of a beautiful girl, for the first time.)

RC: Good God! A woman! You see that, Baines?

RB: Yes, sir. Is she still to be stripped and given a taste of the rope's end, cap'n?

RC: Now don't get hasty. You're always a bit inclined to be hasty. Let's compromise a little, shall we? Let's just take off your oilskins for a start, shall we, my dear?

(He assists her – she reveals the expected charms – dressed in a boy's torn shirt and skin-tight trousers. This is all duly noted by RC.)

RC: Oh, yes. Well! Perhaps not the taste of the rope's end. You probably don't like rope's end, do you – perhaps you'd prefer something else a bit tastier? (Calling) Bring this lady a cheese sandwich! Now, you sit down here and get your breath back. We're both breathing rather heavy. (Catches Baines's scornful eye.) What are you looking at, Baines?

RB: I take it we can leave the girl's plight in your hands, sir.

RC: Exactly, Baines. I shall set her to work for me. She shall be my cabin boy. Don't worry, I shall see that she works her passage, as any stowaway would. What is your name, girl?

GIRL: Ophelia O'Hanaflanagan, sir.

RC: O – what?

RB: Phelia, cap'n. Permission to go aloft, sir?

RC: Aye, buzz off, Baines. I have to instruct my new cabin boy in her duties. (Baines plus the two sailors exit.) But first, my dear, tell me why you stowed away aboard my ship?

OHELIA: I wanted to travel and make a name for myself.

RC: Well, you've come to the right place. If you play your cards right, you can do both at once. Now, it will be your duty to do the dusting, bring me my early morning tea and polish my sextant. Look, come through here and I'll show you where I keep the hammocks ...

(They exit, as we fade to night: a storm at sea. stock film. Long shots of the ship having a tough time staying afloat. Quite a bit of this, then cut to close-up of RB in sou'wester, etc., on the bridge – but too close to see exactly where.)

RB: (shouting) Hoist your missen! Reef the topsail! Batten down all hatches! (About six bucketfuls of water hit him. He gasps and recovers.) Hold her, Mister Granville. Bear over the bowspit!

(Another six bucketfuls hit him. He groans and leaves frame.)

(More stock film, then RB, outside RC's cabin door.)

RB: Cap'n! Are you coming up on to the bridge? The storm's at its height.

RC: (off) I'm afraid I've got much too much to do in here at the moment.

(Cut to: RC, in his bunk. An arm comes into shot and caresses his cheek.)

RB: But we need your experience up there, cap'n.

RC: I'm sorry, but I'm using most of it down here.

(The arms pull him out of shot.)

Stock shots of storm, lightning, etc.

RB: (in close-up on bridge again) Heave to, Mr Granville! Keep her into the wind. (The water hits him again.) Hoist your mainsail!

(The water again – he collapses.)

(Cut to: RB approaching door again, hammering on it.)

RB: Cap'n! I can't keep her upright. She's rolling a lot!

RC: (half smothered by Ophelia) How d'you think I feel?

(More lightning – RB on bridge again.)

RB: Top your rigging! (Water hits him again.) Oh, Gawd!

(Close-up hand banging on door again.)

RB: Cap'n – you gotta come up. It's a filthy night up here!

RC: (beating off an attack by Ophelia) It's pretty heavy weather down here as well.

RB: I tell 'ee, cap'n. It's touch an' go. I doubt if I can hold her on my own.

RC: Don't give up, Baines! I'm not.

(RB in despair, groans and staggers off. A streak of lightning in the sky – then mix to calm, daytime, film of ship.)

Cut to: captain's cabin. (RC, still in shirt and trousers, is seated at breakfast, which consists of rum and ship's biscuits. Ophelia, now only in her shirt, is serving him.)

OHELIA: More rum, cap'n?

RC: No, thanks, my dear, not at breakfast. It's a bit early for me. God, what a night.

OHELIA: I do love you, cap'n.

RC: And I love you, too. And that's the first time I've ever said that to a cabin boy.

(She sits beside him on bench. Suddenly a sound of shouts, cries and a naval gun. Then a banging on the door.)

RC: What's going on?

RB: Cap'n – we're about to be boarded.

RC: Boarded? By whom?

RB: (off) Pirates!

(RC rushes to porthole – looks out. Sounds of muskets, shouts – music over. RC slams porthole-cover over.)

RC: He's right, you know. He's not wrong.

OHELIA: Oh dear.

RC: Don't worry, my love – you're safe in here with me.

OHELIA: Aren't you going out to fight?

RC: No – I shall stay here to protect you.

OHELIA: I'll go out and fight, too.

RC: What, and leave me here on me own? Don't be so daft.

RB: (off) Are you coming out, or aren't you, cap'n?

RC: No, you carry on – I have every confidence in you.

RB: (off) Aye, aye, sir. (Then shouting) Stand by to repel all boarders!

RC: (to girl) Sounds like a landlady I had once. Come, sit down. (They sit. The dreadful cries and clashes of steel and shots continue.) Well, how pleasant this is. How different my life has suddenly become.

OHELIA: Are you sure Mister Baines can manage on his own?

RC: Why not? He saw us through last night without a scratch, didn't he? Which is more than can be said for you, my dear.

OHELIA: Oh, Captain. (She snuggles up to him.)

RC: I shall never forget the first moment I saw you yesterday, when you took off your hat and your hair all fell out over your shoulders.

OHELIA: Were you surprised?

RC: Well, it was a bit of a shock – it usually means an attack of scurvy.

OHELIA: They sound as if they're getting closer.

RC: Don't worry – they'll never get past that door. Baines won't let them. He's not only tough, but he uses his head.

OHELIA: What's it made of?

RC: Solid oak – not a knothole in sight.

OHELIA: No, I meant the door.

RC: Oh, the door – no, I don't know what that's made of—

OHELIA: Listen!

RC: What?

OHELIA: It's gone quiet.

RC: So it has. Perhaps they're fighting on carpet.

RB: (off – knocking on door) It's all over, cap'n.

RC: Ah! Well done, Baines – I knew you'd beat 'em.

RB: They beat us, sir. I'm a prisoner. Are you coming out?

RC: What? No fear. Ophelia and I have got enough rations in here for months. Plenty of rum and ship's biscuits. (She joins him near the door – he puts his arm round her.) Tough bunch, are they?

RB: They are, sir. (Cut to close-up: RB with cutlass at his throat.) Been at sea for months, without setting eyes on a member of the opposite, as you might say, sir. Makes a body a bit edgy, that do. However, they've promised not to kill me if I do as they say.

Cut to: RC and Ophelia.

RC: Then I advise you to agree, Baines. I'm staying in here. The fewer men out there with that lot, the better.

RB: (close-up) Ar. You may be right at that, cap'n.

(Pull back to reveal RB is held by four girl pirates, dark and gypsyish. They gaze at him hungrily. One picks her teeth.)

RB: I'd just like to say if I don't see you again, cap'n, it will have been wonderful.

(He is dragged off by the piratesses. Music up.)

DRESS SHOP QUICKIE

RB: Er – cocktail dresses, please.

GIRL: Certainly, sir – what size is your wife?

RB: No – it's not for my wife – it's for me.

GIRL: For you?

RB: Yes – I'm about an 18, I think. Anything but blue – blue doesn't suit me.

GIRL: Yes – well, I'll just get the manager, sir – he'll deal with you.

RB: No, no – I don't need the manager – I'll just browse around for a while if I may.

GIRL: I'm sorry, sir – I've been forbidden to serve gentlemen with ladies' dresses. It's a rule of the management.

RB: But it's only for fancy dress!

GIRL: Yes, that's what they all say. A lot of your sort come in here. (Calls off) Mr Buller!

RB: What do you mean, my sort?

GIRL: I've got my orders – the manager deals with this sort of thing. (Calls) Mr Buller?

RC: (off) Yes?

GIRL: There's another of those fellahs wanting a cocktail dress.

RC: (off) Oh – I'll deal with him, Miss Jones.

(RC enters – he wears a cocktail dress, covered in sequins.)

RC: Now sir, anything in particular? Something off-the-shoulder? Perhaps in pink – now here's a super little dress …

BAITED BREATH

(A party. RB and hostess talking.)

RB: Well, Harriet, a scintillating crowd here this evening, as usual. How do you do it? You seem to be able to breathe life into any old dull collection of people …

HARRIET: Yes. Talking of breathing life, Roger, have you been on the garlic?

RB: Good lord, you mean my breath? No, not me. (He breathes on her.)

HARRIET: No – well, there's someone polluting the atmosphere round here – I wonder who it can be?

(RC approaches and greets them.)

RC: Hello, Harriet!

(His 'aitches' are very strong, and so is his breath. Harriet reels.)

RC: (to RB) Hello, Hartley! (RB blanches, but recovers.) Harry Hartley.

RB: (trying is best to face RC) How do you do, Mr Hartley.

RC: (He tends to stand rather too close to people.) How do you do. Actually, it's Huntington-Hartley, but who cares about a hyphen?

RB: Quite. (He takes out his handkerchief, and pretends to mop his brow, hiding behind it.)

HARRIET: (staggering slightly) Must look after the guests. See you later!

RC: Bye, Harriet. Hasta la vista. (To RB) Helluva good hostess, Harriet. Hundred per cent. You all right, old chap?

RB: (turned away) Yes – something in my eye, I think ...

RC: Let's have a look. (Peers into RB's eye.)

RB: No – it's all right – just watering a bit. Probably hay fever. (Realises.) No, not hay fever, I didn't mean hay fever ...

RC: Horrible thing, hay fever. I had it at Harrogate on holiday. Horrid. Had to hibernate in the hotel the entire holiday.

RB: (collapses on to settee) Sorry – must sit down. Bit faint.

RC: I can give you the name of a good hay-fever man. Cured mine. (He sits next to RB on settee.)

RB: Oh – expensive?

BOTH: Harley Street.

RB: Yes, I was afraid so.

(Stands up – RC does the same.)

RC: Well, no good waiting for the National Health – hopeless.

RB: (despairs) No, actually I use the old wives' remedy. You twist your neck round and hold your breath for as long as possible. (He turns his head the other way, takes a deep breath.)

RC: Oh – I didn't know about that one. There are some strange old wives' tales about though, aren't there? (RB grunts.) Some fairly strange young wives' tales about, too, especially round these parts. Things they get up to. You married? (RB nods and grunts.) Children? (RB nods.) How many? (RB grunts.) Oh, no, can't answer, holding breath, of course. I've got three. All at boarding school. Gosh, you can hold your breath a long time, can't you? (RB nods in agony.) Yes, all at school now. Helen's at St Hilda's, Harold's at King Henry's in Hertfordshire and Hector is at Harrow-on-the-Hill. (RB's eyes popping out – he finally exhales.) Ah! You're back! Hip hip hooray!

RB: Oh! (Collapses on sofa again, flat out.)

RC: Oh dear! You've overdone it. Lack of oxygen to the brain.

HARRIET: (rushing in) What's happened?

RC: Stand back, everybody—

HARRIET: What are you going to do?

RC: I'm going to give him the kiss of life.

(RB, with a yell, leaps up and runs out.)

RC: (to Harriet) Good gracious! What the hell is up with him, Harriet?

HARRIET: (reeling) I'm sorry, Harry – halitosis!

RC: Had he? I didn't notice. (He takes her arm and walks off with her.) Well, I wouldn't perhaps because I did have a teensy bit of garlic, I think, in the dressing at lunchtime. You know how it is.

(People reel back as they pass on their way out of the room.)

THE BOGLE OF BOG FELL

Night. The interior of a dark, cobwebby Scottish castle. A huge fire-place, with a log fire smouldering fitfully. Chickens strut about and nearby a goat is eating the curtains. Next to the fire sits RB, as an old Scot, covered in red hair and plaid.

RB: Welcome to Cockahoopie Castle. I have a story to tell, so strange that it will make your blood run cold, freeze your gizzard and perish the rubber in your inner tubes. But whisht! Before I begin, let me stoke the fire. (He calls) McWeenie! Put another piece of peat on the fire!

(RC appears, as a replica of RB, same hair and clothes. He carries a wickerwork log basket.)

RC: We're running out o' peat. There's not much of him left now – only his right leg.

RB: Never mind which part – will it burn?

RC: It should do, it's his wooden one.

(He produces a wooden leg from his basket. RB takes it, puts it on the fire.)

RB: Poor old Pete! Home cremation is a tradition in these parts. And so much cheaper. (He picks up large bellows.)

RC: By the by, Andrew, the MacDonalds are here – they've been waiting twenty minutes. Poor wee things are getting awful cold out there.

RB: Well, bring them in, man.

RC: I will, I will. (He starts to go, then turns back.) Do you want mustard on yours or ketchup?

RB: Mustard. Now get out and stop interrupting. Go on, away with ye!

(He puffs at him with the bellows and RC flies away backwards and out of sight.)

RB: Now, where was I? Oh, just here. The story I'm about to tell concerns the Bogle of Bog Fell. Don't worry, it's not all going to be in rhyme, that was by accident. Angus Bogle was a mild-mannered wee man, who came to a tragic end. Finding that his wife was unfaithful to him, he cut her off without a shilling. Whereupon she cut him off with a bread knife, and he died intestate, leaving no money to anyone. And from that day onwards, his ghost haunted the area around his native village of Cockahoopie. The village itself was steeped in history ever since it had been pillaged by McNenemy and his Barbican Hordes, who drank all the whisky and left it alcohol-free.

Cut to: film of mountains and village, etc.

RB: (voice-over) Soon after he died, the Bogle's ghost began to appear to various of the villagers; always at full moon, just after closing time.

(A man walks along a country road – goes behind bush to relieve himself. He stands behind bush. RC, completely white, as the Bogle, rises up from behind bush with a wide-eyed grin on his face. Man reacts in fear – starts to run off, comes back to do up his zip, then runs off. RC disappears. The man runs towards us, and stops near a tree in the foreground. RC appears from behind the tree. Man rushes off again.)

RB: (voice-over) It was a truly terrifying sight. One young man, out with his dog, was so petrified that everything stood on end.

(Young Scot in kilt sees RC scuttling up the road. His hair stands on end (trick wig). Cut to: his dog – the dog's hair is also on end. Cut to: the man's sporran – it stands on end.)

RB: (voice-over) He was a very popular young laddie after that, as he relayed to the lassies the gist of his experiences.

(Young man, surrounded by girls in the heather.)

GIRL: Tell us about when everything stood on end, Jimmy.

RB: (voice-over) Mrs MacMuck, the widow of poor old Mick MacMuck, the sewage worker, had been a bag of nerves ever since her husband died. Before that she'd just been a bag. She would go to enormous lengths to protect herself from the Bogle.

(Widow MacMuck in her bedroom – long (floor-length) nightie. She locks door. Three bolts. Chain. Puts chair under doorknob. Small chest pushes up against chair. Looks under bed, sees chamber pot. Gets into bed, throws back the covers to find RC is there, grinning. She is terrified and frightens him as she screams. She dives through window, lands on a man walking past. Meanwhile, halfway up a Highland road, RC appears, running away.)

RB: (voice-over) The Bogle himself was very timid and always hid himself away in his favourite hiding place – the toilet of his wee cottage. In life, ever since he was a bairn, he had always hid there when he was really frightened ...

(Cut to: RC as Angus Boyle, but when alive. He is at the side of his cottage, gardening. A knock is heard. He cautiously goes to the corner of the house and peers round at the front door. There stands a woman with a tray. A large notice on the tray reads 'Flag day'. Terror on RC's face. He runs into the loo and shuts the door. A puff of smoke from his pipe comes through the little circular holes cut in the door. The chain is pulled.)

RB: (voice-over) And so, even now, as a ghost, when frightened by the widow, he sought retreat and safety in the toilet ...

(RC, as ghost, rushes into toilet as before. This time, a large woman in a nightie emerges, terrified.)

RB: (voice-over) ... which wasn't much fun for the new owners. (The chain is pulled.) And so a plan was hatched to catch the Bogle of Bog Fell. Residing in the village was Professor Monty MacDougal (a shot of a detached house, day), the inventor of the now world-famous MacDougal's self-raising trousers, for people who can't get up in the morning. His brilliant, drink-riddled brain was brought to bear upon the problem ...

(Cut to: RB as professor, white hair and moustache, standing next to a blackboard, on which is his design.)

PROF: (to camera) The idea is this. When the Bogle dashes into the lavatory and pulls the chain, this knocks the large boulder down this specially built ramp and it falls to the ground, rolling to the other end of the toilet. This will cause the whole structure ... (he points to his plan on the blackboard) ... to overbalance, thus trapping the Bogle inside. Any questions?

VOICE: (off) Yes, what time do they open?

PROF: Any minute. Come on, let's have one.

(A stampede is heard, as he rushes out of frame. A door slams.)

RB: (voice-over) And so the plan was put into action. Strangely enough, it was the Professor himself, returning home even drunker than usual one night, that was to be the cause of the Bogle's downfall.

Night. (RB as professor, staggering along the road – houses, etc., in evidence. He leans against a wall, singing. We see a sign on the wall – 'Flour mill'. He staggers along the wall and leans against a barn door. It gives way, he falls inside. Crashes, etc. He staggers out, now white from head to foot. Staggers out of shot. A pair of lovers, hand in hand, walk along the village street. They approach a corner. RC appears from one side, grinning. The couple take flight. Then RB, all white, appears at the other side. RC, terrified, rushes away. RB looks vaguely surprised. RC running up the road, away from us.

RB: (voice-over) And so the Bogle sought to take refuge in his usual place. (The toilet door – RC runs into frame, looks around and goes inside.) What he didn't realise was that the crafty Professor had moved it ...

We now see that the toilet is balanced on the edge of a cliff. The chain is pulled. A rumble is heard. The toilet starts to topple and, in very slow motion, falls onto the rocks of the glen below, shattering to pieces. (The dust settles, we mix to: RB in the castle, by the fire.)

RB: And from that day to this, the village has been known as Bog Fell – because that's where the bog fell, you see. One last thing I'll say to ye – the tale I've told you may seem strange, and almost impossible to believe – but if it's not true, may I be blown to smithereens, and the various parts of my body be distributed and scattered throughout the length and breadth of Scotland, including the Trossachs. Good night.

(The camera widens a little and settles as RB takes a drink. He explodes – his clothes fall to the ground.)

THE SWEAR BOX

(Please note – whenever the word 'farmer' is used, a cuckoo noise is heard. Likewise a 'buzz' for the word 'plonk', and a 'boing' for the word 'clown'.)

A country pub. RB enters, is greeted by barmaid.

BARMAID: Evening, Mr Parsons.

RB: Evening, Dolly. How's the (farmers) beer? Flat as (farmers) usual?

BARMAID: Now watch it, Mr Parsons – you'll have to mind your language in here from now on – look here.

(She points to a box on the counter. It says 'Swear box' on it.)

RB: Oh – a swear box. That's a (farmers) good idea. Is it for charity?

BARMAID: The church fund, five pence a time.

RB: Oh – you'll make a (farmers) fortune out of me.

BARMAID: You're right – you owe it fifteen pence already.

RB: Fifteen (farmers) pence?

BARMAID: Twenty now.

RB: Oh, right. Have you got change for a (farmers) quid?

BARMAID: You won't need much change if you go on like this.

RB: That's true. Too (farmers) right I won't.

(RC enters. Greets RB.)

RC: Evening, Joe.

RB: Hallo, Gilbert.

RC: Coo, it's a bit (farmers) nippy out there tonight. Shouldn't be surprised if we're not in for a (farmers) great fall of (farmers) snow tomorrow. That's all we (farmers) need.

BARMAID: And I need twenty pence, Mr Robbins.

RB: (pointing at box) Got a (farmers) swear box in here. Go on, have this on me. (Puts a few coins in the box.)

RC: Hey, that's a (farmers) good idea.

RB: For the church, five pence a time.

RC: Quite right too. About time this lot in here did something for the (farmers) church. (Puts coin in box.)

RB: Too right. Dozy lot of (plonks).

BARMAID: Whoops – that one costs you ten pence.

RB: You what? You never (farmers) told me that!

BARMAID: You didn't (farmers) ask me. It's five pence for a (farmers) and ten pence for a (plonk).

RC: Look, never mind all that (farmers) rubbish. I'm standing here like a (plonk) without a drink. Pint of best, Dolly. And what will you have, Joe?

RB: Five pounds worth of silver, then we'll take this box over there (picks up swear box), sit down and have a civilised (farmers) conversation. (They sit, the box between them on the table.) So, how's your love life, Gilbert?

RC: (farmers) non-existent, mate. How's yours?

RB: Not all that (farmers) grand. Got in a (farmers) argument with the (farmers) wife about going to the (farmers) dogs on (farmers) Friday night – I (farmers) told her I was (farmers) going anyway and she (farmers) hit me round the (farmers) head with a (farmers) saucepan.

(The barmaid, bringing RC's beer, also carries a bag of silver. She pours all of it into the box and gives RB the empty bag.)

RC: What did you do?

RB: I hit her back – silly old (clown).

BARMAID: (returning) Mr Parsons! That will cost you a pound!

RB: A (farmers) pound? This is getting a bit (farmers) expensive.

RC: I think she's making a (plonk) out of you, charging you a (farmers) pound for a (clown).

(Enter a vicar.)

VICAR: Good evening, Dolly – good evening, gentlemen. A double lemonade and water, please. I say – this swear box seems mighty full. (He lifts it up.)

RC: Yes – and Dolly tells us all that money is going to the (farmers) church!

RB: That's a nice surprise for you, eh, Vicar?

VICAR: Surprise? I'm the (plonk) who (farmers) thought of it.

HOW TO CARE FOR THE SICK

(NB: Dialogue and actions to run concurrently.)

VOICE-OVER: The care of the sick is a very worthwhile subject for study – and a knowledge of first aid is a must for everybody today—

(We see a man, dressed in white coat, standing with first aid box. Tighten slowly onto box.)

VOICE-OVER: And the most important thing to remember in first aid, is to keep the patient calm—

(We see shot of woman with saucepan stuck on her head, rushing around the room wildly. The man grabs her and shakes her vigorously.)

VOICE-OVER: Don't try to remedy the situation yourself—

(Man trying to knock saucepan off with hammer.)

VOICE-OVER: Simply lie the patient down, cover with a blanket and get them to drink plenty of hot, sweet tea—

(Man lies woman on floor, covers with a blanket and tries to pour a cup of tea under the saucepan. Eventually pours tea from teapot down handle of saucepan.)

VOICE-OVER: Calmness is the keynote always when dealing with a patient—

(Man in white coat wheels trolley into room where girl patient is in bed.)

VOICE-OVER: A blanket bath, for instance, can be an unnerving experience if a person is unused to it—

(Man turns away at trolley, girl slips off nightie underneath the blanket and puts it on side table. Man turns, and lifts corner of blanket with one hand. Reacts – the soap in his other hand shoots up into the air. He shakes.)

VOICE-OVER: When bandaging an injured limb, do not do so in such a way that the limb is difficult to cope with—

(Man finishes bandaging male patient with one arm down to his side and the other straight up in the air. Patient departs, having to bend at right angles to open the door.)

(Pan over to reveal another man, his arms bandaged at right angles in front of him. He is holding a cup of tea. He can't get near enough to drink it.)

(Cut to: man in wheelchair, arms stretching straight out, banging on the railings.)

VOICE-OVER: If an arm is bandaged correctly, it can often still be gainfully employed—

(Patient with arm at right angle to his body, lying in bed. Nurse approaches and bends to get something out of cupboard. She suddenly leaps up, outraged. Patient looks innocent.)

VOICE-OVER: Cheerfulness is a great asset, but remember that one must never treat a patient's disability too lightly—

(Patient on bed, lying with both legs bandaged straight up in the air, so that he is an 'L' shape. Man in white coat comes with the trolley, pours out medicine into spoon and suddenly pushes down on patient's legs, causing him to sit up – the spoon goes into his mouth and the man pushes him back down again, then up, then down, like a seesaw.)

VOICE-OVER: Make sure you know how to handle equipment properly, and that it is in a safe condition—

(Two men in white coats carry in male patient on stretcher. They approach the bed feet first. The man at the feet puts down his end, and the man at the head doesn't, so the patient slides straight under the

bed. Another angle – he is hauled out and put on the bed. The two men walk out. The bed immediately folds in half and the patient is doubled up like a jack-knife.)

VOICE-OVER: Finally, be attentive at all times to the needs of the patient, and never be caught off-guard for a moment. Remember, he's in your hands—

(Man in white coat with 'L'-shaped man sitting in wheelchair. The man stops to light a cigarette, letting go of the chair. A long shot – the wheelchair runs down a hill, hits a low wall and the patient pitches straight out of it and disappears from view.)

Songs

Before the final 'late items of news' delivered behind the desks by newsreaders Barker and Corbett (a device constructed by Barker to avoid appearing on the show as 'himself'), each episode of *The Two Ronnies* would usually end with a lavish comedy song written by Barker. Often the pair would perform in the guise of recurring characters, such as Jehosaphat and Jones included here. However, always with an expert comedy ear for trend and taste, Barker would also write pastiches of popular artists. Stars lucky enough to have been immortalized by Barker include Elton John, Kid Creole, Boy George and Cleo Laine. He would also turn out bawdy sing-along medleys to well-known tunes such as 'Amazing Grace' or 'Life on the Ocean Wave', often with full orchestras or brass bands.

Barker has admitted that he never truly enjoyed performing in heavily made-up 'drag' or blackface when singing as busty women, but it is testament to his skilful lyricism and end-of-the-pier eye-rolling camp bravado that these big finales still remain some of the funniest performances and best-loved moments of the series.

JEHOSAPHAT AND JONES

Of all the various musical characters the two Ronnies presented in their show, one of the most popular and enduring was the post-Woodstock, long-haired Country-and-Western duo, Jehosaphat and Jones. They first appeared in the early days of the show and stayed with the duo through to their final series, recorded exclusively for Australia's Channel 9. In 1973 the stool-bound duo even cut an album.

Presented here – beginning with an introductory sketch from the show – is *The Jehosaphat and Jones Songbook* (peddle steel guitar to be imagined).

JEHOSAPHAT, JONES AND GUESTS

RB and RC discovered on stools. Intro into the first number – 'The Muck About Song', which they both sing.

VERSE ONE:
Luella Sue O'Hara is the girl who lives next door,
I've known her since-times I was six
And she was only four
And now that we have both grown up
It's very plain to see
No matter how hard she tries to grow
She's still two years younger than me.

VERSE TWO:
When we was little scruffy kids
I'd play in my back yard
We didn't have no TV set
'Cos times was awful hard
But when she tried to ask me round
To her back yard instead
So we could play together
This is what I always said.

CHORUS ONE:
Don't come around here asking me out
I ain't coming out, just to muck about.
You have to muck about on your own, my dear,
'Cos I'm gonna muck about here.

CODA:
Trundling a truck about, wadding a duck about,
I'm gonna muck about here.

VERSE THREE:
Then ten or twelve years later on
She grew up overnight
Her legs got long and slender and
Her blouse got awful tight
But when I asked her if she'd like
To visit me next door
She only answered 'You're too late,
'Cos now I know what for.'

CHORUS TWO:
Don't come around here asking me out
I ain't going out just to muck about.
You'll have to muck about on your own, my dear,
'Cos I'm gonna muck about here.

CODA:
I'm not struck about
Can't run amok about
Don't give a buck about
Folks here roundabout
Let them cluck about
I'm just tuckered out
– I'm gonna muck about here.

(Applause at end. Mix to pre-VT.)

(Caption 'The Surprises' over long shot of RB and RC, blacked up, with straightened, bouffant hair-do's, identical floor-length dresses. Heavily made up, orange lipstick, etc. RB has his teeth in.)

(They sing the proper words of 'Black Magic', miming two girls' voices. They move identically as they sing.)

BOTH:
That old black magic has me in its spell.
That old black magic that you weave so well.

RC: Those icy fingers up and down my spine.
RB: That same old witchcraft when your eyes meet mine.

BOTH:
That same ole tingle that I feel inside
And then that elevator starts to glide.

RC: And down and down I go.
RB: Round and round I go,

BOTH:
Like a leaf that's caught in the tide.

RC: I should stay away, but what can I do?
RB: (What can she do?)
RC: I hear your name.
RB: (She hears my name.)
RC: And I'm aflame.
RB: (And I'm fair game.) Aflame, with such a burning desire
That only your kiss

(RC kissing noises.)

RB: Can put out the fire.
RC: (Water, water.)

BOTH:
Oh, you're the lover I've been waiting for,
The note that fate had me created for
And every time your lips meet mine
Darling down and down I go
Round and round I go,
In a spin, loving the spin I'm in,
Under that old black magic called love.

(The orchestra then repeats, from the beginning, while RC and RB move without singing, for the first two lines.)

RC: (Third line) (Turns his back and puts his arms round himself, and runs 'icy fingers' up and down his spine.)

RB: (Fourth line) (Three bumps with his hip on 'eyes meet mine'.)

RC: (Fifth line.) (Rattles his bracelets three times, and we hear bells. Squeezes his left boob once, we hear motor horn.)

RB: (Sixth line) (Takes off his earrings and drops them down his bosom – swanee, whistle and splash.)

RC: (sings) And down and down I go.

RB: (speaks) Round and round I go.

BOTH:
In a spin, loving the spin I'm in, under that old black magic
    called Love!

(Applause at end. Mix to pre-VT.)

(Caption – Gary Schmutter over long shot of RB as Gary Glitter, with spangle suit, wig and very high platform shoes.)

RB: (*waves arms about and sings*) You oughta be in my shoes,
My shoes, my shoes
People try and buy shoes
Just like mine
If you pay the price youse
Should get high shoes
When you've got your high shoes
You'll feel fine.
You put your left leg out
You put your left leg in
You put your left leg out
And you shake it all about
You give it all you've got, the whole night through,
And you sometimes put your back out, too.
Ooh!

(He hobbles off.)

BACKING VOICES: (*off*) Get off-get-off, get off-get-off, etc.
(Fading away.)
Mix to pre-VT.

(Caption – 'Elton Bog' over long shot of RC seated at piano as Elton John, with enormous glasses.)

(Intro to song.)

RC: *(sings)* Oh, I have got a woman
I give her this and that
But she's got a taste for all the things
That make her fat.

CHORUS:
Oh baby
Every night she's choc-a-bloc
We do the roll-mop rock cake cheese roll
Peppermint rock.

VERSE TWO:
I rock her to the left,
I rock her to the right
She said, 'I like a man who like a rock all night.'
I took her to the sweetshop
I said it's all for you,
She said I only like my rock when it's
Lettered right through.

REPEAT CHORUS

(Musical break: half-verse and chorus, during which RC changes glasses.)

RC: I took her to the café
For a fancy casserole
The only thing she fancied
Was the luncheon meat roll
I took her for a picnic
I took her for a stroll
We sat among the rocks but she wouldn't
Have a roll.

REPEAT CHORUS

(Applause to end. Mix to studio (live).)

(RB and RC as Jehosaphat and Jones.)

VERSE ONE:
RC: A man said to a bar-maid, now mix me a drink,
A cocktail made up of whatever you think,
RB: She mixed it, he drank it, and went quite cross-eyed,
And three hours later he came to, and cried.

CHORUS:
I'd like to try another like the one
   I had before.
I so enjoyed the last one that I'm coming back for more.
The effect is not immediate, but it's worth waiting for.
So oblige me with another, like the one I had before.
RC: (spoken) ... Only bigger!

VERSE TWO:
RB: A man sat in a drug-store, and he called for the boss.
He said you sold me a pep pill to give to my boss.
I put it on the shelf on the wall near my bed
It fell into the coffee pot and I swallowed it instead.

BOTH:
(CHORUS AS BEFORE)
I'd like to try another like the one I had before.
I so enjoyed the last one that I'm coming back for more.
The effect is not immediate, but it's worth waiting for.
So oblige me with another, like the one I had before.
RB: (spoken) ... Only stronger ...

(Fade.)

UP CAT POLE CAT

BOTH: *(chorus)*
Up cat pole cat juniper tree
Lying in the yard with a bellyful of water melon
Don't pick cotton and I don't plant grass
Out in the open, sitting on my corn patch.

RC: Down in Louisiana where the corn is high
Keep a jumping up to see the gals pass by
Down by the river where the bulrush grows
Watch the gals a-swimming there without no hesitation.

REPEAT CHORUS

RB: Met Mary Ellen by the old barn door
I know just what she's a-waiting for
Up in the loft where the oil lamp flickers
I lost my heart and she lost her parasol.

REPEAT CHORUS

RC: Annie was kissed by the preacher's son
She said, 'Now, what you been and gone and done?'
He said, 'I've been at the end of my wits
Even since the night I grabbed you by the currant bushes.'

REPEAT CHORUS

Town folk come here, try to settle down
Pretty soon it's gonna be a great big town
They build their roads and houses and then
They all have to move to the country again.

REPEAT CHORUS

STUTTERING BUM

RB: Oh, Mary Lou, I'm a-calling you
Up on the telephone
To say thanks for coming to the dance with me
And letting me take you home;
I'm sorry I seemed so nervous
And started to stammer and sweat
But it s-started as s-soon as I saw you

And I ain't got over it yer-yet
I stared at your great big Ber-B-B-Ber-Ber
Beautiful blue-green eyes
I wondered if you Fer-F-F-Fer-Fer
Flirted with all the guys;
When you smiled I nearly Sher-Sh-Sh-Sher-Sher
Shot right out the door
'Cos I'd never seen such pretty little Ter-T-T-Ter-Ter Teeth
    before
I ain't yer-usually a bashful boy
I've took out other gals
I've kissed them on their ber-b-b-ber back-door step
And per per per per promised to be pals but
Since I first caught sight of you
On the Brownsville Buggy ride
Why, I've become a ser-ser-stuttering bum
And my tongue's perpetually ter-tied
My Cer-C-C-Cer Cer Cer C-C-Cer Cer
Collar gets awful tight,
When I Fer-F-F-Fer-Fer feel you close
As I Der-D-D-did last night;
I get a funny feeling in my Ber-B-B-Ber Ber
Ber B-B-B-B-B brain
And I can't Wer-Wer Wer till I per-p-p-per
I Jer-just gotta see you again
(Instrumental break.)
She said she'd see me Saturday
And I put down the phone
My tongue is back to normal now
Now I'm once more alone.
But next time that I meet her
On Saturday night around ten,
You can ber-bet your ber-bottom dollar I'll be
A ser-stuttering bum again.
I'll grab her by the Ber-b-b-ber-ber barn
And per-p-p-push her inside
I'll take my cer-courage, in both hands,
And ask her to be my ber-bride.
And if she holds my cer-cer-clammy hand
And tells me that she would,

I'll Fer-fer-fer-fer-fer fetch a preacher right away
And that'll cure my stutter for good.
That's good! That's Ger ger, ger-ger-ger, g-g-ger-ger
Ger-ger, ger-g-ger ger good!

RAILROAD MAN

BOTH:
They told me when I left the jailhouse
'Now try to go straight if you can.'
Now I'm doing fine, 'cos I'm on a straight line
A-working for the railroad man, oh Lord,
A-working for the railroad man.
RB: They said, 'Lay tracks for the railroad
'Cos steam means speed and power,'
So I'm doing by best and I'm travelling west
About fifteen feet an hour, oh Lord,
About fifteen feet an hour.
RC: Oh I crouched all night laying track down
And the wind on my back made me choke
And I felt that the bottom had fell out o' my life
Till I found that my braces had broke, oh Lord,
I found that my braces had broke.
RB: Someone had stole my hammer,
But I still got to earn my bread
And life ain't so grand, when you're standing on your hands,
And driving in the rivets with your head, oh Lord,
And driving in the rivets with your head.

BOTH:
There's a curve in the track up yonder
I think it's the beginning of the end;
I've tried going straight, but sad to relate
I think I'm a'going round the bend, oh Lord,
I think I'm a'going round the bend.

BLOWS MY MIND

BOTH:
The river's flowing, up the hill
It keeps moving, I keep still
Some folks say that thinking makes you blind
And when the wind is blowing from behind
It blows my mind.
Questions filter through my brain.
Who makes water? What makes rain?
Is bakin' powder made from bakin' rind
And when the wind is blowing from behind
It blows my mind.
Painted girls and neon light
Lord, you made the darkness bright
The hole in my blue jeans is hard to find
But when the wind is blowing from behind
It blows my mind.
I'll go home and change my clothes
Brush my hair and blow my nose
A barrel-organ's life is one long grind
And when the wind is blowing from behind
It blows my mind.

WE KNEW WHAT SHE MEANT

RC: My cousin Pauline was a Tennessee Queen
As pretty a critter as you've ever seen
But she was so dumb that no matter how she tried,
When she opened her mouth she'd put her foot right inside.

BOTH:
(chorus) We knew what she meant
We knew what she meant
We heard what she said
But we knew what she meant.
RC: She invited the preacher to her house, they say
She said, 'It's a party, I'm 19 today
Ma's bought me a dress and a bonnet so cute,
So come up and see me in my birthday suit.'

REPEAT CHORUS

RC: She went to a dance hall one night on her own
And she smiled at a young man who stood all alone
He remarked that he'd not had the pleasure before
And she answered, 'Come on then, let's get on the floor.'

REPEAT CHORUS

RC: One day she went into a department store
And she said to the guy who was stood by the door
'I need some material to make a new belt.
Perhaps you can tell me where I can get felt?'

REPEAT CHORUS

RC: She said, 'I once met a guy with dark wavy hair
So we rushed off to Alaska for a quick love affair
But I came back disappointed with a cold and a cough
We were both frozen stiff and I just broke it off.'
BOTH:
We knew what she meant
We knew what she meant
We heard what she said
But we knew what she meant.

SHE AGREES

VERSE ONE:
I got myself a gorgeous gal
She lives just out of town
She's always most agreeable
Whenever I'm around
We never ever quarrel and
She sees my point of view
She just agrees with everything
(Well, that's not strictly true).

CHORUS ONE:
('Cos) She agrees we're like the bees
And the birds up the trees
She agrees that love is
Wonderful and right –
She agrees in every way
With everything I say
But she won't agree to do
What I asked her to last night.

VERSE TWO:
She's such a healthy sort of gal
She plays all kinds of sports
She's a wonderful all-rounder when
She's wearing tennis shorts
She's great upon the golf-course, she's
An expert rifle shot;
And when she plays a game she gives
It everything she's got.

CHORUS TWO:
(Oh) She plays baseball, she plays pool
She plays hockey for the school
She can ski, and swim, and fence

And fly a kite –
Throw a dart or bounce a ball
She'll play any game at all
But she wouldn't play the game
I asked her to last night.

CODA:
RC: She agrees that I'm sincere,
And she thinks that I'm a dear.

BOTH:
But she won't agree to do
What I asked her to last night.

(REPEAT CODA)

RB: She agrees that I've got class,
And she thinks that I'm a gas.

BOTH:
But she won't agree to do
What I asked her to last night.
No, she won't agree to do
What I asked her to last night!

GAL FROM ARKENSAW

VERSE ONE:
She was a big, fat, welcome on the mat,
True blue Southern gal,
Met her down in Arkensaw, never saw the
Gal before, but she seemed a real cool pal
She could rustle cattle and her sister
From Seattle, she used to do it as well
She was a big, fat, what d'you think of that?
Uptight downtown belle.

VERSE TWO:
She was a huge, tall, really on the ball
Great big loving dame
Travelled with the rodeo, working in the
Stripper show, no two shows the same
Country show or cattle fair, she would drop
Her underwear, everyone enjoyed it, you could tell
She was huge, tall, no complaints at all,
Uptight downtown belle

VERSE THREE:
She was a great, proud, say it out loud
Bubbling ball of fire
To the guys who came to see, she would always guarantee
Temperatures would shoot up higher
Didn't have to prove it 'cos when she began to move it,
Boy, how the crowd would swell.
She was a great, proud, wonderfully endowed, uptight down-
    town belle.

VERSE FOUR:
She was a large, fine, try one of mine,
Rattling big success
Seemed to be the one for me, seemed a lot of fun to me,
But she made my life a mess
Took my gold, left me in the cold, didn't even
Leave me my heart
She was a large, fine, lay it on the line,
Regular downtown tart.

IN THE SUMMER TIME

VERSE ONE:
BOTH (*throughout*):
What I mean
There's a dream

Of a queen
Who I've seen
In New Orleans
In the Summertime

VERSE TWO:
She's so lean
So serene
And she's clean
I've never seen
Such a Queen
Of seventeen
In the Summertime

MIDDLE EIGHT: In the Summertime
There will come a time
At the moment I'm
Working overtime
For a pal o' mine
So I'll have a dime
To git to New Orleans.

VERSE THREE:
Her eyes are green
Just like a bean
Her legs are lean
And just between
Ourselves, I mean
To love that queen
In the Summertime.

VERSE FOUR:
Her name is Jean
It's Jean Christine
Her boyfriend Dean
Is really mean
He's a Marine
And so obscene
Nearly all the time.

VERSE FIVE:
I mean
To steal the scene
I'll win his Jean –
The old routine
Will melt that Queen
Like margarine
In the Summertime.

VERSE THREE *(repeated)*:
Her eyes are green
Just like a bean
Her legs are lean
And just between
Ourselves, I mean
To love that Queen
In the Summertime.

IT DON'T MEAN THAT I
DON'T LOVE YOU

VERSE ONE:
Now just you listen to me, darling
What I say to you is true
If you really want to leave me
That's entirely up to you
But believe me when I tell you
I am really not to blame
All your silly fears are groundless
I still love you just the same.

CHORUS:
It don't mean that I don't love you
Just because I never speak
And I never give you presents –
Take you swimming in the creek;
Just because I hate your cooking

Oh, please don't get in a stew –
Just because I'm not your grandma,
Doesn't mean I don't love you.

VERSE TWO:
It don't mean that I don't love you
When I punch you in the nose
And go out with other women
Never buy you any clothes.
How can we remain together
With so many ifs and buts?
It don't mean that I don't love you –
But my wife – she hates your guts.

NEIGHBOURS

RC AND RB: (*chorus*) Heat up the coffee
Serve up the stoo,
Pull up a chair
'Cos we're neighbours, me and you.
You take the golf-clubs
I'll take the car
What's yours is mine
'Cos that's what neighbours are.

VERSE ONE (*spoken*):
RB: John and Joe were neighbours
They lived side by side
Joe, he was a bachelor
John, he had a bride
They borrowed from each other
Just like neighbours do
Said Joe, 'Why keep two lawn-mowers
When only one would do?'

REPEAT CHORUS

VERSE TWO *(spoken)*:
RC: Young John drove home to Joe's house
And returned his neighbour's car
Then popped in through Joe's back door
To borrow a good cigar;
On the couch lay his own wife, Molly
With her cheeks so blushing red
She said, 'Poor Joe's
TV don't go,
So he switched me on instead.'

REPEAT CHORUS

VERSE THREE *(double verse, spoken)*:
RB: 'I wish we had a baby,'
Said John to his wife one day
''Cos neighbour Joe's got a baby-carriage
He wants to give away.'
So they both looked under the gooseberry bush
And telephoned the stork
But it never came, and it seemed a shame
To take an empty pram for a walk.
RC: John went away on a business trip
And he spent a year at sea
When he came back he found his wife

With a baby on her knee
She said, 'Joe brought it over
One night as I lay asleep
The stork left twins at Joe's house
So he gave me one to keep.'

REPEAT CHORUS

DIMPLES

Oh, the dimples in her cheeks
And the ribbons in her hair
And the rosebuds on her lips
And that lacy underwear
(spoken) Oh, the dimples in her cheeks!
There's a gal who lives near me
Pretty as a pin
Whenever I go by her place
She always lets me in
She's a gal without no brains
She's simple, so they say
But when I take her in the woods
She always knows the way.
Oh, the dimples in her cheeks
And the sunburn on her knees
And the music in her voice
And she tries so hard to please
(spoken) Oh, the sunburn on her knees!
When first we met she was wearing pants
And pushing an old iron plough
At first I thought she was a boy –
But I don't think so now.
Sometimes we go for buggy rides
And other times we walk
I'd like to ask the gal her name
But we don't get time to talk.
Oh, the dimples in her cheeks

And the freckles on her back
And the starlight in her eyes
And she loves my brother Jack
(spoken) What a shame she married Jack.

THE GIRL WHO'S GONNA MARRY ME

She can sow, she can hoe,
She can read, she can write,
She can cook a man a breakfast in the middle of the night,
She can cut up a chicken,
She can cut down a tree,
Wow! That's the gal who's gonna marry me.
She can dig, she can jig,
She can juggle, she can jump,
She can drive a fella crazy with a wiggle of her rump,
She can stand in the saddle,
She can sit on your knee,
Wow! That's the girl who's gonna marry me.
She can joke, she can smoke,
She can drink a dozen beers,
She can move a grand pianner, she can move a man to tears,
She can pour out her heart, or
She can pour out your tea,
Yep! That's the gal who's gonna marry me.
She can roast, she can toast,
She can boil, she can bake,
She can cut a fella dead and she can cut a slice of cake,
She can cook a fella's goose, and
She can fry a fricassee,
Yep! That's the gal who's gonna marry me.
She can sweep, she can weep ,
She can giggle, she can grin,
She can play a little poker, she can play a little gin,
She's as spicy as a pickle,
And sweeter than a pea,
Hup! She's the gal who's gonna marry me.